Luce Irigaray and Prem

The essays in this groundbreaking collection stage conversations between the thought of the controversial feminist philosopher, linguist and psychoanalyst Luce Irigaray and premodern writers, ranging from Empedocles and Homer to Shakespeare, Spenser and Donne. They explore both the pre-Enlightenment roots of Luce Irigaray's thought, and the impact that her writings have had on our understanding of ancient, medieval and Renaissance culture.

Luce Irigaray has been a major figure in Anglo-American literary theory, philosophy and gender studies ever since her germinal works, *Speculum of the Other Woman* and *This Sex Which Is Not One*, were published in English translation in 1985. This collection is the first sustained examination of Irigaray's crucial relationship to premodern discourses underpinning Western culture, and of the transformative effect she has had on scholars working in pre-Enlightenment periods. Like Irigaray herself, the essays work at the intersections of gender, theory, historicism and language. This collection offers powerful ways of understanding premodern texts through Irigaray's theories that allow us to imagine our past and present relationship to economics, science, psychoanalysis, gender, ethics and social communities in new ways.

Theresa Krier is Professor of English at Macalester College, and is author of *Gazing on Secret Sights: Spenser, Classical Imitation, and the Decorums of Vision* and *Birth Passages: Maternity and Nostalgia, Antiquity to Shakespeare*. She is the editor of *Refiguring Chaucer in the Renaissance*. **Elizabeth D. Harvey** is Associate Professor of English and Director of Graduate Studies, University of Toronto. She is the author of *Ventriloquized Voices: Feminist Theory and English Renaissance Texts*, the co-editor of *Women and Reason* and *Soliciting Interpretation: Literary Theory and Seventeenth-Century English Poetry*, and editor of *Sensible Flesh: On Touch in Early Modern Culture*. She is currently completing a book on early modern literature and medicine, *Inscrutable Organs*.

Routledge studies in Renaissance literature and culture

Luce Irigaray and Premodern Culture

Thresholds of history

**Edited by Theresa Krier
and Elizabeth D. Harvey**

LONDON AND NEW YORK

First published 2004
by Routledge

2 Park Square, Milton Park, Abingdon, Oxfordshire OX14 4RN

Simultaneously published in the USA and Canada
by Routledge

711 Third Avenue, New York, NY 10017

First issued in paperback 2014

Routledge is an imprint of the Taylor & Francis Group, *an informa company*

© 2004 Theresa Krier and Elizabeth D. Harvey for selection and editorial
matter; individual contributors their contribution

Typeset in Times by
GreenGate Publishing Services, Tonbridge, Kent

British Library Cataloguing in Publication Data
A catalogue record for this book is available from the British Library

Library of Congress Cataloging in Publication Data
A catalog record for this book has been requested

ISBN 978-0-415-32340-6 (hbk)

ISBN 978-0-415-75869-7 (pbk)

Contents

Illustrations

Notes on contributors

Elizabeth Jane Bellamy is the author of *Translations of Power: Narcissism and the Unconscious in Epic History* (Cornell, 1992), *Affective Genealogies: Psychoanalysis, Postmodernism, and the "Jewish Question" after Auschwitz* (Nebraska, 1997), and many essays on Renaissance literature and contemporary theory; she is co-editor of *Imagining Death in Spenser and Milton*. She is Professor of English at the University of New Hampshire.

Harry Berger, Jr. is Professor Emeritus of Literature and Art History at the University of California, Santa Cruz. He has written many essays and books on ancient and Renaissance literature and art, including *The Absence of Grace: Sprezzatura and Suspicion in Two Renaissance Courtesy Books* (Stanford, 2000), *Fictions of the Pose: Rembrandt Against the Italian Renaissance* (Stanford, 2000), *Making Trifles of Terrors: Redistributing Complicities in Shakespeare* (Stanford, 1997), *Imaginary Audition: Shakespeare on Stage and Page* (California, 1989), *Revisionary Play: Studies in the Spenserian Dynamics* (California, 1988), *Second World and Green World: Studies in Renaissance Fiction-Making* (California, 1988), and *The Allegorical Temper* (Yale, 1957). He is the editor of *Spenser: A Collection of Critical Essays* (Prentice-Hall, 1968). Another volume of essays, *Situated Utterances: Texts, Bodies, and Cultural Representations*, edited and introduced by Judith Anderson, is forthcoming from Stanford University Press.

Rosi Braidotti is Professor of Women's Studies in the Arts Faculty of Utrecht University and scientific director of the Netherlands Research School of Women's Studies. She co-ordinates ATHENA, the European Thematic Network of Women's Studies for the European Commission's SOCRATES programme, as well as the NOISE inter-European University exchange programme. In the academic year 1994–95 she was a fellow in the School of Social Science at the Institute for Advanced Study in Princeton. In 2001 she was awarded a Jean Monet fellowship in the Robert Schuman Centre of the European University Institute, Florence. Her publications include *Metamorphoses: Toward a Materialistic Theory of Becoming* (Polity Press, 2002), *Nomadic Subjects: Embodiment and Sexual Difference* (Columbia University Press, 1994), *Women, the Environment and Sustainable*

Development: towards a Theoretical Synthesis (together with Sabine Hausler, Ewa Pluta, and Saskia Wieringa), and *Patterns of Dissonance: a Study of Women in Contemporary Philosophy* (Polity Press/Routledge, 1991). Her work has been translated into several languages. She has published extensively in feminist philosophy, epistemology, poststructuralism, and psychoanalysis. She serves as an adviser to the journals *Signs, differences, Feminist Theory,* and *The European Journal of Women's Studies.* She is currently concentrating her philosophical research on the concept of difference and the notion of 'Europe.'

Jonathan Crewe is the Willard Professor of English and Comparative Literature at Dartmouth, and Director of the Leslie Center for the Humanities. His publications include *Trials of Authorship* (1990), *Hidden Designs: The Critical Profession and Renaissance Literature* (1986), and *Unredeemed Rhetoric: Thomas Nashe and the Scandal of Authorship* (1982). He is the co-editor, with Mieke Bal and Leo Spitzer, of *Acts of Memory: Cultural Recall in the Present* (1992), and has recently edited Shakespeare's *Coriolanus, Narrative Poems, Twelfth Night, Measure for Measure, Troilus and Cressida,* and *Henry VIII* (1998–2002) for the new Pelican Shakespeare. He is currently working on a book on the genealogy of Elizabethan romance.

Barbara L. Estrin is Professor of English and Department Chair at Stonehill College where she specializes in early modern literature and modern poetry. Her books include *The Raven and the Lark: Lost Children in Literature of the English Renaissance* (Bucknell, 1985), *Laura: Uncovering Gender and Genre in Wyatt, Donne and Marvell* (Duke, 1994), and *The American Love Lyric after Auschwitz and Hiroshima* (Palgrave, 2001). Currently, she is working on a book-length project, "Orphan Envy," a study that reads backwards from contemporary fiction to Shakespeare. She has published numerous articles on Renaissance and contemporary writers.

Elizabeth D. Harvey is the author of *Ventriloquized Voices: Feminist Theory and Renaissance Texts* (Routledge, 1992), co-editor of *Women and Reason* (Michigan, 1992) and *Soliciting Interpretation: Literary Theory and Seventeenth-Century English Poetry* (Chicago, 1990), and editor of *Sensible Flesh: On Touch in Early Modern Culture* (Penn, 2002). She is Associate Professor of English at the University of Toronto, and is currently completing a book on early modern literature and medicine, *Inscrutable Organs.*

Amy Hollywood is Professor of Theology and the History of Christian Thought at the University of Chicago Divinity School. Her book, *The Soul as Virgin Wife: Mechthild of Magdeburg, Marguerite Porete, and Meister Eckhart* (Notre Dame Press, 1995), received the International Congress on Medieval Studies Otto Gründler Prize. She is more recently the author of *Sensible Ecstasy: Mysticism, Sexual Difference, and the Demands of History* (University of Chicago Press, 2002) and is now working on a book about meditation, memory, and mourning in late medieval mysticism.

Ann Rosalind Jones, Esther Cloudman Dunn Professor of Comparative Literature at Smith College, is the author of *The Currency of Eros: Women's Love Lyric in Europe, 1540–1620* (1990) and (with Peter Stallybrass) of *Renaissance Clothing and the Materials of Memory* (Cambridge, 2000), which won the MLA's James Russell Lowell Prize in 2001. She has written numerous articles on gender, ideology, and women's writing in early modern Europe, and she is now completing a translation, with Margaret Rosenthal, of Cesare Vecellio's Venetian costume book, *Degli habiti antichi et moderni di tutto il mondo*.

Theresa Krier, Professor of English at Macalester College, is the author of *Gazing on Secret Sights: Spenser, Classical Imitation, and the Decorums of Vision* (Cornell, 1990), *Birth Passages: Maternity and Nostalgia, Antiquity to Shakespeare* (Cornell, 2001), and essays on ancient and Renaissance poetry. She has edited *Refiguring Chaucer in the Renaissance* (Florida, 1998) and co-edited a special issue of the annual *Spenser Studies*. She is a former editor of *The Spenser Review*.

Grant Williams teaches at Nipissing University, Canada. He has published articles in *English Literary History, Exemplaria, Rhetoric Society Quarterly, Dalhousie Review*, and *SubStance*. He is co-editor of *Forgetting in Early Modern English Literature and Culture: Lethe's Legacies*.

Acknowledgments

In "What Is Called Thinking?" Heidegger famously meditated on the etymological links between thinking and thanking. His own extensive remarks and the wide popularity of this link notwithstanding, we make no claim to resolve its enigmatic nature. But we've found that the collaborative adventure of this book – the long, sometimes exhilarating hours in which we thought with each other, with our contributors, and with the writers to whom we try to listen – answers to Heidegger's notion of grateful memory (Heidegger 1968: 141), as well as his notion of thinking as grateful releasement (Heidegger 1959: 83–5). We can hardly overstate our gratitude to the contributors to this volume, and to sponsors of conferences in Cambridge and Toronto – the International Spenser Society and the Renaissance Society of America respectively – which promoted sessions on Irigaray and premodern writing.

Elizabeth D. Harvey would like to thank Sophie Levy for her skill and flexibility as a research assistant, her colleagues at the University of Toronto for their intellectual generosity, and Theresa Krier for friendship, brilliance, extraordinary patience, and for conceiving this collection. She gratefully acknowledges awards from the Social Sciences and Humanities Research Council of Canada, a Chancellor Jackman Research Fellowship in the Humanities from the University of Toronto, and an Andrew W. Mellon Fellowship from the Folger Shakespeare Library, all of which made the research and preparation of this volume possible. Her greatest debts are to Anthea and Nicholas, who are always becoming in new ways, and to Mark Cheetham, whose sustaining generosity makes thinking possible.

Theresa Krier is grateful to her new colleagues and students at Macalester College, to her family, and especially to Elizabeth D. Harvey, without whose intelligence, wit, drive, professional canniness, and endless reserves of friendship this project would never have come to fruition. Pepper and Bran, the two grandest members of her household, died at the beginning and end of a single winter when we were working hardest on this book. Thinking of them, it becomes easy to understand that thinking and thanking originate in the same gesture, and that Heidegger's originary word "thanc" is, as he says, "imbued with the original nature of memory: the gathering of the constant intention of everything that the heart holds in present being" (Heidegger 1968: 141).

We wish to thank the National and University Library, Prague, the Schnütgen Museum, Cologne, the Pierpont Morgan Library, New York, the Cloisters Museum, New York, the National Gallery of Art, Washington, DC, and the University of Virginia Library for permission to reproduce illustrations.

1 Future anteriors

Luce Irigaray's transmutation of the past

Elizabeth D. Harvey and Theresa Krier

> What is realized in my history is not the past definite of what was, since it is no more, or even the present perfect of what has been in what I am, but the future anterior of what I shall have been for what I am in the process of becoming.
>
> Jacques Lacan (1977b: 86)

Luce Irigaray has been called a philosopher of change (Whitford 1991: 15), and the essays in this collection demonstrate the metamorphic power of her work in general and its applicability to classical, medieval, and early modern literature and culture in particular. To suggest that her writings have the capacity to illuminate premodern culture might seem on the face of it to be a counter-intuitive claim because Irigaray does not appear to be overtly interested in the specificities of history. Yet it is precisely her training as a philosopher, linguist, and psychoanalyst that has given her the variety of resources necessary to challenge the fundamental structures that shape our sense of who we are in relation to the present and the past. Her interrogations of language, her critiques of rational and philosophical thought, and her use of the explosive potential of a psychoanalysis turned on the disciplines that subtend our inherited cultural realities allow us to see the past through the lens of a powerfully gendered ethical theory. She scrutinizes the nature of knowledge, our sensory faculties (especially the hegemony of the visual), what it means to be embodied, and what the nature of divinity is. She is a subversive philosopher, a term that calls up not only her ability to overthrow or fundamentally disrupt philosophy, but, in its root sense, to turn to its underneath, what it suppresses in order to function. If philosophy, especially metaphysics, employs a language shorn of affect, gender, and historical specificity, as Irigaray charges, her project is to re-embody this neutral discourse, to resituate it within a world attentive to sexual difference and material origins.

The title of her book on Heidegger (*The Forgetting of Air in Martin Heidegger*) is symptomatic of a tactic that informs her work generally: her sustained engagements with philosophy seek to activate memory, to recover a past or substratum that has been lost or forgotten. Her rereading of such philosophers as Plato, Plotinus, Descartes, and Spinoza opens their texts to the historical and cultural contexts in which they were embedded, rendering accessible new ways of understanding pre-Enlightenment culture. Irigaray's animation of the past, making the mute speak, is also always a transmutation, a way of changing our understanding of our histories. This volume thus explores both the historical roots of Irigaray's thought and the impact that her writings have had on our own understanding of premodern cultures in order to appraise her work's capacity to transform our reading practices and our modes of knowing. As these essays demonstrate, while Irigaray's thinking has the capacity radically to reshape how we conceive of gender relations and women in history, the topics and ways of reading that her work offers scholars of early literatures also catalyzes dialogue among medical and scientific discourses and ideologies, religion, cosmology, rhetoric, politics, philosophy, and psychoanalysis, allowing us to imagine our relationship to economics, ethics, and social communities in fundamentally different ways.

Luce Irigaray has been a major figure in Anglo-American literary theory, philosophy, and gender studies ever since her germinal works, *Speculum of the Other Woman* and *This Sex Which Is Not One*, were published in English translation in 1985. Initially controversial, she fascinated and outraged feminists because of her putative biological essentialism, her apparent belief that the essence of woman was located in her bodily nature, and her so-called psychic essentialism, her supposed misreadings of Lacanian psychoanalysis. Margaret Whitford's 1991 book-length study *Luce Irigaray: Philosophy in the Feminine* requited these charges in ways that not only ensured Irigaray's permanent place in the history of feminist thought but that also set the stage for a range of newly sophisticated theoretical interpretations of Irigaray's writings. Subsequent engagements with her evolving thought and prolific writings by such theorists as Judith Butler, Rosi Braidotti, Martin Jay, and Elizabeth Grosz have confirmed her importance as one of the leading feminist theorists of the late twentieth and early twenty-first century.

While Irigaray is a prominent presence in Anglo-American and European feminist theory, no large-scale appraisal has yet been undertaken that examines either the historical origins of her thought or the transformative effect she has had on scholars working in pre-Enlightenment historical periods. Yet her theories are themselves demonstrably rooted in historical ideas, and she ceaselessly reads, questions, and unpacks the major philosophers from the very earliest to the most recent; she is in fact most engaged with those philosophers who themselves write densely layered palimpsests of earlier thinkers. Her critique of Platonic and Neoplatonic thought, her radical reconception of the body, her theory of mimeticism, her redefinitions of religion and science, her understanding of the exchange of women, and perhaps most importantly, her writing on the relationship between women and language, have profoundly altered the way we think about gender in history. She is a writer analytical, critical, lyrical, riddling at once. No reader familiar with the major contributions, interventions, personae, strategies, and challenges of women writers or characters of early periods throughout Europe is unequipped to read Irigaray, because she employs strategies of reading and methods for challenging dominant discourses that are derived from and reminiscent of these premodern tactics. The essays in this collection demonstrate the fruitfulness of her unsettling, provocative writings, for they, like Irigaray herself, work at the intersections of gender, theory, historicism, and language practices in philosophy, poetry, drama, religious writing, science and medicine.

In classical, medieval, and early modern studies, historicism continues to be a dominant force, although its centrality is being challenged and augmented by a revitalized psychoanalytic theory, a renewed interest in formalist approaches, the prolific growth of gender and queer theory, and by the methodological variety generated by the productive commerce among and between disciplines. Many recent studies that examine discursive practices in the light of historicism, gender studies, and psychoanalysis evince the potent influence of Foucault and Lacan (Carla Mazzio and David Hillman, *The Body in Parts*, Valeria Finucci and Regina Schwartz, *Desire in the Renaissance: Psychoanalysis and Literature*, and Carla Mazzio and Douglas Trevor, *Historicism, Psychoanalysis, and Early Modern Culture*, to take a few examples), but where Lacan is often understood as conservative, with theories of subjectivity and the symbolic which offer little hope for change, there are crucial conversations yet to be staged between Foucault and Irigaray, between materialist historicism and Irigaray's movements in feminism and philosophy, and above all between Irigaray's work and pre-Enlightenment texts. Change, as we have suggested, is what Irigaray presses toward in all her work on becoming, on metamorphosis, on as yet unimagined forms of gendered relationships and political and communal structures.

IMAGINARY HISTORY, SENSIBLE SPEECH

The nature of the affinity between Irigaray's writings and premodern culture may be explained in part through her radical and increasingly supple notion of the imaginary.[1] Although her use of the term inevitably evokes Lacan's psychoanalytic Imaginary, famously elaborated in "The Mirror Stage" (Lacan 1977a: 1–7), Irigaray transmutes the concept through her intricate rereading of Freud, and she infuses the idea with renewed flexibility and scope through her dialogue with philosophical, literary, and political influences that include the pre-Socratics, Gaston Bachelard, phenomenology, and the Marxist-psychoanalytic writings of Cornelius Castoriadis (Whitford 1991: 54–6).[2] This redefined imaginary lies at the heart of her writings and the ethical project she develops in *This Sex Which Is Not One* and *An Ethics of Sexual Difference*. We can witness the beginning of Irigaray's reconceptualization of the imaginary in *Speculum*, where, as Whitford argues, she interrogates Lacan's use of the mirror and its role in constructing subjectivity (Whitford 1991: 65). Irigaray implicitly confronts Lacan by converting his flat mirror into a speculum, a tactic that enacts her concept of mimicry (repetition – or reflection – with a difference), "*crossing back though the mirror that subtends all speculation*" (Irigaray 1985a: 77). Whitford's point can be usefully extended to consider the specifically historical dimension of Irigaray's rewriting of Lacan's mirror, a revision that reveals her cultivation of a linguistic and historical imaginary.

The speculum, as the *Oxford English Dictionary* records, was integral both to the history of optics, telescope lenses in particular, and to surgery, where in the late sixteenth century it was used initially to dilate the eye and subsequently developed as an instrument designed to examine the concavities of body, especially the mouth and the womb "so that the eye can enter, to see, notably with speculative intent" (Irigaray 1985g: 144). Irigaray's playful activation of the different meanings of "speculum" calls up the word's history, beginning with its Latin etymological roots and diverging into the historical record of its significations, and provides an exemplary instance of her sense of language in general. Words for Irigaray contain a kind of imaginary, a set of cultural associations and a historical past that can be evoked but not regulated. As she reminds us in *Sexes and Genealogies*, analysis liberates the patient's energy through the "creation of language," and puns and etymologies that free "unrealized potential" are forms of linguistic play directly linked to the imaginary (Irigaray 1993d: 157, 161–3). Her etymological pun on speculum thus sets a male oculocentric philosophical genealogy against the "view" from the concavity of the female body, juxtaposing patriarchal vision with literal and historical embodiment, what philosophy must jettison in order to instantiate itself as universalizing discourse. The evocation of etymology replicates in miniature *Speculum*'s structure, which foregrounds history through its inversion of temporality: that it begins with Freud and ends with Plato allows us to see the development of Western culture and philosophy backwards, a defamiliarized and distorted optic. The long sections on Freud and Plato flank the central section with its brief history of philosophy – as if time itself were the mobilizing force in this deconstructive architecture – and dramatize the way the present and recent past function as lenses through which we understand the remote past, "disconcerting," as she puts it, language and the logic of Western thought (Irigaray 1993g: 136–44).

Like Castoriadis, who in his 1964–65 essay "Marxism and Revolutionary Theory"[3] introduced the "imaginary" as a term that expanded Lacan's definition into the social and political realms (Castoriadis 1997: xv), Irigaray uses Freud to challenge Lacanian orthodoxies and widen the social and cultural implications of the imaginary. Castoriadis asserts that Freud's essential contribution consisted in the "discovery of the imaginary element in the psyche – in revealing the most profound dimensions of … the radical imagination" (Castoriadis 1987: 281), and both Irigaray and Castoriadis work to recover the potential in Freud's formulation, unearthing a primordial imaginary that predates Lacan's construction. The radical imagination for Castoriadis has both an individual psychic and a social dimension, and for him, the social is always historical; indeed, he asserts that history "is impossible and inconceivable … outside of … the *radical imaginary*" (Castoriadis 1987: 146). Irigaray's history is analogously derived from the cultural imaginary, not only from linguistic roots and elided contexts that generate the history of Western philosophy, but also from economic structures, the history of science, and the fabric of metaphor they bequeath.

For Irigaray, science means the method of objective inquiry that subtends practices as diverse as physics, linguistics, and psychoanalysis, and her analysis seeks continually to destabilize the certitudes of knowledge on which these sciences rely (Weed 1994: 81). Irigaray draws on the epistemological structures of science, converting them to tropes in a move that Elizabeth Weed sees as homeopathic (Weed 1994: 83), that is, a cure that is based on ingesting minute doses of the pathological agent. Irigaray invokes the Copernican revolution in *Speculum*, for example, arguably *the* fundamental rupture in the history of astronomy and an epistemological crisis that left a powerful imprint on the early modern imagination, in order to fashion an extended conceit about man and his abjuring of matter (Irigaray 1985g: 133–4). We expect her analysis to confirm scientific "truth": because man identifies with – even becomes – the sun in his quest for transcendence and power, woman is characterized by the inert materiality associated with the earth. Irigaray cites Copernican theory first to establish how gender relations are based on supposedly stable scientific paradigms (man as the centre of the universe, woman as the planet orbiting around him), but then she uses the specifics of Copernican theory to unsettle conventional gender hierarchies by emphasizing Copernicus's discovery that the earth moved: in its annual orbit around the sun, in its diurnal rotation on its own axis, and in its motion of declination (Coffin 1958: 68). Woman, far from being a predictable, motionless body tethered to its orbit around the (male) sun, is "restless and unstable," "never exactly the same," "whirling closer or farther from the sun whose rays she captures and sends curving to and fro in turn with her cycles" (Irigaray 1985g: 134). This formulation not only inverts the active/passive male/female binaries and the heliocentric structure of Copernican theory, but it also uses Copernicus's own discoveries of the earth's movements to disrupt the interpretations of these "facts" and the gendered implications based on them. Irigaray's analogy is a catachrestical elaboration, a paradoxical figure almost metaphysical in the elaborateness of its metaphorical dilation. It exposes science to the history of its own uncertainties and changes and undermines science's steady progression towards truth. Irigaray's conversion of science to metaphor interrogates the mechanism by which seemingly objective knowledge supports often unquestioned cultural assumptions, such as analogies of gender. Her gendering of Copernican astronomy calls up Donne's *Anniversaries* or Milton's *Paradise Lost*, revealing the reciprocal complicity between science and the cultural imaginary and illustrating in the process her central project in *To Speak Is Never Neutral*: the "questioning of the language of science, and an investigation into the sexualization of language, and the relation between the two" (Irigaray 2002b: 5).

Elizabeth D. Harvey's essay on John Donne in this volume explores a wide range of such processes, encouraged by Irigaray's work to rethink Donne's poetic practice in light of major epistemological shifts in the fields of medicine and physics. Subtended by the earliest Western philosophers' thinking on the elements and their interactions, Harvey, like Irigaray reading Nietzsche or Heidegger, unfolds the implicate order of the elements, the humoral body, the gendered body in Donne's work. Hewing closely to Empedocles' proposals on elemental motions, Harvey links these with Donne on embodiment, on separation, on union, on the sense of touch, on color, and above all on the passions. Harvey moves between Irigaray's critique of philosophy and science, on the one hand, and Donne's engagement with erotic poetry, physics, and physic, all in order to demonstrate the magnitude and pervasiveness of the link between elemental and emotional. The sweep of Harvey's essay indicates how open Irigaray is to the pre-Enlightenment past, and how often, how complexly even short forms of poetry are traversed by other discourses. For if we find it relatively easy and rewarding to think of shifted discourse, particularly of the sciences, in the large works of Chaucer, say, or Milton, short poetic forms engage these discourses more elusively. This is one reason that William Empson's brilliant work on Donne and science, in "Donne the Space Man," for instance, has always sounded not only bold but peculiar. Given the wide expanse of Harvey's essay and the reading rubrics opened up by Irigaray in her endless passages among multiple discourses, Empson's ways of reading seem prescient.

The association between women and matter that shapes the Copernican analogy is the subject of Jonathan Crewe's essay, which explores one of the most enigmatic of *Speculum*'s chapters, "Une Mère de Glace." Made up entirely of quotations from Plotinus's Sixth Tractate in the *Enneads*, this chapter exemplifies Irigaray's strategy of mimicry or "radical citationality" (Weed 1994: 83), which in turn opens into a vertiginous perspective on the past because, as Crewe argues, Irigaray's ventriloquism recalls Plotinus's own reworkings of Plato. As Irigaray's practice shows, replication reveals difference, and Plotinus's representation of Matter is distinguished from Plato's through prosopopeia, his endowing of apparently inanimate Matter with affect and desire. Crewe's intricate argument develops from Judith Butler's reading of Plato's chora (hypodoche) as a catechresis; the feminized receptacle is a disfiguration because of Plato's refusal to admit the feminine, to acknowledge the *mater* in matter (Butler 1994: 156). Where Butler focuses on Irigaray's miming of Plato as a tactic that exposes what Plato excludes, Crewe reads Plotinus's chora, and Matter itself, as threshold figures that inhabit the boundary between the human and non-human. The hybridity of Plotinian Matter, the union of incommensurable orders, illuminates the idea of the in-between that is central to Irigaray, as Rosi Braidotti's Deleuzian reading in her Afterword clearly shows. Whether in the figure of the shore or coast, the border between fluid and material that Bellamy and Williams examine, the angel that joins corporeal and incorporeal states, which Harvey discusses, or Krier's analysis of the veil as mediator, thresholds and figures of liminality populate Irigaray's theory as images of intervention, communication, and possibility.

Where Plotinus personifies Matter, literally making a face or human form (prosopon-poeien), as Crewe persuasively suggests, Irigaray's conversations with the philosophers she mimes is similarly animating, as if through her quotation and direct address she made dead men speak. Her resuscitations are even more complex than Plotinus's vitalization of Matter, however, because her citations are always at least double, incorporating both the philosopher's voice (and sometimes the ghostly presence of other philosophers to whom he is responding) and her own. The implications of this cohabitation are theorized obliquely by Irigaray in *To Speak Is Never Neutral*, where she discusses the phantasm and verbs. She suggests that the infinitive, a verb form "devoid of any mark of person or number," implying neither subject nor object, has a kind of phantasmatic presence that subtends discourse and that is irreducible to words (Irigaray 2002b: 55, 60). Of particular interest to her is the infinitive "to absorb," which she sees as elucidating the transference and counter-transference dynamic. "Absorb," to suck up or swallow, is a transferential phantasm that summons a variety of verbs associated with eating and being devoured, words that Irigaray contends describe the phantasmatic register of analytic relations.

The idea of incorporation, of ingesting another person, is pivotal to Theresa Krier's essay on Homer's and Virgil's maternal sea-nymphs and their marine homes – epic characters, settings, and episodes that she reads in light of a contrast between the familiar epic theme of mortality and Hannah Arendt's great contrary notion of *natality*. She invokes the mythic origin for *mêtis* – that cunning resourcefulness seen by the ancients as an ideal quality of mind – a narrative recounted by Hesiod and Apollodorus in which Zeus swallows his first wife, Mêtis, who was then pregnant with Athena. The myth juxtaposes male and female pregnancies and births, and mental "conception," suggesting a cultural anxiety about maternal reproductive power, that can in ideal circumstances, Krier argues, be transformed into long-term processes of cultural nurturance that mime pregnancy and birth. Scenes of emergence from watery caves and Odysseus's concealment beneath maternal veils thus take on resonances that Krier reads through Irigaray and Arendt's important theories of natality and becoming. In the placental relation we can see the materiality of the signifying process layered upon the concepts of conscious and unconscious, and perhaps understand why representations of mothers and the relevance of maternal environments slip persistently from the view of interpreters of philosophical, poetic, and narrative texts. Linking the temporality of natality with narrative and with Mêtis (and what she represents in the way of intelligence, thinking, positing projects for a livable future) allows Krier to speculate about why and how Irigaray's own work resists narrative and reduces it when it crosses her path.

Irigaray not only recounts the myth of Mêtis in *Marine Lover* (Irigaray 1991: 150–3), she also performs it. If absorption or incorporation is her metaphor for transference relations in the analytic context, it also informs her bonds with the philosophers she engages in dialogue. *Marine Lover* begins with an extended apostrophe to Nietzsche, a philosophical and poetic address that is intensely intimate, as if Irigaray were, or had been, inside Nietzsche: "I was merely the drum in your own ear sending back to itself its own truth." "I am your hearing. Between you and yourself, I ensure the vocal medium. A perpetual relay between your mouth and your ear." "You fold the membrane between us in your own way. ... The membrane was not yours to have. We formed it together." "But [I] no longer wish to return into you. As soon as I am inside, you will vomit me up again" (Irigaray 1991: 3, 7, 12). In Irigaray's subsequent discussions of Apollo, she makes Mêtis a foundational myth for Western culture:

> Just as Zeus swallows Mêtis the fluid daughter of the man and woman of the sea so as to give birth to Athena, his thought, so Apollo takes into and upon himself the mirror that is his sister so that he can give birth to the dream of beauty ...
>
> (Irigaray 1991: 153)

The notion of incorporation informs Irigaray's discursive and therapeutic swallowing of Nietzsche, a process of absorption through which she produces thought. As Krier's deft analysis of Homer and Virgil through Irigaray shows, this internalizing movement implicates pregnancy and childbirth, but it also operates in a metaphoric register to designate the complex mental operations that bring psyches and mind into the fullness of their becoming.

Incorporation is sometimes signaled in Irigaray's writing through references to skin, both as the membrane that bounds the body, rendering it integral, and through breaches in its layers, which frequently figure communication. In *Marine Lover*, Irigaray fastens on the twinship of Apollo and Artemis as an image of a unity that contains two singularities, just as her writings on the placenta argue for a union that does not obliterate difference, but rather joins the separate maternal and fetal skins. Artemis's "glory," she says, "will always consist in bringing children into the world, bringing each one into his own skin." But because "she endlessly gives their/her skin to others, leads them to wrap themselves in their/her appearing, irrevocably, Artemis will lack a skin" (Irigaray 1991: 153). Artemis, a hybrid of the sort that Crewe theorizes, wears borrowed animal skins, and thus subsists "between the animal and the divine kingdoms," an intermediary between beast, human, and divine, and a patron of that most liminal act, childbirth.

Irigaray's sense of skin derives in part from Freud's notion of a bodily ego, an idea that Didier Anzieu elaborates in *Le moi-peau* (*The Skin Ego*). Anzieu's theory of the body as bounded by a "skin envelope" meshes well with Irigaray's own sense of the skin's ability to establish a limit and a human identity. In her chapter on Dionysus, she says of this hybrid "man-god" – who is twice born because his mother, Semele, is killed by a thunderbolt, and he is then sewn into Zeus's thigh until he ready to be delivered – that as a god, he "lacks boundaries, limits – a skin." She characterizes him as the "god of desire," who will "have place everywhere and nowhere, inhabiting nothing" (Irigaray 1991: 123). This formulation echoes the early modern representation of the sense of touch, which is both ubiquitous and lodged in no single place, since tactility is for Irigaray both linked to the mother, as it is for Anzieu, and to the skin, a tactile anchoring that Dionysius is denied because he is not of woman born: "Deliverance by a woman in labour is a thing unknown to this hybrid infant. ... And the doubling of their bodies, the difference in their boundaries – the coming into appearance in one's own skin" (Irigaray 1991: 123). The instantiation of human subjectivity is irretrievably linked to the mother's touch, a connection that is permanently inscribed on the skin and harbored in the faculty of touch, and Irigaray repeatedly returns to this sense as the foundation of her ethics.

Amy Hollywood's essay treats the breaching of the skin envelope in another hybrid, part-man, part-god, figure: Christ. When Irigaray mimes Angela of

Foligno in "La Mystérique" section of *Speculum*, she also necessarily calls up the whole tradition of reverencing the piercing of Christ's side that Angela herself drew on, as if a wound or passage into earlier discourses had been opened. Indeed, George Herbert's invocation of this tradition in his poem "The Bag" makes the laceration a kind of bag or mail pouch, a receptacle for messages that Christ will carry to his father's "hand and sight," an image of mediation between human and divine registers (Herbert 1974: 160). Irigaray's reading of the incision in Christ's side is, like her reading of Descartes, double; her engagement in *Speculum* is augmented by her return to the vulnerable Christ figure in *Marine Lover*. As Hollywood points out, Irigaray's understanding of the wound in both texts is shaped by her desire to interrogate Lacan's designation of woman as lack, a categorization that situates women within the inextricable logic of castration. In refusing to valorize Christ's laceration, with all the vulvic/vaginal resonances that the illustrations and textual descriptions elicit, Irigaray privileges what Judith Butler calls an "eros of surfaces," an erotics that eschews the penetrability that sustains the heterosexual matrix. Hollywood argues that Irigaray forecloses on the radical ways in which Christ's feminization in medieval texts destabilizes the conventional gendering of penetrating and penetrated bodies. She suggests that the chain of reasoning that associates the masculine with penetration, containment, and plenitude and the feminine with being penetrated, fluidity, and lack is disrupted by medieval depictions of Christ's bleeding, pierced body, its ability to nourish or offer refuge in the clefts of its wounds, and the erotic implications of sucking the aperture in Christ's side. Hollywood's claim may indeed allow us to apprehend not only medieval depictions but also such texts as Aemelia Lanyer's blazoning of Christ's crucified body in *Salve Deus Rex Judaeorum* in new ways. Yet we must not be too quick to dismiss Irigaray's subtly pervasive challenges to philosophical and psychoanalytic paradigms, for as both Hollywood and Butler acknowledge, Irigaray's radical reading practices, her infiltration of other texts, and her notions of incorporation also suggest that she is continually redefining and disrupting how we think of the body's boundaries, what we mean by an inside and an outside, and what defines gender.

The body is, of course, one of Irigaray's great tropes, one reason for the enormous appeal she holds for scholars of premodern culture. For Irigaray, the body is always a historical and metaphorical body, which is not to say that it is not also a physical body, but it is not, as was charged by her first feminist readers, an essentialized body. Bourdieu's notion of the *habitus* supplies a useful way of understanding her sense of corporeality:

> The *habitus* – embodied history, internalized as second nature and so forgotten as history – is the active presence of the whole past of which it is the product. As such, it is what gives practices their relative autonomy with respect to external determinations of the immediate present. This autonomy is that of the past, enacted and enacting, which, functioning as accumulated capital, produces history on the basis of history, and so ensures the permanence in

change that makes the individual agent a world with the world. The *habitus* is a spontaneity without consciousness or will ...

(Bourdieu 1990: 56)

If the *habitus* is a set of bodily dispositions or practices that have become objectified or naturalized over time, an incorporation of somatic history, then these habits will continue to reproduce themselves until they and the mechanism of their transmission are questioned. Irigaray's critique of Freud and the logic of sameness and her interrogation of Lacan's idea of lack as human impotence displaced onto femininity rely on paradigms of Western thought that do not, of course, originate with Freud. Indeed, the same charges that Irigaray levels against Freud could also be employed to question the predominance of the Galenic model in the early modern period. Galen's homology, which saw the female body as isomorphically identical to the male body except that female reproductive organs were retained inside the body instead of being extruded, relies, as Freud's does, on vision, and its effects are apparent in the hierarchical privileging of the male body, a subordination of the female body to the form and function of the masculine paradigm. Galen's ideas subtend Freud's, an enactment of a cultural *habitus* that continues to shape our understanding in phantasmatic and explicit ways.

Irigaray's tactic in *Speculum* and *This Sex Which Is Not One* is to fashion a new imaginary through apprehending the body and its tropes differently, a project that she performs in the famously outrageous lyrical text, "When Our Lips Speak Together." Ann Rosalind Jones provides an important theoretical and historical context for a new understanding of this widely debated and influential essay by reading it in relation to Irigaray's engagement with Marxist theory in the two preceding chapters of *This Sex*, "Women On the Market," and "Commodities Among Themselves." She argues that the three essays can be read as a kind of suite, moving from a critique of patriarchy's commodification of women to utopian remedy. Whereas economic systems collude with symbolic and psychoanalytic interpretations of femininity to make women exchangeable commodities who circulate in order to sustain male privilege but who never have sexual value outside of the economic or reproductive cycle, "When Our Lips Speak Together" seeks to imagine a sexuality and a language outside of the restrictive, obliterating commodity culture. The movement from Marxist critique to a lyrical imaginary is reproduced in Jones's insightful analysis of the French sixteenth-century vogue of blazoning the female body, a practice that not only partitioned and commodified the female body, but became a medium for rivalry and male display. Jones suggests that these fashionable poems were countered by a female-authored dialogue, which, like Irigaray's "When Our Lips," takes female erotic pleasure and female speaking as coextensive.

DIRECT ADDRESS: IRIGARAY AND READING PRACTICES

Through her own revisionary reading and in much of her explicit theorizing, Irigaray brings to light practices and protocols of reading that may begin in, but resonate well beyond, feminist adversarial readings against the grain.[4] Reading is more complex than ideas about it in any one period; Irigaray's work suggests to us how the readerly psyche acts with processes that psychoanalysis has identified with the dream work and unconscious processes more broadly: free association, condensation, dissemination, substitution, projection, introjection, negation, destruction, generation. ... These processes of reading – and writing in response to reading – occur not only in specific authors and readers, who are often of most interest to literary scholars, but also in whole discourses, which are of most interest to Irigaray. Thus in *This Sex* she argues,

> This process of interpretive rereading has always been a *psychoanalytic undertaking* as well. That is why we need to pay attention to the way the unconscious works in each philosophy, and perhaps philosophy in general. We need to listen (psycho)analytically to its procedures of repression, to the structuration of language that shores up its representations ... What is called for ... is an examination of the *operations of the 'grammar'* of each figure of discourse, its syntactic laws or requirements, its imaginary configurations, its metaphoric networks, and also, of course, what it does not articulate at the level of utterance: *its silences*.
>
> (Irigaray 1985a: 75)

In the more than three decades since Irigaray first wrote these words, readers have of course done just this kind of reading of what remains unsaid in discourses, with vigor, anger, challenge. Here, meditating on the essays in this collection, we emphasize how much new creation and generativity emerge from the most negating of readings. Reading is a combination of actions at once social, isolate, explicit, tacit, conscious, preconscious, and unconscious, all in constant mobility. Moreover the liveliness of reading processes involves, paradoxically, both life drives and death drives. The binding or activating of many threads of cognition and affect in a moment of reading will give way to unbinding, release, the yielding of conscious to unconscious recombinations of the text's "psychic intensities," to borrow Freud's phrase from *The Interpretation of Dreams*. Freud also contributes the notions of binding and unbinding, which we use here, in his discussion of the death drive, in *Beyond the Pleasure Principle* (Whitford 1994: 390–5). Irigaray herself, provoked by psychoanalysts' ways with the death drive, accuses them of being in thrall to it and links it and the life instincts to writing and narrative: insofar as the death drive involves a repetition compulsion, the death drive is evident in Freud's and Lacan's "telling the same story over and over again" (Irigaray 1985a: 115). Irigaray's own long-term reading of certain philosophers with relentless inversions and reversals, reading for their inevitable burying and forgetfulness of their debt to the feminine, can sound suspiciously like telling the same story over and over again. Yet even repetition and the death drive she can revise to make manifest the drive toward life that fuels them:

> Would *repetition compulsion* not be that which remains of an insistent left-behind? And the death at work there, does it not really mean that it/the id [*ça*] is still, and always, repeated, or that it/the id is still, and always, trapped in the mirror-surface of a present, leaving life drives left-over, or behind?
>
> (Irigaray 2002b: 202)

Irigaray's shake-up of the relations between life and death drives opens up ways of thinking about the works that Grant Williams engages in his essay for this volume. Blazons, those poetic and visual inventories of a lady's beauties which Renaissance poets deploy repeatedly even when they recognize the exhaustions of the form, commodify, dismember, depersonalize the lady, as Ann Jones's essay also makes clear. Critiquing this impulse in blazon is the aim of the influential array of recent gender scholarship that Williams surveys; we suggest that the blazon gives offense now, as it roused skepticism and concern in major Renaissance poets, precisely because its form devitalizes the very lady for whom it expresses desire. Is this desire a drive toward life or toward death, then? But Williams also shows that the Renaissance blazon allows, and sometimes achieves, a different relation to the desired object. Far from pursuing a death drive through repetition, the blazon *may* mark a male subject's encounter with feminine alterity, and release him into a condition of wonder; it proceeds not by the repetition compulsion, always naming and seeking the self-same, but by a rhetorical defamiliarization of the beloved and acknowledgment of otherness – impulses that free the life drives for unpredictable encounters.

One point we take from Irigaray's complex recurrences to the death drive and the repetition compulsion is that she allows us to explore how the work and pleasure and life instincts of reading involve something like a death drive, which has its own exhilarations and even its own drive toward life. So, on the one hand, Irigaray notes the alienation of the subject's entry into language: "We will be the void, the blank, the place of exclusion permitting the functioning of combinations, articulations, and differences, as well as network, bundle, sedimentation of differences" (2002b: 103). On the other hand, a few sentences later she starts a new paragraph by listening to herself differently or showing that she's been entertaining a notion, not owning it: "One might, no doubt, understand castration in that way." The fact is, rather, that in psychoanalysis, in reading, in seeking meaning,

> we resist explosion, fragmentation, nothingness, death. Animality, the body … loathe ex-centricity and spatial and temporal dispersion. They continue always to strive toward restoration at some center, which can happen only when an original, or a supplemental, unity, whether it is called return, reappropriation,

communion, narcissistic delegation, or jouissance, is projected as an end. Those are some of the other names of the object of desire that will (a)rouse us as speaking subjects ... and engaging us in some impossible communication with the other.

(Irigaray 2002b: 103–4)

Irigaray's reading practices are nothing if not strenuous, and she insists on the reader's constant, active presence. The locution "engaging with Irigaray" has become a topos since the wonderful essay collection of that title; we might think of the energetic range of connotations of "*engagé*" in French, and to think of readers as moving freely among psychic activities not only of absorption but also of challenge, wrestling, provoking, and even courting. As early as *Speculum*, she calls for reading actions by "woman" which in their energy, exhilaration, violence expand the possibilities of resistance:

Turn everything upside down, inside out, back to front. *Rack it with radical convulsions*, carry back, reimport, those crises that her "body" suffers in her impotence to say what disturbs her. Insist also and deliberately upon those *blanks* in discourse which recall the places of her exclusion and which, by their *silent plasticity*, ensure the cohesion, the articulation, the coherent expansion of established forms. Reinscribe them hither and thither *as divergencies*, otherwise and elsewhere than they are expected, in *ellipses* and *eclipses* that deconstruct the logical grid of the reader-writer, drive him out of his mind, trouble his vision to the point of incurable diplopia at least. *Overthrow syntax* by suspending its eternally teleological order, by snipping the wires, cutting the current, breaking the circuits, switching the connections, by modifying continuity, alternation, frequency, intensity. Make it impossible for a while to predict whence, whither, when, how, why.

(Irigaray 1985g: 142)

This manifesto about gender, voice, and agency argues readerly actions that extend beyond questions of gender, and allow literary scholars to extend the scope of our thinking about readerly reception. Irigaray begins "The Rape of the Letter," one of her most sustained arguments about reading and writing processes, with the bold claim:

To read a text is to fold it into a foreign network, to expatriate, dispossess, and disapppropriate it. Even if the reader were nothing more than a blank page exposed to the text's writing, she or he would already be defined topologically, already inscribed, if not in black and white, then at least in relief. ... There is no reading or writing that is not subversion. Furthermore, the text's imprint or writing, even unaware and unwilling, can operate indiscriminately because it does not convey, but rather *produces*.

(Irigaray 2002b: 121)

We teach our students protocols of literary or philosophical or critical interpretation, and rightly so, even when we know that these change over time; tracing the history of interpretive protocols in our various disciplines is one of the core ways of doing a discipline. But we also know that reading has freedoms and surprises outside our protocols:

> For whoever has entered into articulation, there are no landmarks or road signs indicating a straight pathway, no rest stops along the way that would allow him or her to assume that the development could one day be surveyed, recapitulated, summed up in some unity.
>
> (Irigaray 2002b: 127)

This possibility of surprise is one of the reasons that scholars value interdisciplinarity, hard as it is to do well. The contributors to this volume, all based in specific disciplines, try to listen for the surprises of their texts, paradoxically to listen vigorously – to discern a new future in old, well-known texts, even those texts against which we have railed for their blindnesses. None of these processes of reading is intrinsically irresponsible to history. Indeed such practices open up a history richer and, paradoxically, more unpredictable (a temporal reversal that Irigaray would appreciate) than any one discipline, discourse, or reader can imagine.

Even within the traditions of a single discipline – literary history, say – there is room for surprise, as Elizabeth Jane Bellamy's essay on the poet's work of transforming past poems into new futures demonstrates. Her meditation on Edmund Spenser's narrative of the knight Marinell, child of a sea-nymph, dweller on a seacoast, in light of Irigaray's "When the Gods Are Born" from *Marine Lover*, generates the notion of a coastal unconscious revealing Spenser to be a creative forgetter of a crucial precursor poet. Marinell has long been read in relation to his pampering sea-nymph mother as a mama's boy who, entering her oceanic element, gets to regress to uterine passivity. But Bellamy begins with the surprisingly apt observation that Marinell never in fact seems other than ill at ease in and around water. She turns her attention to a poetic history richer, more unpredictable and riddled with gaps, suppressions, and forgetfulness than we have yet imagined, arguing that Spenser deploys a gothic seacoast style borrowed from Ariosto while excluding (misreading? repressing?) Ariosto's tightly controlled expulsion of the Mediterranean coasts of the Sannazaran marine eclogue. Thus, Spenser's Faerie "strond," listened to for its unspoken, becomes the Irigarayan child-god's least prosperous of islands; and Marinell uncannily anticipates her disaligned coastal child-god as a foreigner in all parts.

Listening is a complex enterprise for Irigaray, and readers in literary and philosophical disciplines can afford to profit from at least two aspects of psychoanalysis. First, the clinical psychoanalytic setting, Irigaray argues in "The Utterance in Analysis," "can be a technique for subverting the utterance" (2002b: 95). *There is always a listener*, though the listener, unlike the clinician, speaks in response. Reading is always a conversation, a charged and often sparring conversation. The expressiveness of the listener (not only the presence of the listener, as in reader-response criticism) is a capacity or a subject position for which scholars of literature and philosophy and historians of ideas have not often made room; once we say this, it strikes us as odd that we haven't made room, since it's a space that we ourselves inhabit. We can think of hardly a paragraph in which Irigaray is not at pains to create that space, or to create the persona of an expressive, expert reader; reading is exchange between such expressive positions – "Don't you think so? Listen" (Irigaray 1985a: 205; see Harvey 1992/95: 136–9). The reader posited as a woman refuses to be deprived of speech and articulate thought.

Again, with his characteristic attunement to the debate of discourses within individual works, Harry Berger, Jr. argues in this book that misogyny masks the deeper anxiety of gynephobia. Through his appropriative deployment of Irigaray's thesis about the "hom(m)osexual monopoly" of patriarchy, in which "women, signs, commodities, and currency always pass from one man to another" (Irigaray 1985a: 171, 192), Berger stages a densely populated conversation among readers and writers, juxtaposing the strong objections by others that Irigaray's is an ahistorical, universalizing, totalizing view, with his own awareness that she rather mounts a critique of a specific critical discourse, namely modern social theory's model of precapitalist social formation. By persisting in her engagement with, say, Marx, Weber, Lévi-Strauss, Malinowski, Mauss, Irigaray makes manifest the ideological fantasy – the imaginary – underlying social theory, as well as the vertiginous, productive pleasures of revealing hidden and unconscious motives of entire discourses. Berger's layering of voices includes none from premodern periods, but provides a rich array of positions from which to read, in specific texts, for critiques of discourse, for the structural unconscious, for what is there but not said.

The constant, active presence of the expressive listener keeps our attention on the *event* – or to put it more strongly with one of Irigaray's favoured words, the *advent* – of exchange between reader and writer. This advent constantly modulates and varies, as the tenor of the exchange varies. Sometimes the stake of the exchange is winning:

> In the processes of language, and not only just in language, are affirmed the intention and the desire, to *master* between games, cause of all liaisons, copulations, associations, accords, combinations, groupings, etc. To get the better of them through manipulations, multiplications (and also divisions, and other calculations and operations), spacings, intervals, separations
>
> (Irigaray 2002b: 134)

But equally, reading might be experienced not as mastering an object of study, or invading or penetrating it that it might yield its secrets – major concerns of early modern epistemology and sciences – but as nearing a person, and not a person speaking into a void but a person attending to the listener. "Is it not because I do not know you that I know that you are?" she asks in *To Be Two*.

> Only love consents to a night in which I will never know you. Between those who love each other, there is a veil. ... Does such a night correspond to blind faith or to respect for the one I will never know? Is it not this unknown which allows us to remain two?
>
> (2001b: 9).

We suspect that much of what Irigaray's later work posits as ideal relations between the two of the couple actually originates in her earliest, longest-lasting, radical reading practices, the model for a relationship of intensity and wonder which allows for nearing the unknown of a person, as a mode of knowledge. This would be knowledge based on the premise that writings we've known and studied for a long time enfold or conceal within them much that we may know but haven't yet been able to think. From very early on, her figures for love between two are also figures for reading: "Between our lips, yours and mine, several voices, several ways of speaking resound endlessly, back and forth" (Irigaray 1985a: 209).

The second aspect of the psychoanalytic setting informing the reading position that Irigaray expands is that the clinician listens for what is not said, and does so with knowledge of a wide repertoire of the ways that the unsaid can signify:

> there was something taking place in this discourse that was, in spite of the patient, worth listening to – its emptying. Because itterance of utterance – retelling oneself, retelling the other – hems in if taken up as text, but reopens and empties out, if received by another ear ... [Then] some act, different from avoidance or emptying, is shaping up, and some other is taking shape. The point is that the patient perceives the place where she or he is called, sought, denied as other. ... he or she discovers his or her right to be implicated in [the inquiry]
>
> (Irigaray 2002b: 96, 98).

These psychic actions of the patient, as well as the actions of the clinician who listens, model reading for Irigaray, and the emptying of which she speaks is not only like the repressions of discourse but also like temporal intervals and formal spaces in written and literary texts.

Many kinds of readerly and writerly expressiveness go on in such gaps and spaces. Literary scholars might put more pressure, for example, on formal intervals: caesurae, spaces between lines and stanzas, between cantos, between chapters, and on temporal gaps, breaks, and tempi. The texts we study in this book are both filled with and/or emptied by what Irigaray enumerates as "always retraced frameworks, spaces, spacings, intervals." Irigaray is often suspicious of formal breaks and their temporal impositions on readers, hence also suspicious of narrative: "Time is cut up, over and over again, and lost in all kinds of caesuras and scansions that will be forced to toe the party line by deceptive plays of relationships" (Irigaray 1985g: 290). Yet she also makes room for the bold reader, who can break into and generate new forms in the music of what happens in narrative, poetry, drama. "Their regularity, stereotypicality, coding and privileges are susceptible to innumerable remanipulations, deviations, detours, angles, biases, transgressions, subversions, stories. If one risks it" (Irigaray 2002b: 134). Narrative may itself be a way for the unconscious to engage or become conscious of temporality. Such a notion may provide leads to understanding packed, enigmatic passages like Irigaray's call for the analysis of space and time in creation myths:

> In the beginning there was space and the creation of space, it is said in all theogonies. The gods, God, first create *space*. And time is there, more or less in the service of space. On the first day, the first days, the gods, God, make a world by separating the elements. This world is then peopled, and a rhythm is established among its inhabitants. God would be time itself, lavishing or exteriorizing itself in its action in space, in places.
>
> Philosophy then confirms the genealogy of the task of the gods or God. Time becomes the *interiority* of the subject itself, and space, its *exteriority* ... The subject, the master of time, becomes the axis of the world's ordering ... He effects the passage between time and space.
>
> Which would be inverted in sexual difference? Where the feminine is experienced as space, but often with connotations of the abyss and night ... while the masculine is experienced as time.
>
> (Irigaray 1993e: 7)

But if it is *time* which is the unthought known, the unexamined, the interior or the concealed, then perhaps articulating the peculiarities of narrative temporality would make manifest or unfold energizing ways in which the feminine is associated not only with space but with time. Certainly this book's essays on temporality in Homer, Virgil, Spenser, and Shakespeare allow us to think so. Barbara Estrin's essay here on *Othello*, for instance, reads both Desdemona and Othello for the respective modes of temporality they inhabit, and finds Desdemona's the more complex and mobile. If Irigaray's own linkage of the masculine with dramatic catastrophe – a predetermined path to temporal finality – risks sounding alarmingly essentialist and increases her resistance to drama as a form, Estrin demonstrates how catastrophe may be a property of Shakespearean tragic masculinity, not of masculine subjectivity generally. And if philosophical discourse has, according to Irigaray, relegated the feminine to an association with space and denied her an association with time, Estrin reveals the surprising hope that Desdemona might bring to readers and viewers, insofar as she discovers the temporality implicit in rhetoric's figures of temporal reversal and mobility. Especially in the great willow song exchanges, Desdemona discovers the strengths of her shuttling among past, present, and future, weaving a new cultural elaboration.

It is not only psychoanalysis or Derrida that allows Irigaray to read for the unspoken; she draws this practice as well from the pre-Socratics and from Heidegger, who makes much of revealing and concealing. Irigaray beautifully and surprisingly transforms many objects, chief among them the placenta, angels, and the curtain in Freud's account of the *fort-da* game, into veils. As Irigaray's meditations on the placental imply, the veil, as Krier's essay shows, functions as a linkage of language and the material. The veil also figures whatever lies between conscious and unconscious reading process, or for the to-and-fro passage between conscious and unconscious, the endlessly fascinating movements of revealing and concealing. The veil becomes a figure for the readerly process of unfolding and making manifest that which has remained implicit, invisible, even unthought in a passage – which suggests that many premodern allegorical works, especially those vivified by indomitable personifications of Nature, discover a new and transformative member of their genre in Irigaray's works. We are reminded of Jorie Graham's lines and blank spaces from her poem in *Swarm* on Calypso, Odysseus, the sea, the veil, "Underneath (Calypso):" "What must be inferred under/the blemished mantling shimmers" (Graham 2000: 42). So the complex Irigarayan figure of the veil unfolds ways to think about all reading as revisionist thinking. For Irigaray, the placental "veil" participates in the literal creation of the formative unconscious; in the placental relation we can see the materiality of the signifying process layered upon the concepts of conscious and unconscious.

In the enigmatic and beautiful passage that we use as an epigraph to this Introduction, Lacan proposes that psychoanalysis shakes up the chronology of the patient's narrative, disconcerts the logic of tenses. As Harry Berger, Jr. glosses this idea in an essay on Shakespeare called "The Fight for the Future Perfect," in psychoanalysis:

> the future perfect is the tense of *undoing*, not only the pathological negation of the past Freud isolated as an obsessional symptom ... but also its homeo-pathic antidote, the undoing that occurs during the process of analysis ('If I believe this story, then I will have been other than I was, or thought I was').
>
> (Berger 1989: 121)

This future anterior, negotiating between past and present, past and future, is less a tense than a daimonic energy, negating with the sometimes ferocious, some-times mischievous destructiveness of daimons like Eros or Hermes. But like those intermediaries between heaven and earth – or Artemis, or the Irigarayan angel, or the Spirit in Christian theology – the future anterior also generates new pasts by transforming our protocols of interpretation of past documents. Thus Rosi Braidotti's Afterword to our volume calls for a "nomadic itinerary" crucial to the creativity of theory, and she starts to imagine the future for which the volume's earlier essays have proposed new anteriors, by surveying our own time and the changes that it heralds. Like Irigaray, Braidotti carries "the aporia of deconstruc-tion" into affirmative gestures at once intellectual, activist, affective, and speaks for the hopeful possibilities of an affirmative, vitalist materialism outside the binaries of phallogocentrism. The creativity of the psychoanalytic, Irigarayan look to the past is like the generativity of Lacan's future anterior as Catherine Clément buoyantly describes it:

> But it is true that the locution "I will have been," oddly twisted as it is, con-tains seeds of the future that one finds retroactively. It is a memory curious

about its own future. A memory with a gift for science fiction, which refuses simply to repeat the old saw, "once upon a time," over and over again. Everything is different if we say, "It will have come to pass ...". The fairy, whether good or bad, wins in advance: the story is already sketched out, but it changes as it is being told. As if nothing had happened, the future anterior alters history: it is the miraculous tense.

(Clément 1983: 123)

We hope that readers of this volume, and the writers we study in it, will be glad – will have been glad – to say that new discourses, metaphors, narratives, readings will have come to pass.

Notes

1 See Berry (1994), Mueller (1993), Hollywood (2002), Parker (1987), Meakin (1998), Corthell (1997), Krier (2001, 2003), Harvey (1992/1995).
2 See Whitford's enumeration of these influences (1991: 53–70). One source for Irigaray's reconceptualization is phenomenology, which allows her to move fluently between the psychoanalytic idea of the unconscious and the social and poetic products of the imagination, to examine, in other words, the traffic between volitional acts of fantasy and a prediscursive substratum to which we have incomplete access. Whitford suggests that Bachelard, particularly his work on the elements, furnished an elemental vocabulary that allowed Irigaray to write about the passions, the affective dimensions of our being and the way pathos interacts with systems of knowledge. These two sources converge with a third, the confluence of psychoanalytic and political theory in the writings of Althusser and Castoriadis.
3 This essay became the first part of *The Imaginary Institution of Society*.
4 In this section our thinking is informed by writers like Freud on dreamwork and on the death drive (1900, 1920), Christopher Bollas on the unconscious and free association (1987, 1995), Stanley Cavell on women in film (1981, 1996), Heidegger on thinking (1954, 1959), Angus Fletcher (1991) and Gordon Teskey (2003) on thinking in poetry, Ross Chambers on reading (1991).

2 Mère marine

Narrative and natality in Homer and Virgil

Theresa Krier

> Why should the exile   return home?
> Era?   Period?
> Discover: Calypso has shuffled the deck.
> Has veiled the early with the late.
> Has veiled sequence.
>
> Jorie Graham (2000)

The last narrative episode in Virgil's great four-book philosophical poem the
Georgics recounts how Aristaeus the shepherd, who has lost his precious bees to
sickness, calls on his sea-nymph mother Cyrene, in her home beneath the ocean,
in a lament that includes long complaint against her for having brought him into
the world:

> "mater, Cyrene mater, quae gurgitis huius
> ima tenes, quid me praeclara stirpe deorum
> (si modo, quem perhibes, pater est Thymbraeus Apollo)
> invisum fatis genuisti? aut quo tibi nostri
> pulsus amor? …
> en etiam hunc ipsum vitae mortalis honorem …
>   … te matre relinquo.
> quin age et ipsa manu felicis erue silvas,
> fer stabulis inimicum ignem atque interfice messis,
> ure sata et validam in vitis molire bipennem,
>   tanta meae si te ceperunt taedia laudis."
>
> (*Georgics* IV.321–32)

["O mother, mother Cyrene, that dwellest in this flood's depths, why, from
the gods' glorious line – if indeed, as thou sayest, Thymbraean Apollo is my
father – didst thou give me birth, to be hated of the fates? Or whither is thy
love for me banished? … Lo, even this very crown of my mortal life …
though thou art my mother, I resign. Nay, come, and with thine own hand tear
up my fruitful woods; lay the hostile flame to my stalls, destroy my crops,
burn my seedlings, and swing the stout axe against my vines, if such loathing
for my honour hath seized thee."][1]

Cyrene and her sister nymphs, spinning while listening to narratives sung by one of their number about the gods and their loves, hear Aristaeus' outcry, and open their waters to him. He enters their marine realm, where they feast and comfort him; then Cyrene instructs him how to find, seize, and wrest an explanation of his trials from the sea-god, shape-shifter, and seer Proteus. When he achieves this heroic task and Proteus does speak, it is to tell Aristaeus that he himself is the cause of the bees' destruction: Aristaeus had pursued Eurydice, who while fleeing him had stumbled upon and been bitten by a venomous snake; this was the cause of her death, which caused Orpheus all that pain to seek her in the underworld. Orpheus, raging, has evoked vengeance against Aristaeus. When Proteus plunges back into the deep sea, Cyrene takes over, revising a crucial detail of Proteus' account.

> "nate, licet tristis animo deponere curas.
> haec omnis morbi causa, hinc miserabile Nymphae,
> cum quibus illa choros lucis agitabat in altis,
> exitium misere apibus."

(IV.531–4)

> ["My son, thou mayest lay aside thy heart's sorrow and care. This is the whole cause of the sickness; hence it is that the Nymphs, with whom she was wont to tread the dance in the deep groves, sent this sore havoc on thy bees."]

Cyrene has scant interest in Orpheus, and her proposed ritual focuses on propitiating the nymphs, Eurydice's friends who have suffered a loss and to whom Aristaeus owes something, with ritual sacrifice. Only then does Cyrene speak of Eurydice herself, and only after that of Orpheus. When Aristaeus carries out her instructions, promptly and correctly as he always does, a miracle happens: from the rotting flesh of sacrificed cattle, swarms of bees emerge, earnest of future hives' flourishing, of the wax and honey by which bees figure agricultural bounty.

In this essay I read Virgil's episode in light of the Homeric episodes to which Virgil pays homage: the *Odyssey*'s tale of the encounter between Proteus and Menelaos, made possible by the instruction of the nymph Eidothea (Book IV); Ino's aid to the sea-soaked Odysseus in Book V; the *Iliad*'s meetings between Achilles and his sea-nymph mother Thetis, who educates him in his stance toward his own mortality (Books I and XVIII). In the process I want to engage two problems that emerge among readers of ancient texts involving representations of the feminine-maternal, and offer alternatives to them.

The first problem is specific to classicists who study Virgil's poetry and have remained uninfluenced by any feminist kind of reading, much less an Irigarayan one. As a consequence they simply do not ask the right questions, and do not imagine how details of a narrative about gender might signify. The *Georgics* belongs to a great tradition of poetry on natural philosophy, which always involves issues of origins and endings, matter and first matter, birth, maternity and paternity, and the movement toward death; this kind of poetry is laced with allusions to earlier poets

– including Homer – understood as allegorists of nature, their work understood as exemplars of natural bounty.[2] One would think that a long tale of maternity, a maternal realm of waters and caverns, sacrifice and mortality, would arouse intense questions about gender. But it does not. Commentators focus much more on Proteus' inset narrative of Orpheus and Eurydice, in part because they find the Aristaeus/Cyrene story odd and that of Orpheus familiar, in part because they can marginalize the tale of the nymph and her son as a framing device for the presumptively more important tale of Orpheus. Traditional literary criticism from classicists has been almost entirely helpless to attribute significance to Cyrene. In a construction that sounds illogical to a reader of Irigaray, R. A. B. Mynors says in his commentary that Cyrene "is no more than an essential intermediary in the story" (301); Farrell's superb discussion marks her only insofar as she "introduces an episode of allegorical cosmogony" (270). As Andrew Wallace shows in an elegant essay, the marginalization of Cyrene, which begins with Ovid's *Fasti* (ca. 8 CE), continues into sixteenth-century editions of Virgil's work; she puzzles even modern editors.[3]

The second problem arises within feminist criticism, insofar as it follows one version of Irigaray's critique of phallogocentric discourses for their unconscious disavowals of the mother. Of course a narrative about a mother who dwells in the sea and a son's recourse to her for aid virtually summons some interpretation along Irigarayan lines, so perfectly does it match Irigaray's own favorite topoi. It would be possible to adduce from Irigaray's work principles for criticizing myth's forging of links between maternity and death. As she scolds Nietzsche in *Marine Lover*, "If birth amounts to a beginning of death, why drag out the agony? ... 'Heavy is life,' you go around telling anyone willing to listen. ... If the taste of eternal life eternally haunts you, why prolong this passage through death?" (Irigaray 1991: 23). In a related vein Sheila Murnaghan (1992) surveys Archaic Age poetic works – Homer, Hesiod, the *Homeric Hymns* – to argue for a pattern of an "unequal and unsought bargain by which women, by virtue of their capacity for motherhood, are assigned a disproportionate share in bearing the burden of mortality."[4] Women characters and feminized elements like earth or sea, Murnaghan argues, carry a burden not only in giving birth but in anticipating, then having to mourn, the deaths of their own offspring; in speaking of death to their children; above all in bearing responsibility for the mortality of those whom they birth. This is such a pervasive cluster of myths about the feminine, running through all early periods of Western literatures, that it might well seem to adumbrate an inevitable relationship between the maternal and death.[5] It is true, as I've argued elsewhere, that the allure of the maternal, desire for the mother as well as fear of her, is strong and seemingly constant in Western cultures; we face a constant challenge to recognize and transform this nostalgia into something that liberates rather than imprisons. Thus Adriana Cavarero, among others, uses Penelope, Demeter, and other figures from ancient myth to make good on what Irigaray tirelessly argues is the symbolic debt owed the mother, and to think out how mythopoeic representatives of the maternal-feminine enable strong alternatives to the idea of a phallogocentric symbolic order.[6] But poets too, among them

Homer and Virgil, also carry out this critique of a nostalgia for the maternal. Poets do not simply transmit benighted narrative motifs and figures, but interpret, transform, invent new ways of taking old representations. Murnaghan is not much interested in these transformations, and neither is Irigaray.

Some passages in Irigaray's own work, written in rhetorical circumstances that called for strong polemical positions and building on her own rigorous and exhaustive earlier readings of the philosophers, continue to sponsor feminist literary critics' indictments of texts, and perhaps lead to Irigaray's own, problematic dualisms. Thus in the 1984 essay "Divine Women" we find this passage, which could be advanced as a brief against Virgil's episode of Cyrene and Aristaeus:

> We [women] are still and always guardians of the phylogenesis of the human race … we are still and always between different incarnations, and devoted to the task of assisting man in his incarnation: a terrestrial and marine place for man's conception and gestation, with the mother feeding him, guiding his steps, fostering his growth, aiding him to develop in relation to his established gender, his Man-God. Thus women are traditionally the guardians of the multiform embryo, of the growing child, of the suffering man.
>
> (Irigaray 1993c: 55–72, at 66)

This passage could work as a perfect plot synopsis of Virgil's narrative, and an Irigarayan kind of reader might be tempted to lament the episode and leave it behind. I, however, will linger with it, because an Irigarayan reader can also find positive features in it and because Irigarayan thinking needs supplementing by literary thinking. For a writer so engaged with ancient texts' deployment of the elements – texts deeply interwoven with mythic narrative – Irigaray shows surprisingly little interest in actual texts of ancient myth or for that matter in narrative or poetry more generally.[7] Her interest in the elements as posited by the ancients does allow her to remark environments and motions within her texts – vital practices for readers of narrative – and her elemental materialism coincides with a sphere of knowledge and inquiry widespread in premodern writing. But – to take just one example – Irigaray's famous reading of Plato's *Symposium* falters when she neglects the fictive, rhetorical situation within which Diotima instructs Socrates; that is, Irigaray takes Diotima's passage as a set of philosophical propositions stripped of its narrative aspects.[8] Or again, her important essay "Divine Women," in which she discusses how she came to study the four elements, begins with an attempt to engage versions of the Melusine narrative. But she takes premodern narrative as primitive, opaque, and unenlightened, in that it needs to be transposed into an analysis of elements, senses, and movement before the narrative structure manifests its true worth. Otherwise she resorts to distressing banalities about early periods:

> I understand now that this relationship [between humans and the elements] has never been decoded and has therefore remained a matter of fables and

monsters (particularly in the etymological meaning of the word), revealing
and hiding something of our identity ... something of the dramas and spells
that captivate us, capture us, bind us, and separate us. ... Is it not true that in
this age of sophisticated technical apparatus we still frequently turn to the
Middle Ages in search of our images and secrets?

Is this because we still need a little time to dream? ... When we take a close
look at the myth of Melusine, its range of diffusion, its different versions, we
are in fact investigating something that attracts us, fascinates us even, like a
mystery, a key to our identity. ... I am far from suggesting that today we must
once again deify ourselves as did our ancestors with their animal totems.

(Irigaray 1993c: 55–72, at 57–60)

Fables and monsters do have serious functions of revealing and concealing, functions that Irigaray, like Jorie Graham in the epigraph to this essay, attributes also
to the sea; I will be discussing these very functions of the Virgil narrative and its
predecessors.[9] So I don't wish to jettison Irigaray's remarks here, nor the example
of her powerful deconstructive interpretive ventures. But insofar as she's
remained with philosophical and psychoanalytic modes, narrative kinds make her
uneasy, and she even castigates literary scholars for their insufficiently rigorous
use of her work:

I think that in the United States my books are read mainly in literature depart-
ments. But they are philosophical books and I think that there is a great deal
of misunderstanding about them because the heart of my argument is philosophical, and literary scholars are not always prepared to understand this
philosophical core. ... I resist genres because in Western tradition to pigeon-
hole oneself in a genre is to accept a hierarchy. ... I resist genres because, and
above all, what matters to me is opening new ways of thought.

(Irigaray 1995b: 3–4)

I daresay Irigaray is right about literary readers' insufficiencies in philosophy, but
she perhaps underestimates the degree to which strong works like her own create
and educate their readers; furthermore her objections to genre, while plausible to
someone reared on the French literary tradition since neo-classicism, carry less
force for those who know the melée of pan-European medieval and Renaissance
genres. In any case, there is no such thing as a pure genre, nor for that matter a
pure discipline. But this should simply serve to preserve a certain humility before
all that we have not mastered of Irigaray as other (other discipline, other language,
other discourses), say a way to keep an attitude of multiculturalism from slipping
into an imperialist kind of consumerism.

Irigaray's own positions and interpretive acts could bear further investment in
narrative, and this investment is something that literary readers bring to her work.
As Irigaray's own practice shows, new concepts can wrest from old texts new
possibilities for changing lives, rather as Virgil's Aristaeus does in wrestling with
Proteus, in a recapitulation of Menelaos' Homeric struggle. In what follows on

the Virgil episode, I bring together insights from non-feminist and feminist classicists, address their blind spots, and suggest alternative interpretive guides from Irigaray and Hannah Arendt. I argue, as against classicists' and earlier feminists' readings, that in the fourth *Georgic* Virgil recognizes the allure of linking the maternal with death through his own reading of Homer, and transforms Thetis' maternal orientation toward mortality into Cyrene's maternal orientation toward *natality*, the ongoing life of her son as a thinking adult in a community, which entails among other things learning to acknowledge his participation in another's death and to fashion projects that carry him into a livable future. Cyrene accomplishes this in her scenes of instruction and interpretation of the material received from Proteus. I argue further that the strange narrative episode of Aristaeus the beekeeper and his sea-nymph mother constitutes Virgil's argument for the usefulness of narrative to philosophical poetry. The *Georgics* ends, as William Batstone suggests, "with a story of interpretation which becomes part of the labyrinth of thought."[10] It is Irigaray's own intensive readings of the philosophers, her engagements with their tropes and topoi, that make it possible to see this, even though Irigaray herself never discusses Homer or Virgil, or philosophical poetry for that matter. Not coincidentally, I argue that Irigaray's liberatory philosophical achievement might be transformed, its impasses broken through, by others bringing narratives into engagements with Irigaray's work.

Among the mythic clusters associating the maternal with death, as Murnaghan's survey makes clear, is that of the mother who instructs her own child about his mortality. Perhaps the earliest, certainly the most formative, of these in Western narrative is Homer's Thetis, who tells her child Achilles of the prophecy concerning his choice between a short and glorious life or a long, quiet one, and whose exchanges with Achilles mediate the crucial decisions that move him toward his own death and prepare for his sending many others to their deaths (*Iliad* I and XVIII). These episodes generate many later sea-epyllia, seashore laments, and elaborations of sea-nymph life in narrative poetry.[11] Before the action of the epic Thetis has already transmitted the prophecy about Achilles' choice to him; she accedes to his destiny, knowing beforehand that he will choose a short, glorious life; her function is to make manifest and articulate, with characteristically Homeric fullness, the choice, its pathos about parents and their young, and its consequences for the tragic in epic. It is when Achilles cries out on hearing of the death of Patroclus that Thetis mourns her own son:

> He cried out
> terribly, aloud, and the lady his mother heard him
> as she sat in the depths of the sea at the side of her aged father,
> and she cried shrill in turn, and the goddesses gathered about her,
> all who along the depth of the sea were daughters of Nereus.
> For Glauke was there, Kymodoke and Thaleia,
>
> …
>
> and the rest who along the depth of the sea were daughters of Nereus.
> The silvery cave was filled with these, and together all of them

> beat their breasts, and among them Thetis led out the threnody …
> "Ah me, my sorrow, the bitterness in this best of child-bearing,
> since I gave birth to a son who was without fault and powerful,
> conspicuous among heroes; and he shot up like a young tree,
> and I nurtured him, like a tree grown in the pride of the orchard."[12]
>
> (*Il.* XVIII, Lattimore lines 34–57)

Thetis, one of many mourning mothers in the *Iliad*, actually furthers rather than resists Achilles' commitment to death, his hostility to community, and his approaching murderous frenzy, by procuring the divine armor crafted for him by Hephaistos.[13] Homer consolidates Thetis' nurturant and lamenting features, and makes them aspects of her maternity.

But elsewhere, in an Orphic tradition which Homer may or may not have known, Thetis is a cosmogonic goddess, possibly present at the beginning of all things, and, most relevant for this essay, she is identified with *mêtis* or cunning intelligence, improvisational planning, wise counsel, resourceful knowledge borne of experience. The goddess Mêtis, first wife of Zeus, was the mother of Athene; Athene in turn is the patron of Odysseus, the *polymêtis* hero. Scholars have documented the tantalizing traces by which, in the Orphic tradition, Mêtis was a creatrix, a cosmogonic power preceding even Kronos and Rhea, and by which she became associated with feminine marine deities, including Thetis, who has, like Mêtis, shapeshifting powers.[14] *Mêtis* is also a quality of mind held by or urged on many divine and human beings, the particular ability to think resourcefully and cunningly, to plan, to improvise in urgent circumstances, to know when and how to conceal, when and how to make manifest.

The fact that Mêtis and her daughter *in utero* Athene are swallowed by Zeus (as Hesiod and Apollodorus tell it, Hesiod in *Theogony* 886–900 and Apollodorus in *Library* 1.3.5), and the fact that Athene inherits and becomes deity of her mother's quality of mind after her double birth from her mother's womb and then her father's head, clearly evince a masculine envy, fear, and appropriation of female procreative power; this much seems unexceptionable after three decades of feminist analysis. But are male characters' skills with *mêtis* only and always a refusal to acknowledge the specificities of female reproductive capacity? To argue that would be, like Irigaray, to posit implicitly an Ur-myth subtending all myths – here, all the specific, surviving, written narratives and characters involving *mêtis*. In the episodes I consider in this essay, those of Cyrene and Aristaeus, Aristaeus and Proteus, Ino and Odysseus, Eidothea and Menelaos, *mêtis* is not violently seized from the female; nor is it aggressively disembodied. Rather *mêtis* saturates all alike – male and female characters, and the environing elements – as figure for surrender to long-term processes of formation and transformation modelled by pregnancy, *in utero* life, birth. These physiological events immerse the participants in a precisely characterized temporality of becoming: active and passive at once, enclosed and protected but also urgently mobile, full of struggle and endurance, with marine settings that mean at one moment life, at another death. *Mêtis*, originally linked with pregnancy, gestating, and cosmogenesis, is a temporal span of passion, something undergone but requiring or eliciting the exertion of energies. (Perhaps this much is what even Hesiod's or Apollodorus' Zeus wishes in seizing Mêtis' powers: he absorbs but also redoubles the parental body and his own experience of biological parenthood, fusing male and female procreative power, and changes his own internal structure: he could perhaps be imagined to seek a capacity for immersion in formative, shape-shifting, agonistic temporal process. That poetic narrative has yet to be written.) *Mêtis* belongs not only to the mother and her corporeal structure, but also to the child who undergoes a process of becoming; thus Aristaeus' immersion in maternal waters and caves but also his passionate cleaving to the shape-shifting matter of Proteus, as the return to infantine forms makes possible a re-emergence into responsible adult forms of culture and relationship. As we will see when we turn to Hannah Arendt, this cleaving to the temporal process of becoming, the struggle from concealment in salt waters to the revelation of life in air and light, is what makes narrative possible at all.

Homer either precedes or suppresses the tradition of Thetis' intelligence and capacity for fluid thought, but Virgil certainly knows it, and restores it to the marine mother Cyrene in *Georgics* IV, emphasizing less a Greek cunning or shapeshifting than a Roman *auctoritas*, orderly resourcefulness, practical innovations in interpretation. At the same time he tamps down the Iliadic maternal inclination to accept the sacrifice of her son to war. He does all this by modeling Cyrene not only on the Iliadic Thetis but on the Odyssean Eidothea, the nymph who helps Menelaos; on Proteus himself, who provides knowledge and instruction; and on Ino, who instructs Odysseus as he is reborn from the threatening engulfment of the sea. Eidothea, in *Odyssey* IV, possesses the *mêtis* associated with Thetis, now inflected toward practical plans of survival, navigation, orientation toward the human world. She brooks no nonsense from Menelaos, stuck on the isle of Pharos, who has failed to gather his own *mêtis* to help himself and his immediate community:

> Are you so simple then, O stranger, and flimsy-minded,
> or are you willingly giving up, and enjoying your hardships?
> See, you are held so long on the island, and can find no way
> out of it, while the heart in your companions diminishes.

She tells him about Proteus' range of knowledge, lays a plan to capture him, and ensures that Menelaos will carry out her instruction: "There I will take you myself when dawn shows and arrange you/orderly in your ambush .../Now I will tell you all the devious ways of this old man" (*Od.* IV, Lattimore lines 371–410). Homer's Eidothea has no patience for tragic fatality or for an infatuation with death on the part of suffering men; what she teaches him is not that he must die, nor how to die, but how to live, to think, to have a future, and how to do so in community. Menelaos learns not of mortality – from which his marital kinship to Zeus will spare him, as Proteus tells him – but of his own natality.

As Hannah Arendt articulates this notion in contradistinction to the fascination with mortality cultivated by warrior cultures, natality is a condition of birth as entry into a "web of human relationships which is, as it were, woven by the deeds and words of innumerable persons, by the living as well as by the dead" (Arendt 1987: 40).[15] The uniqueness of personal identity starts with being born of a particular woman, belonging to the world, and entering into an unknowable but specific future in community. Irigaray addresses similar issues in more dispersed fashion throughout her work; many of the pieces on the mother/daughter relationship, chiefly "Daughter and Woman," sketch what Arendt would recognize as her concept of natality, as do some instances of Irigaray's "becoming" (Irigaray 2001a: 30–9). Arendt would also say, as Irigaray says of the sea and of "fables and monsters" in her remarks on the Melusine narratives, that natality is a matter of moving from hiddenness or concealment to being manifest, joined to the world of appearance. The orientation of natality is toward the world and a life elaborated in it by thinking, action, and manifestation, not toward mortality and its end or the invisibility of life *in utero*. Natality's best emblem might be the moment in the *Odyssey* when the sea-nymph Ino throws an ambrosial veil to Odysseus as he struggles in a violent sea, after leaving his long concealment with Kalypso. Ino sees the tempest-tossed Odysseus and encourages him not to give in to his own fatigue or the waves' engulfment, but to fight his way toward a new manifestation of himself to a human community, first by accepting the veil which an Irigarayan reader cannot but see as maternal, placental, mediating his transformative motions from water to land:

> She took pity on Odysseus as he drifted and suffered hardship,
> and likening herself to a winged gannet she came up
> out of the water and perched on the raft and spoke a word to him:
> "Poor man, why is Poseidon the shaker of the earth so bitterly
> cankered against you, to give you such a harvest of evils? ...
> But do as I say, since you seem to me not lacking in good sense.
> Take off these clothes, and leave the raft to drift at the winds' will,
> and then strike out and swim with your hands and make for a landfall
> on the Phaiakian country, where your escape is destined.
> And here, take this veil, it is immortal, and fasten it under
> your chest; and there is no need for you to die, nor to suffer.
> But when with both your hands you have taken hold of the mainland,
> untie the veil and throw it out in the wine-blue water
> far from the land; and turn your face away as you do so."
>
> (*Od.* V, Lattimore lines 336–50)

This is nearly the end of *Odyssey* V. At its start, Dawn has risen to make herself manifest to the world. Its narrative is that of Odysseus' departure from Kalypso, whose name itself means "concealment." When he reaches land after accepting the sea-nymph's aid, he promptly buries himself with leaves and brush as if protecting and concealing fragile embers of life, and sleeps concealed and exhausted. When he wakes, he is naked, salt-encrusted, ready to manifest himself as on his natal day, as he steps back into human community by supplicating Nausikaa.

Birth, Arendt says, has a "world-creating faculty" (*The Human Condition*, 242). Natality is an apt orientation for philosophical poetry, which aims to teach its readers how to live, aligned with the truth of how things are; in Virgil's episode of Cyrene and Aristaeus, philosophical poetry fused with narrative is offered as a major alternative to the maternal pathos of the *Iliad*, with its insistence on the sacrifice of sons to a warrior economy of death.[16] Classical scholarship not influenced by feminist critique, steering clear of Cyrene and her marine home, misses the relevance of Virgil's anti-Iliadic insistence on *natality* rather than *mortality* as the condition or orientation that launches the subject – both Aristaeus and Cyrene – into knowledge and ethical action. Virgil's evocations of Homer in the *Georgics* serve a Virgilian argument for the heroism not of exalting death but of seeking knowledge to make possible a condition of natality and ongoing life. It serves a Virgilian argument for the role of the mother as well as the father in the life of the youthful hero, and indeed suggests an independent life of thinking and creative action for the sea-nymph.

The most startling of Virgil's transformations of Homer, having the son re-enter the usually closed maternal waters and caverns in a trajectory reversing his original birth rather than having the nymph-mother come to the shore to aid her son, bespeaks the importance of natality to Virgil's philosophico-narrative poem. Aristaeus' movement into aquatic birth passageways which open up to him is a swift journey of sensuous marvel:

> simul alta iubet discedere late
> flumina, qua iuuenis gressus inferret. at illum
> curuata in montis faciem circumstetit unda
> accepitque sinu uasto misitque sub amnem.
> iamque domum mirans genetricis et umida regna
> speluncisque lacus clausos lucosque sonantis
> ibat, et ingenti motu stupefactus aquarum
> omnia sub magna labentia flumina terra
> spectabat diuersa locis ...
>
> (*Georgics* IV.359–67)

> [Whereat she bad the rivers part to admit the passage of the youth. The waves like curving precipices reared all around him, gathered him into the vastness of their bosom and sped him down beneath the flood. And now, marvelling at his mother's home, the aqueous realms, the pools immured in caverns and resonant groves, he moved, and in a daze at the mighty motion of waters there beheld all rivers gliding each in due direction under the massy earth.]

Aristaeus' marveling journey into a maternal marine element condenses several episodes from the *Odyssey*, the Homeric poem of births, in order to posit a condition of natality. These include multiple Odyssean instances of hospitality and nurture provided Telemachus and Odysseus on their respective journeys, but here I focus on Homer's Cave of the Nymphs, with its mysterious combination of shelter and signs of absent, independently creative nymphs. Homer says:

There is a harbor of the Old Man of the Sea, Phorkys,
in the countryside of Ithaka. There two precipitous
promontories opposed jut out, to close in the harbor
and shelter it from the big waves made by the winds blowing ...
At the head of the harbor, there is an olive tree with spreading
leaves, and nearby is a cave that is shaded, and pleasant,
and sacred to the nymphs who are called the Nymphs of the Wellsprings,
Naiads. There are mixing bowls and handled jars inside it,
all of stone, and there the bees deposit their honey.
And therein also are looms that are made of stone, very long, where
the nymphs weave their sea-purple webs, a wonder to look on;
and there is water forever flowing.

(*Od.* XIII, Lattimore lines 96–109)

In the earlier episode of Ino's aid to Odysseus by means of her immortal veil, Odysseus resists both veil and advice, suspicious of nymphs who, as it seems to him from his recent and partially willing sojourn with Kalypso, threaten to engulf him in their watery realms and conceal him from life with others. Even when he decides to accept Ino's help, stripping off the clothes provided by Kalypso and tying Ino's placenta-like veil around his chest, he undergoes days in the stormy sea, convinced of his imminent demise, until Athene inspires him to risk clinging to a rock face. Again and again during this travail Odysseus has to decide to live by entrusting himself to the advice of Ino and Athene. Yet this trust requires not passivity but action, even aggression, in order that he fight his way free of the concealing waters. When he tosses the veil back to the sea, he acknowledges his definitive emergence from oblivion into the elements that humans inhabit, earth and air. His arrival at the Cave of the Nymphs on the coast of his own island seems Homer's elaboration of a safe, maternal space not exactly within uterine depths that threaten oblivion – not, that is, within the mother as physical environment – but rather in a space of creative activity that the mother provides for a child now external to her. The space of the Cave and the fact of its absent nymphs together articulate in the world of appearances the sense of space sketched by Christopher Bollas when he describes dream as "an intelligence of form that holds, moves, stimulates, and shapes us" – what the mythological poets call *mêtis*, that maternal capacity of formative mind:

> Gathered and processed by the dream space and dream events, I live in a place where I seem to have been held before: inside the magical and erotic embrace of a forming intelligence that bears me. ... [in] a continuous reminiscence of being inside the maternal world when one was partly a receptive figure within a comprehending environment.[17]

When Virgil brings together passages from the *Odyssey*, he therefore condenses several stages of the subject's relation to the mother. Aristaeus gladly enters welcoming waters, thus reversing Odysseus' struggles against the hostile sea and creating the possibility of a benign reversion to the womb; Aristaeus is not absorbed but remains distinct, within an environment full of partitions and demarcated spaces. Once there he is tended and strengthened, yet parental figures also give him complex information and then provide an arena in which his action will show his ability to grow into manhood, a kind of education that Telemachus also receives from his mentors.

The poetic resonances of Homer in Virgil's episode thus gain thematic relevance as the familiar trope of sonic maternal resonance, here expanded from an original thought of sounds heard from an intra-uterine, aquatic site into a sense of sounds that open out to communities and mutual obligations, as in Arendt's notion of natality. First, the nymphs' realm of water and rock, cave and vaulting, receive, contain, or amplify the sounds that pervade this episode. "Mater, Cyrene mater" (IV.321) calls Aristaeus in grief and rage; "At mater sonitum thalamo sub fluninis alti/sensit" [but his mother heard the cry from her bower beneath the river's depths] (IV.333–4); there follows immediately the catalogue of nymphs that foreshadows the groups of nymphs whom Aristaeus has offended and neglected, and this is followed by acknowledgment of the communities of nymphs and natural objects – that is, the world of natality in which Aristaeus must manifest himself:

> pars epulis onerant mensas et plena reponunt
> pocula, Panchaeis adolescunt ignibus arae.
> et mater "cape Maeonii carchesia Bacchi:
> Oceano libemus" ait: simul ipsa precatur
> Oceanumque patrem rerum Nymphasque sorores,
> centum quae silvas, centum quae flumina servant.
>
> (*Georgics* IV.378–83)

[Some laid dishes on the table and cups in turn refilled, while on the altars Arabian incense flared. Then said his mother: "Raise up your goblets of Maeonian wine and pour in honour of Ocean"; and she prayed Herself to Ocean, father of the world, and to the sisterhood of Nymphs that guard a hundred forests and a hundred rivers.]

All these features – Cyrene, her sister nymphs, the singing Clymene (whose name Virgil borrows from Homer), and the setting taken from Homer's cave of the nymphs in *Odyssey* XIII – have long been properly understood as aspects of Virgil's exaltation of Homer as poet of natural philosophy and, like Ocean, father of the world. In the context of my concerns here, they signify Virgil's insistence (in an argument directed both to Lucretius and to the Iliadic Homer) on the value of natality and narrative, and the function they both have of bringing into the world of appearances that which has been concealed.

Maternal sonority is relevant as well for the content of its speech. It is not just that the nymphs' home resounds with echoes of poetry celebrating the fullness of the world, as the uterus transmits haunting and resonant sound to the unborn infant, although Virgil contributes grandly to that topos; it is not just that the voice of the mother soothes her child, though that is one function of Cyrene's prayers to Ocean and to "Nymphas ... sorores" (IV.382).[18] Like a mother with an older child, she also speaks words of truth to him, directing, instructing, challenging, warning, advising. (Cyrene has direct speech in 49 lines and also prays aloud; Aristaeus speaks 15. This fact alone should put paid to the long tradition of dismissing Cyrene and her signifying powers.) As with the nymph Eidothea advising Menelaos how to take Proteus in *Odyssey* IV, her speech makes possible their joint venture to find an explanation. When Proteus has spoken and disappeared, Cyrene speaks again, refining and revising Proteus' knowledge with her own thinking, to teach Aristaeus how to put knowledge to practical and ethical use. Aristaeus will apparently achieve natality only because of his immersion in the waters of a maternal realm: safe but also risky, enclosed and deep underground but also open and moving, in the company of a mother who welcomes and anoints him as she would an infant but steadily requires adulthood of him and thinking of herself.

That it is natality as orientation to the world in its manifestations through community and the living of a life explains why the fantasy of regression to uterine fusion with an archaic mother does not compel Virgil, though it would be an easy choice to make. Fusion with the maternal would be another infatuation with mortality like that of Homer's Achilles. Rather Aristaeus and Cyrene think, speak, and act toward a future, ongoing life; Aristaeus' marine experiences are delineated as specific, separable events rather than an undifferentiated immersion. David Quint's alternative understanding of Aristaeus' visit to Cyrene's domain will make this clear. For Quint,

> [Proteus'] transformations can be understood as the words and figures of poetic language. The displacement of Proteus from Cyrene's cave would then stand for the temporal distance between poetic representation [i.e. Proteus] and a timeless source of meaning [i.e. Cyrene]. ... As nature advances watery prime matter – which the eye cannot observe in its original state – into form and the different orders and species of creatures, so a timeless originary meaning is differentiated in time by language and representation. In Cyrene's cave, Aristaeus arrives at a pure origin which, because it is undifferentiated, cannot represent itself and is inaccessible to his understanding.
>
> (Quint 1983: 38)

But what could it mean to say that Cyrene's origin is undifferentiated? This would make sense only if Quint assumes an anterior fantasy of mother/child fusion in pregnancy and birth, in which case Proteus becomes the Oedipal father who ushers the child Aristaeus into language and meaning by offering him difference, differentiation, and language. But in Virgil, it is Cyrene herself who offers language, differentiation, and meaning; nothing in the passage links her to undifferentiation. Cyrene's highly articulated marine home and the diverse forms of mobility within it – the mobility of the waters and the sea animals, the journeys of both Aristaeus and Cyrene, the wrestling with Proteus, Proteus' sudden disappearance, and especially Aristaeus' reemergence into the elements of air and earth – suggest that the marine mother presides over differentiation in both time and space.[19] Natality launches thinking and acting in the world, thought and action which, in philosophical poetry which Virgil here puts forward as an alternative to heroic epic, specifically do not require the sacrifice of sons in an economy of death nor the suffering of mothers as they accede to their children's deaths.

With birth a new being *appears* – emerges into manifestness – and spends its life in projects that move between the poles of the manifest and the concealed. With Aristaeus' reentry into Cyrene's waters he returns to the concealment of intrauterine life: a reconcealment that will permit further manifestations of meaning. Proteus, in Virgil's sea episode, may be said to draw out of the past facts that were concealed; Cyrene in her interpreting or rethinking draws out of Proteus' account that which remains concealed in it, that which still calls to become manifest: Aristaeus' own part in the death of another, the wood-nymphs' loss, the practical and ritual requirements for action in order to live harmoniously with the nymphs. Then the sacrifice itself serves, in part, as a making manifest of Aristaeus' part in death, a repetition or imitation of an earlier death – but in order that he may go on with a commitment to living.[20] This property of making manifest in birth and in thinking is a consequence of Virgil's working through the Homeric epics to move away from an Iliadic orientation to mortality, by transforming the character type of Thetis, the *mater dolorosa*, into a complex sea-nymph who also shares the thinking and acting qualities, the concealing and revealing qualities, of Kalypso and Ino in the *Odyssey*.

Luce Irigaray's abjuring of the magics of narrative and poetry seems to me, a literary scholar, a curious fact, a phenomenon that needs thinking about; after all, other prominent continental theoretical writers about gender trained in philosophy and psychoanalysis discuss or write both narrative and poetry. She insists on cleaving to the intransigencies of discourse; thus when an imagined interlocutor at the end of "The Utterance in Analysis" asks her, "but what about Oedipus and the oedipal complex?" – for she has not addressed these – she replies, "The synchronic function of discourse puts into play what the myth stages" (Irigaray 2002e: 108). Her disinclination to narrative sequence is part of what makes her early work difficult to read, for she does not much engage sequence – of thought, of image, of unconscious assumption – within the philosophers she addresses, and so at first (and for a long time) a reader may have the sense that one could just open a book of hers anywhere and begin at random. But her declining, if that is what it is, to take up narrative doesn't imply any refusal on her part to take up natality. If she veers from the temporality of narrative, she gives attention instead to structure of discourse, and proposes new figurations of embodiment and embodied process – a focus that contributes to the widespread sense of her lyricism. She might even be said to be a curiously *modernist* lyricist, in her focus on image and metaphor of structure. Irigaray often prefers notions of developmental or organic process over more narrative temporalities. The placental veil, for instance, which Irigaray uses to figure the complex, infolded web of union and separateness between pregnant woman and foetus, or to figure movement and mediation (as in her discussions of angels, or her discussion, in "Divine Women," of the curtain in Freud's account of the *fort-da* game), also contains the potential for arcs of more narrative urgency and risk, as when Homer's Ino offers Odysseus her veil and he responds to its liminally threatening status: it offers now life, now death.

Furthermore, for Irigaray it may be more urgent to *disarticulate* figures of divine splendor – angels, Dionysus, Apollo, Christ, the Virgin – from their narratives and from verse – from the sphere of "fables and monsters" – in order to make them heralds and models of new, yet unthought identities, relationships, and plot trajectories. Thus the great meditations on the gods in "When the gods are born," in *Amante marine*, always engage with the myths completely abstracted and generalized from their specific texts. Irigaray is uninterested in poets' *versions* of myths, uninterested in the specific arcs of language and thought offered by Homer as against Hesiod, or Virgil as against Lucretius or Homer. Instead she adumbrates – not exactly new stories for the gods, for that would entail fiction-making – but new invitations to her readers to imagine differently: "The Christ thus makes manifest a new way to overcome the pain of living" (Irigaray 1991: 164); "This divine is still to be revealed" (Irigaray 1991: 171); "This aspect of Christ is still to be discovered" (Irigaray 1991: 182); "But perhaps a certain kind of divine has never taken place, even though it has been heralded" (Irigaray 1991: 182). These proffers of new horizons shimmering within divine symbols accompany her critique of the toxic fantasies that undergird traditional – and abstracted – mythic narrative. Irigaray's lyrical and critical modes of analysis intertwine powerfully in *Amante marine*. There she seems to imply, as in her reading of Nietzsche's *Zarathustra*, that his hortatory fiction keeps him trapped within himself. "And you [she says to Nietzsche] will pitch yourself to a higher creation not by devouring the other so it is reduced to your own substance, but rather by letting different bodies be and their fortune multiply" (Irigaray 1991: 18). In spite of her declining of fiction, which the literary reader may always regret, she has always been passionately committed to projects of natality: to thinking, interpreting, planning, proposing, liberating; carrying messages of mobility, transformation, and hope. Perhaps her refashioning of mythic beings and her jettisoning of narrative are commitments to helping the narratives of others multiply.

Notes

1 I use R. A. B. Mynors' Latin text and commentary throughout (*Virgil: Georgics*, Oxford: Clarendon Press, 1990), and the English translation of L. P. Wilkinson (*Virgil: The Georgics*, London: Penguin, 1982). The epigraph to this chapter is from Jorie Graham, "Underneath (Calypso)," section 2, from *Swarm*, New York, Ecco Press, 2000.

2 For placement of Virgil's *Georgics* in this tradition, see commentary by D. Clay, *Lucretius and Epicurus*, Ithaca: Cornell University Press, 1983; J. Whitman, *Allegory: The Dynamics of an Ancient and Medieval Technique*, Cambridge: Harvard University Press, 1987; J. Farrell, *Vergil's* Georgics *and the Traditions of Ancient Epic: The Art of Allusion in Literary History*, Oxford: Oxford University Press, 1991; R. Lamberton, *Homer the Theologian: Neoplatonist Allegorical Reading and the Growth of the Epic Tradition*, Berkeley, University of California Press, 1986; M. Murrin, *The Allegorical*

Epic: Essays in Its Rise and Decline, Chicago: University of Chicago Press, 1980; D. O. Ross, Jr., *Virgil's Elements: Physics and Poetry in the* Georgics, Princeton: Princeton University Press, 1987; D. Sedley, *Lucretius and the Transformations of Greek Wisdom*, Cambridge: Cambridge University Press, 1998; R. F. Thomas, *Reading Virgil and His Texts: Studies in Intertextuality*, Ann Arbor: University of Michigan Press, 1999.

3 Partial exceptions to the lack of curiosity include Ross, 221–2, who recognizes the generative force of Clymene's *umida regna*; D. Quint, *Origin and Originality in Renaissance Literature: Versions of the Source*, New Haven: Yale University Press, 1983, p. 38, and especially W. Batstone, "Virgilian Didaxis: Value and Meaning in the *Georgics*," in *The Cambridge Companion to Virgil*, ed. C. Martindale, Cambridge: Cambridge University Press, 1997, pp. 125–44, and A. Wallace, "Placement, Gender, Pedagogy: Virgil's Fourth *Georgic* in Print," *Renaissance Quarterly* 56, 2 (Summer 2003), pp. 377–407.

4 S. Murnaghan, "Maternity and Mortality in Homeric Poetry," *Classical Antiquity* 11, 2 (October 1992), pp. 242–64 at 264. See also M. Kitts, "The Wide Bosom of the Sea as a Place of Death: Maternal and Sacrificial Imagery in *Iliad* 21," *Literature and Theology* 14, 2 (June 2000), pp. 103–24; S. Wofford, *The Choice of Achilles: The Ideology of Figure in the Epic*, Stanford: Stanford University Press, 1992, pp. 25–96; G. Nagy, *The Best of the Achaeans: Concepts of the Hero in Archaic Greek Poetry*, Baltimore: Johns Hopkins University Press, 1979.

5 There is a vast literature on maternity and its various relationships to death, both figuratively and historically. On mothers and death in early modern writing, see e.g. G. A. E. Parfitt, "Renaissance Wombs, Renaissance Tombs," *Renaissance and Modern Studies* 15 (1971), 23–33; J. Adelman, *Suffocating Mothers: Fantasies of Maternal Origin in Shakespeare's Plays*, Hamlet *to* The Tempest, London and New York, Routledge, 1992; T. Krier, *Birth Passages: Maternity and Nostalgia, Antiquity to Shakespeare*, Ithaca: Cornell University Press, 2001.

6 Krier, *Birth Passages*; A. Cavarero (1995a).

7 Irigaray's recurrent attention to Antigone is perhaps the exeption that proves the rule. Her luminous discussion of Dionysus, Apollo, Artemis, and Christ in *Marine Lover*, a different kind of exception, I will return to at the end of this essay.

8 Irigaray, 1993g: 20–33. Qualifications and disputes with Irigaray's reading, as well as a reprinting of Irigaray's own essay, appear in *Feminist Interpretations of Plato*, ed. N. Tuana, University Park: Pennsylvania State University Press, 1994. Even Irigaray's gestures toward specific treatments of myth invariably transpose into discussions of a generalized, abstracted myth. See e.g. "The Forgotten Mystery of Female Ancestry" (1989), in her *Thinking the Difference: For a Peaceful Revolution*, trans. K. Montin, New York: Routledge, 1994, pp. 89–112: she doesn't like to hew closely to these ancient mythopoeic texts.

9 Graham, "Underneath (Calypso)."

10 Batstone, "Virgilian Didaxis," 128. In this essay I focus on Virgil's responses to Homer, and exclude all other precursors to Virgil, including those we more easily take to be philosophical, e.g. Hesiod, Nicander, Lucretius, Aratus, Varro. In spite of these exclusions, I should say that I think Virgil's argument about the inclusion of mythic narrative is a direct response to Lucretius' emphatic dismissals of the gods from the way things are.

11 J. Nohrnberg, *The Analogy of* The Faerie Queene, Princeton: Princeton University Press, 1976, sketches the sea-epyllion genre from the vantage point of Renaissance poetry: "These poems feature a myth of erotic connoisseurship or erotic possession … a rich sensual preoccupation; a theme of metamorphosis (often in connection with the metamorphic element of water); and frequent erotic pietàs. Subfeatures are a deliberate mythopoetic digressiveness and the accommodation of extended 'monodramatic' complaints by the narrative" (592n.436). See also E. J. Bellamy's essay in this volume,

Murnaghan, "Maternity and Mortality," and especially L. Slatkin, *The Power of Thetis: Allusion and Interpretation in the* Iliad, Berkeley: University of California Press, 1991.

12 Passages from the *Iliad* and the *Odyssey* are cited from the translations of R. Lattimore, *Iliad*, Chicago: University of Chicago Press, 1951; *Odyssey*, New York: Harper and Row, 1967.

13 The latter is devoted to Thetis, and happily indebted to her, for when Zeus cast him out of Olympos, Thetis rescued him and succored him in the sea depths; there, under her protection, he began his work in metals. So Hephaistos too is frequently associated with *mêtis*. See *Iliad* XVIII.395ff.

14 Thetis is said to have changed shape repeatedly to escape Zeus' overtures; she also fled the advances of her husband Peleus by metamorphosing: in Ovid's *Metamorphoses* XI, into a bird, a tree, a tigress; in the scholia *ad* Lycophron 2.175, 178, into a cuttlefish or *sepia*. On *mêtis*, see M. Detienne and J.-P. Vernant, *Les Ruses de l'intelligence: La mêtis des grecs*, Paris: Flammarion, 1974; on Thetis' relationship to this quality of mind, pp. 127–64; for Thetis' metamorphic flight from Peleus, p.159n. 129. See also I. E. Holmberg, "The Sign of Mêtis," *Arethusa* 30, 1 (1997), pp. 1–33.

15 H. Arendt, "Labor, Work, Action," in *Amor Mundi: Explorations in the Faith and Thought of Hannah Arendt*, ed. J. W. Bernauer, Dordrecht and Boston: Martinus Nijhoff Publishers, 1987, pp. 29–42, at 40; see also Arendt, *The Human Condition*, Chicago: University of Chicago Press, 1958, pp. 7–9, 176–8. I am indebted to expositions of Arendt by Cavarero (1995b); C. Mazzoni, *Maternal Impressions: Pregnancy and Childbirth in Literature and Theory*, Ithaca: Cornell University Press, 2002; H. Jonas, "Acting, Knowing, Thinking: Gleanings from Hannah Arendt's Philosophical Work," *Social Research* 44 (Spring 1977), pp. 25–43, at 30–1.

16 Besides Murnaghan's account, cited above, of Archaic works linking mothers with mortality, see also the analysis of filial sacrifice in the *Aeneid*, in D. L. Miller, *Dreams of the Burning Child: Sacrificial Sons and the Father's Witness*, Ithaca: Cornell University Press, 2003.

17 C. Bollas, "Aspects of Self-Experiencing," in *Being a Character: Psychoanalysis and Self Experience*, New York: Hill and Wang, 1992, pp. 11–32, at 14.

18 See J. Kristeva, "Place Names," in her *Desire in Language: A Semiotic Approach to Literature and Art*, trans. T. Gora, A. Jardine, and L. Roudiez, New York: Columbia University Press, 1980, 271–94, at 282; K. Silverman, *The Acoustic Mirror: The Female Voice in Psychoanalysis and Cinema*, Bloomington: Indiana University Press, 1988, pp. 72–140; D. Anzieu, *The Skin Ego: A Psychoanalytic Approach to the Self*, trans. C. Turner, New Haven: Yale University Press, 1989, pp. 157–73.

19 To put it another way, in terms of feminist and psychoanalytic discussions of the trope of the sonorous cavern of the maternal body: Virgil pays tribute both to the moment that instigates what we know as the emotional resonance of the fantasy of intrauterine life and the environmental mother, and to the mother's later labor of inducting the child into the world of language and differentiation. Silverman argues that "identifying the sonorous envelope trope as a fantasy" allows her to "stress the ways in which the fantasy functions as a bridge between two radically disjunctive moments – an infantile moment, which occurs prior to the inception of subjectivity, and which is consequently 'too early' with respect to meaning and desire, but consequently 'too late' for fulfillment. The first of those moments, which can be imagined but never actually experienced, turns upon the imaginary fusion of mother and infant, and hence upon unity and plenitude. The second moment marks the point at which the subject introjects a preexisting structure, a structure which gives order, shape, and significance to the original ineffable experience" (*The Sonorous Envelope*, 73). Although I take issue with her final formulation – an ineffable experience is still an experience, and we can usefully think of the compelling fantasy of the maternal cave as evincing what Bollas calls the "unthought known," a shape of experience and proprio-affect that comes to us

through our utterly unique emergence into being through gestation – Silverman allows us to articulate the powerful double temporality that Virgil's narrative represents and to discern why it is so satisfying.

20 For lack of space I refrain from detailed analysis of Aristaeus' sacrifice, though a full argument about natality in the episode would call for it.

Many thanks to Elizabeth D. Harvey, Andrew Wallace, and John Watkins for reading diverse versions of this essay.

3 What does Matter want?

Irigaray, Plotinus, and the human condition

Jonathan Crewe

Plotinus in the Sixth Tractate of the *Enneads*, "The Impassivity of the Unembodied," implicitly poses the strange question "What does Matter want?" That question arises from Plotinus's seemingly contradictory, if not oxymoronic, personification of Matter. The relevant parts of his text are quoted verbatim under the title "*Une Mère de Glace*" in Luce Irigaray's *Speculum of the Other Woman* (Irigaray 1985g: 168–79).[1]

In the Sixth Tractate, while claiming only to summarize and logically expound Plato's argument regarding Matter, Plotinus elaborates and even fancifully improvises on a key passage in the *Timaeus*.[2] Indeed, his ventriloquism of Plato anticipates and even "sanctions" Irigaray's own, while his personification of Matter gives his discussion of the topic the character of an extended *prosopopoeia*. As soon as Matter is personified, there are things it can want, or want to be. I hesitate to say that Matter thus takes on the character of a desiring subject in Plotinus, since the phrase "desiring subject" may carry us a little too far, but Plotinus certainly imputes wishes to Matter. That personification isn't wholly unanticipated in the *Timaeus*, as we shall see, but Plotinus goes a good deal further than Plato.

The point of asking "What does Matter want?" in the context of Irigaray's *Speculum* is that Plotinus's personification of Matter inevitably reveals certain assumptions about *human* wants and the human condition. As represented by Plotinus, the human condition turns out to be a fractured one, the divisions and contradictions of which he displaces on to maternity or, more broadly, on to femininity. *Speculum* certainly draws critical attention to that displacement.

Yet Irigaray does not directly address the wants of Plotinus's personified Matter, nor does she pursue certain questions raised by the Plotinus passage about the implication of the feminine in the human and vice versa. In fact, Irigaray "says" nothing about Plotinus. She quotes him verbatim, even if she does so in a context she has created. Her feminist point may seem too obvious to require more than quotation – a view apparently taken in many commentaries on *Speculum* – but we should not too hastily assume that Irigaray's point is or can be self-evident. Nor should any such presumption forestall further inquiry into the feminism of *Speculum* or the human condition as Plotinus conceives it. Nor, finally, should it forestall further inquiry into the relation of Woman – or women – to the human condition. Those are the questions I shall take up in this paper.

I am well aware that this proposal will raise the hackles of many who are wary of regression to a pre-feminist humanism, or about the loss of feminist specificity in submerging the condition of women in a larger, but more nebulous, human condition. I can only ask readers to bear with me since I believe I am raising this question from the vantage point of feminism (or at least of Irigaray's feminism), and in the interests of contemporary feminist thought. I do not accept that engaging with the question of the human is inimical to feminism. On the contrary, as I hope to suggest, persistent refusal to engage with the question may do more to incapacitate feminism than enable it today.

To begin in a feminist register, then, the question "What does Matter want?" is not for a moment gender-neutral. Given that Plotinus features in Irigaray's *Speculum* as an exemplar of the Platonic tendency to conflate maternity with materiality – Mother with Matter – the feminine is implicated in the question from the start. As I have posed it explicitly, which Plotinus does not, the question also clearly echoes the notorious Freudian one "What does Woman want?"[3] That question in turn emerges from, and keeps on returning to, Freud's view of Woman as the great unknown of psychoanalysis – as its unexplored Dark Continent. That is the view on which Irigaray dwells with so much sardonic amusement and ironic indignation in the opening section of *Speculum*.

We may of course dismiss "What does Woman want?" as a pseudo-question that does no more than expose the gender-bias of what poses as a disinterested scientific inquiry. The related question "What does Matter want?" could similarly be dismissed as a prejudicial one in what poses as philosophical inquiry. Yet summary dismissal is not the only option or necessarily the best one. Even if the questions are not accepted in their own terms, their contexts, implications, varying formulations, and, above all, interrelations are ones with which, following Irigaray, we may choose to engage critically. That is the choice I am making here.[4]

Before proceeding, I should like to outline some contexts in which I am posing the question. First, to recapitulate briefly, at the time *Speculum* was published, feminism had created a novel, "alien" frame of reference in which historic male pronouncements on Woman needed only to be quoted in order to be rendered comic. In the case of Freud, the "mystery" of woman and her desires needed only to be transported from Freud's texts and contexts of address into *Speculum* to be seen as a risible mystification, internal to psychoanalysis as a gendered cultural discourse with antecedents going back at least to Plato. Irigaray's *Speculum* is itself a historic text in the sense that its powerful "alienating effect" had become available, so to speak, at that particular historical moment, although it was Irigaray who took brilliant advantage of it. The same alienation effect was available to Irigaray for citations from Plato and Plotinus, and, indeed, from male Philosophy in general.

Almost from the start, feminist commentators have recognized the power of comic displacement in *Speculum*. As Moi (1985: 31) puts it:

> In this context (or, more appropriately, *con-texte* – con in French means "cunt"), seemingly straightforward quotation undermines Plotinus's discourse: these are, after all, no longer Plotinus's words but Irigaray's expert

(literal) imitation of them. Her perfect mimicry manages subtly to expose his narcissistic phallocentrism.

Yet the effect of comic exposure, a gift of history as well as of targeted feminist endeavor, was also seen almost from the start as a complex effect rather than one of simple, revolutionary demystification or undermining. The question of Irigaray's relation to the discourses she "alienates" – recites, mimes, parodies, ironizes, performs – has occupied a good deal of attention, as have the erotics of Irigaray's relation to the philosophers she has been seen as "romancing" (Burke 1989: 226–40). The specular interplay of *Speculum* certainly cannot be wholly oppositional. In effect, it would seem, Irigaray acknowledges the constitutive precedence enjoyed by patriarchal gender-discourse and thus engages in a critique that remains bound, affectively as well as cognitively, to its objects. At least for this European feminist, there is apparently no real outside – no habitable, self-sufficient, or truly imaginable alternative – to the gendered discourse of Western culture, phallocentric if you will, especially in such privileged articulations as Platonism and Psychoanalysis.

Whatever separatist/alternative impulses *Speculum* may manifest – ones that can capitalize, for example, on the enabling features of female anatomy and same-sex erotics, or on the cultural counter-discourse of female mystics[5] – Irigaray also seizes gleefully on what might be called the tolerances of certain antipathetic discourses, here the Platonic and psychoanalytic ones. The capaciousness, porousness, inventiveness, and engaging seductiveness of those discourses – the seductiveness being nowhere more apparent than in Freud's asides to women as the reluctant bringer of bad news – renders them provocatively enabling as well as oppressive.[6] In spite or because of themselves, those oppressive discourses afford many opportunities to play, of which Irigaray takes advantage.

Feminist philosophical commentaries on Irigaray's critique of Platonism supply an additional context for my question "What does Matter want?" As I have already mentioned, the questions "What does Matter want?" and "What does Woman want?" are not unrelated, since one of the major topics of *Speculum* and of feminist commentaries on it is the conflation of maternity and materiality – of Mother with Matter – that has been a feature of Western philosophy (or of patriarchal ideology) at least since Plato's *Timaeus*. Here is the *locus classicus* in the *Timaeus* for Plato's influential thematization of the *hypodoche* as a material "receptacle" – and of the material *as* a receptacle:[7]

> We may liken the receiving principle to a mother, and the source or spring to a father ... the matter in which the model is fashioned will not be duly prepared, unless it is formless and free from the impress of any of those shapes which it is hereafter to receive from without. For if matter were like any of the supervening forms ... it would take the impression badly. Wherefore, that which is to receive all forms should have no form ... wherefore the mother and receptacle of all created and visible and in any way sensible things is not to be termed earth, or air, or fire, or water or any compounds of these, but is

an invisible and formless being which receives all things and in some mysterious way partakes of the intelligible, and is most incomprehensible.

(Jowett 1931: 470–1)I[8]

If anything, the conflation is even more apparent and decisive in Plotinus than it is
in Plato:

> The Ideal Principles entering into Matter as to a Mother affect it neither
> for better nor for worse.
> Their action is not upon Matter, but upon each other; these powers con-
> flict with their opponent principles, not with their substrata ...
> This, I think, is why the doctors of old, teaching through symbols and
> mystic representations exhibit the ancient Hermes with the generative organs
> always in the active posture; this is to convey that the generator of things of
> sense is the Intellectual Reason-Principle; the sterility of Matter, eternally
> unmoved, is indicated by the eunuchs surrounding it in its representation as
> the All-Mother.

(Irigaray 1985g: 179)

Insofar as the feminine is equated with the maternal, and both are conflated with
the material, asking what each wants can merely seem like two ways of asking a
single question, the implication being that there is no answer.

Rigorous, informed feminist commentaries on Irigaray suggest, however, that
although the questions are related they are not quite the same one. As Judith
Butler emphasizes, for both Plato and Plotinus the mother is only an analogy for
the material. That hardly makes it a random or innocuous figure of comparison,
yet according to Butler, glossing Irigaray, the analogical *difference* is at least as
important as the resemblance:

> The figure of the nurse, the mother, the womb cannot be fully identified with
> the [Platonic] receptacle [*chora, hypodoche*], for those are specular figures
> that displace the feminine at the moment they purport to represent the femi-
> nine. The receptacle cannot be exhaustively thematized in Plato's text,
> precisely because it is that which conditions and escapes figuration and
> thematization. *This receptacle is not a metaphor based on likeness but a dis-*
> *figuration that appears at the boundaries of the human, both as its very*
> *condition and as the insistent threat of its deformation; it cannot take a form,*
> *be a morphe, and, in that sense, cannot be a body.*

(Butler 1994: 154)[9]

In Irigaray and some feminist commentary, then, something remains as an irreducible "surplus" even after analogical conflation of the material with the
maternal. It is thus a resource for critical appropriation, resistance and even
deconstructive subversion.[10] To cite Butler again:

Irigaray [argues] that the feminine exceeds its figuration, just as the receptacle does … significantly, Julia Kristeva *accepts* this collapse of the *chora* and the maternal/nurse figure … Irigaray [in contrast] asks how the discourse that performs this conflation invariably produces an "outside" where the feminine *not* captured by the figure of the *chora* persists.

(Butler 1994: 154)[11]

Insofar as woman remains "unembodied" she remains radically heterogeneous to patriarchal logic and evidently beyond capture. Differently put, the counterpart to the embodied mother is always the unembodied other woman, perhaps "*une mère de glace*," but only in the sense of being the invisible not-mother behind the mirror.

If, in a sense, that "other" location merely deepens the inscrutability of Woman, it also raises an important question about whether Woman is, or can be, the definitive referent or subtext of the Platonic discourse of Matter. Butler already anticipates that question when she writes that the Platonic receptacle is "*a disfiguration that appears at the boundaries of the human, both as its very condition and as the insistent threat of its deformation*." The question of how the feminine is implicated in the human and vice versa may be one that arises from Platonism generally, yet it can be posed with particular clarity in relation to Plotinus's work. To that end, it is necessary to separate Plotinus from Plato in a way that has not, as far as I know, been attempted in feminist philosophical commentary.[12]

Admittedly, since Plotinus claims to do no more than rehearse Plato's *Timaeus* argument in the quotations that comprise "*Une Mère de Glace*," such a separation may seem redundant.[13] Even when it is recognized, as Butler does, that Plotinus occupies a distinctive place in the history of philosophy, that fact does not necessarily change the point for feminists. It certainly doesn't change the point for feminists to say, as standard histories of philosophy do, that Plotinus rereads Plato through an Aristotelian lens while trying to reclaim Plato from Aristotle's strictures.[14] If anything, that project would only strengthen the biological and teleological underpinnings of Plato's argument.[15]

Nor, strictly speaking, does Plotinus change the basic terms and conditions of the Platonic argument. Insofar as the terms are set by the fact that the Idea (Idealism) is constitutively opposed to Matter (Materialism) in a binary that cannot be surpassed, the conditions of the argument will include keeping Idealist hierarchies and priorities in place, and continuing to subjugate the Matter that potentially threatens them. The radical immobilization and disempowerment of Matter – and of maternity to the extent that it is implicated – must and do remain conspicuous imperatives of Plotinus's argument.[16] That holding action includes treating Matter as the "base" conceptual and even material support of a system of thought that in no way essentially depends on it, and remains utterly heterogeneous to it. Plotinus explains, for example, that:

The reflections in the mirror are not taken to be real, all the less since the appliance on which they appear is seen and remains while the images disappear, but Matter is not seen either in the images or without them. But suppose

the reflection on the mirror remaining, and the mirror itself not seen, we
would never doubt the solid reality of all that appears.
(Plotinus, Sixth Tractate, as cited by Irigaray [1985g], 174)

The quasi-concept of matter thus seems to function in a manner analogous to visible appliance of the mirror in de-realizing appearances, ones which might otherwise be taken as "solid reality." Without the notion of the omnipresent, impalpable, material substrate, there would be no ground on which appearances could emerge, so to speak, nor, it would seem, would it be possible to get "behind" those appearances. Matter thus has at least a "base" cognitive function with respect to the system that repudiates it, but it remains excluded from any part in reality.

Plotinus can legitimately be treated for certain purposes, then, as an extended footnote to Plato, but there are specific features of Plotinus's Sixth Tractate that distinguish it strikingly from the *Timaeus*. The difference is partly a matter of elaboration and continuous rephrasing, albeit in the guise of mere restatement. Plotinus says "the same thing" as Plato does, but at considerably greater length and not in identical terms. Plotinus even adds, without any clear warrant from the *Timaeus*, that the perpetual recalcitrance of Matter with respect to the Good additionally makes it Evil (*to kakon*). A notable addition that may represent, among other things, an implicit mutation in gender-discourse with consequences for women living in later times.[17] From one point of view, all the elaboration and continuing approximation merely confirm Butler's point that the receptacle cannot be definitively thematized in Platonic thought. It is less a concept that can be "thought" in Platonism than the marker of a limit to what is thinkable in it. Yet if the contradictoriness and intractability of the "concept" Matter make it, on one hand, a stumbling block, they also, it would seem, function as a provocation to extend the capacities and boundaries of philosophical argument. Building, no doubt, on Platonic precedent, Plotinus steps, first, into the role of Platonic ventriloquist, and then into the role of Matter's poet-mythographer. The baffling "absence" of omnipresent Matter requires that it be summoned into existence and rendered accessible to (re)cognition by an extended *prosopopeia*.

How, then, does Plotinus animate and characterize Matter? First, as we already know from his title, Matter is "impassive." That trait precludes it from agency as well as participation. Could it also confer on Matter a "massive," potentially threatening, self-sufficiency? That possibility is soon undercut when we learn that this impassivity belies "a bare aspiration towards substantial existence" (168). Evidently, animate Matter can't be imagined, or possibly allowed, *not* to want something. In the first instance, it must want to exist *as* something.

Plotinus's inventory continues. Since Matter is unembodied and not numbered among the Real Existents, it is not surprising to learn that it is an "invisible phantasm." It is nevertheless a phantasm that "lives" in its own strange location, on "the farther side of all these categories." Its invisibility turns out to be chosen, since it "elud[es]" all effort to observe it. Perversely, it "presents contraries in [all] the things that are based upon it." It additionally possesses the power of "utterance," even though all its utterances are "lies," and can never be anything but lies. In that respect, it is consistent and predictable, yet it still bedevils truth, perhaps (although Plotinus does not say this) by confronting it with the liar paradox. Despite its seeming abjection, Matter "pretends to be great." It "masks" itself and "makes trickery" of all that seems to be present in it, yet its theatrical unreality renders it absolutely void. Its incapacity to participate in the Good in any way that can ever change its own nature – to participate in any way but that of "bare seeming" – renders it "essentially evil" (171). This means that it is "not amenable to modification by the Good; but that means simply that it is subject to no modification whatever" (172).

Plotinus elaborates further:

> [Matter offers] a base to that which never enters, something which, by its presence, by its insistence, by its cry for help, in its beggardom, strives, as it were, by violence to acquire and is disappointed so that its poverty is enduring, its cry unceasing.
>
> (175)

"This alien base exists and myth represents it as a pauper to exhibit its nature, to show that Matter is destitute of the Good." The name too (Poverty) conveys that Matter's need is never met. The union with Poros, Possession, is designed to show that Matter does not attain to Reality, to Plenitude, but to some bare sufficiency.[18] Nevertheless, "all that impinges on this Non-Being is flung back as from a repelling substance; we may think of an echo returned from a repercussive plane surface." "Matter ... wears Magnitude as a dress thrown about it by its association with the image of magnitude" (178). Nevertheless, "destitute of all resisting power ... [it] can but accept all that an active power may choose to send."

On the strength of this inventory, we might still infer that Matter is feminine, since many if not all items in the bill of indictment are ones historically leveled at Woman from what might be called a "classic" phallologocentric viewpoint. If nothing else, (feminine) Matter is recognizable as a negative and strenuously negated function of that mindset. That does not mean, however, that the personification of Matter definitively conflates Matter with the Mother; there is both more and less to Woman than that, as Plotinus is at pains to make clear. Having spoken of the All-Mother as a "representation" (179) of Matter, he adds:

> This too-exalting title is conferred on it in order to indicate that it is the source of things in the sense of being their underlie: it is an approximate name chosen for a general conception; there is no intention of suggesting a complete parallel with motherhood to those not satisfied with a surface impression but needing a precisely true presentment; by a remote symbolism, the nearest they could find, they indicate that Matter is sterile, not female to full effect, female in receptivity only, not in pregnancy; this they accomplish by exhibiting Matter as approached by what is neither female nor effectively

male but castrated of that impregnating power which belongs only to the unchangeably masculine.

(Plotinus, cited by Irigaray [1985g], 179)

"Of course," as Irigaray often has occasion to say in *Speculum*, "as you would expect." It's not about women, after all, but about men, or rather about masculinity. But then, of course, about "castrated" masculinity, for which the feminine is the always-available stand-in. So the discourse of masculinity takes a familiar detour through the disempowered feminine, to which, however, it speedily returns.

Beyond the "of course," however, something remains to be said that isn't necessarily a matter of course. If Plotinus's discourse of Matter both is and isn't about the Mother, that is not only because it is really about men, but because Matter is figured in his argument as a *barred* maternity, forever arrested on the threshold of whatever empowerment or potency the maternal affords, or may even be *thought* to afford. What is evident in Plotinus's finale, as it is throughout his personification, is a continuous drama of empowerment and disempowerment. Matter is summoned as needed, yet practically any contradictory trait ascribed to Matter, from impassivity through ghostliness to trickery, masquerading, aspiration, presumption, and Evil itself, threatens to empower it. As soon as any trait is disclosed, its potential therefore has to be arrested immediately.

Plotinus's characterization and periodic ventriloquism of Matter is always inseparable from his attempt to master it, cognitively and otherwise. Insofar as mastery requires that the psyche of Matter be penetrated, the revelation of Matter's wants (merely to be something, to do something, to own something, to partake of the Good) can be apprehended only as a threat to those in possession. (If it should appear that these wants are ordinary, hardly a mystery, Matter nevertheless remains inscrutable, so who knows what it really wants?) Indeed, any change in the status of Matter would undermine the very system of oppositions that constitutes the Good. It belongs to the Evil character of Matter that it aspires, however weakly, to change.

Despite or because of the defensiveness and willed lack of sympathy in Plotinus's characterization of Matter, his capacity to recognize its wants implies a degree of identificatory participation in its feminized otherness. Plotinus is at least capable of a degree of empathy, arising, no doubt, from his own psychic participation in Matter's "castrated" condition. Plotinus is thus (at least) doubly positioned in his text: on one hand as Plato's legatee and propagator of the philosophical master-discourse; on the other, as part of an incapacitated mass. Procreative self-actualization, the model for any actualization in Plotinus, lies so far beyond the bounds of possibility that any liberation of "desire" seems almost unreal. Matter is barred on one hand from "full" maternity and devoid on the other of the inseminating potency repeatedly and definitively assigned to masculinity in Plotinus. It is doubly "sterile."

Can this personification of Matter be other than a projection of the speaker's own disempowered and endlessly contradictory condition, of his own "character?" A "character" that has, however, fully internalized the rationales and imperatives if its own subjugation? If the answer to this question is affirmative, Plotinus's personification of Matter may count as, among other things, an unofficial portrait of the philosopher in late antiquity, a learned Greek living under the Roman Empire. (A portrait distinct, needless to say, from the admiring one drawn by Plotinus's disciple Porphyry [Trumbull 1934].) His privilege all too tenuously separates him from the mass.

As well as humanizing Matter, this projection may "humanize" Plotinus, yet we still seem quite far from anything that could be called the general human condition. It would certainly be incongruous to consider Plotinus as anything like representative man, or, for reasons of gender and/or class among others, as an exemplar of the general human condition.[19] Nor does he necessarily have much to "say" about that condition. Yet to *exclude* him tacitly from the human condition and disqualify his representation on that score would be to draw the human boundary in much the same place as he draws it, between the privileged and the deprived, merely reversing his valuations. If we follow Butler's lead, it is not enough to perform such an inversion while leaving the question of the boundary, or, more broadly, of the human threshold unconsidered. When Butler speaks of the *chora* [*hypodoche*] not as a human figure but as a liminal disfiguration, she implicitly raises the question of where that threshold is located and what transpires at it.

To forestall any misunderstanding, I do not take Butler's point to be a simple one, of which the meaning is self-evident. At one level, to speak of the *chora* [*hypodoche*] as a "disfiguration" is to say little more, in deconstructive terms, than that it is a figuration. No full or proper figure of the human, or of anything else, is to be expected under deconstructive logic, nor, perhaps, is any "central" location to be anticipated for any figure (disfiguration). The force of Butler's comment depends, however, not just on perceived disfiguration, but on how the particular threshold is conceived and what, precisely, is located there.

Insofar as the *chora* [*hypodoche*] constitutes a "disfiguration" of Woman, it does so partly by displacement and partly by the synecdochic reduction of Woman to the maternal body, ultimately to the womb. It also constitutes a disfiguration, however, by splitting Woman into the maternal and something Other. The barely apprehended potentialities of this alterity may be ones feminism seeks to conserve, but it remains radically inaccessible to "human" understanding.[20] Perhaps that is something Irigaray intimates when she writes of "*Une mère de glace*": a sea of ice.[21] While Irigaray may feel bound to conserve the feminist potentialities, or even the threatening power, of this otherness, its determination as feminine remains unalterably problematic. For Plotinus, this radical alterity is that of the material. In both Plotinus and Irigaray, the *chora* [*hypodoche*] can mark the point of arrival and/or disappearance of the human into what might be called the non-human, or, in a more threatening register, the Inhuman.[22] Yet the location of the *chora* [*hypodoche*] on the threshold makes it something of a hybrid figure (a disfiguration in that sense) in which two incommensurable orders are united. In this hybrid guise, the *chora* [*hypodoche*] seems almost like a metaphysical conceit, in which heterogeneous terms are yoked by violence together. If so, however, it is a conceit that indicates both the disconcerting proximity of the human to, and its participation in, that which is notionally heterogeneous, even threatening, to it; it also indicates the disconcerting tenuousness of the boundary separating the human from that which is notionally other than human.

From the standpoint at least of Western feminism, it obviously matters that Western culture has been predisposed to feminize the reduced and/or divided figure that hovers on the human threshold, thus implicitly securing the full humanity of the masculine. That abiding predisposition, especially when coupled with the Western predisposition to locate Woman on the threshold between human and animal, would be quite enough to warrant a continuing critique and secure its feminist specificity.[23] Although the category Woman has all but ceased to be viable for purposes of feminist critique (for *all* the reasons that will be familiar to readers), there are nevertheless certain contexts – that of Western classical philosophy and its legacy, for example – in which the term Woman, or perhaps the feminine, may retain an important, non-essentialist, critical function. The point is not necessarily to reclaim the term as foundational for feminism but rather to take it (at least) as a discursive category of which the critical and even political potentialities are not necessarily exhausted. In this instance, the potentialities include those of reconnecting the condition of Woman to the human condition, a connection paradoxically facilitated by Plotinus.

The fact that the *chora* [*hypodoche*] marks the point of human emergence and/or disappearance in Plotinus – the "condition" of humanity being that of its unalterable proximity to, and even its participation in, the inhuman – makes the feminine the chosen yet endlessly repudiated figure (disfigurement) for the insecurity, liminality, and limitation of the human. The feminine thus "represents" a general yet disavowed condition of human existence. Plotinus's personification of Matter does not, however, confine itself to the level of logical generality. More accurately, it cannot, or does not, conceal the psychic and socioeconomic dimensions of this liminal precariousness of the human. What Matter wants seems to be what humans can be presumed to want, at least from the standpoint of the possessor: to be something, to do something, to own something, to partake of the Good. These forever denied wants apparently pose a threat of dispossession, not only as if the sharing of goods will impoverish everyone, but as if dispossession would entail a loss of "full" human status to those who possess and defend it as an exclusive privilege. While the human mass may be ubiquitous, it is tantamount to the inhuman, and the *de facto* boundary, widely given *de jure* effect, runs between it and that which constitutes humanity, always insecurely, through gender, agency, possession, rank, visibility, etc. The effective boundary is not that between humankind and something else but is drawn internally to the species. The location of the *hypodoche* in Plotinus draws attention to material conditions of the human that may apply unequally to women but do not apply to them alone.

Ironically, in fact, Plotinus ends up by saying quite a lot in spite of himself about the human condition. The mediating perspective is always that of privileged possession; from that perspective the human mass as Matter remains invisible, ghostly, inscrutable. Its huge "impassivity" poses the threat that it has no recognizable wants, its condition thus being one of almost unimaginable, object-like security and self-sufficiency. At the same time, Plotinus must impute to the mass the minimum human wants that he cannot imagine as wholly absent. Presuming those denied wants, the masses must then be suspected of endless perversity, resistance, trickery, dissimulation, and misrepresentation. While their "base" abjection and impotence render them despicable, their poverty constitutes an endless demand on ownership. A "shared" humanity thus appears strictly unthinkable. Is it wrong to suppose that feminism might have a special stake in attending to these boundary conditions of the human, both metaphysically and materially? To be especially vigilant about the shifting placement of this boundary, in law and in fact? To keep in view the horizon of a shared and shareable humanity?

Perhaps counter-intuitively, attention both to the figure of Woman and to the metaphysical contexts in which it is precipitated does not necessarily come at the expense of the historico-political, nor does it necessarily obscure the overdetermined differences of women's lives. On the contrary, it may facilitate recognition of these differences: not all women stand in quite the same precarious material relation to the human threshold, however it is conceived or constructed. Socioeconomic privilege, global location, ethnicity, historical experience, and a host of other factors affect at least women's degree of proximity to the threshold. Perhaps the most drastic instance, in which women are formally located on the side of Matter while still called upon to perform the maternal function, belongs to the history of slavery. Indeed, the prevalence of slavery in the Roman Empire is not necessarily irrelevant to Plotinus's personification of Matter.[24] The next gradation is that of conditions tantamount to formal slavery, to which innumerable women are now exposed. Worldwide, at all events, women are at varying degrees of risk, circumstantially and endlessly, of being either reduced to maternity or exiled to the far side. Or both, as will generally be the case.

Invoking the term Woman as a feminist one does not necessarily result, then, in the denial of differences, and it may additionally promote feminist reflection, both critical and self-critical, on the human condition. Or, inseparably, on human *conditions* in the pursuit, ultimately, of an "impossible" shared humanity. This is not a question of re-idealizing the human. Donna Haraway, for example, has suggested the anti-humanist, feminist potentialities of another liminal disfiguration, namely the Cyborg that marks the threshold between the human and the technological; she has also heralded science's virtual erasure of the boundary between the organic and the inorganic at the molecular level, thus undermining one traditional precondition of humanity. Feminism is in no way bound to an essentializing humanism by attending to boundary conditions. Nor is it in any way incapacitated by acknowledging that the human is always a liminal, hybrid figure, although subject to highly variable, historically contingent, understanding as such.

Starting with *hypodoche* offers the advantage of enforced, perhaps even unwanted, attention to one disturbing point at which we may say, following Butler, that the human barely emerges and/or disappears. Partly enabled by Plotinus, to whom she at once yields place and replaces in the fluid medium of "*Une mère de glace*," Irigaray identifies this site as one of reserve feminist power, so to speak, although it can't be that alone. Even Plotinus makes it implicitly a site of imaginative reflection on the human in the guise of reflection on Matter. The troublesomeness of the category for him imports more than just a logical impasse in Platonism. The human is in question.

To what, then, does a reading of *"Une Mère de Glace"* conduce in feminist reflection or feminist politics? The whole point cannot be that it exposes Plotinus's "narcissistic phallocentrism." Even if we thought that was Irigaray's intended main purpose – and she is far from saying that, or saying anything in as many words about Plotinus – the next question could be "so what?" Powerful, complex answers have been provided by Irigaray's best commentators and continue to be implicitly provided by feminist activists around the globe (ones who, as often as not, reject "feminist" as an exclusive or privileged designation). I suggest no more than that a reading of Plotinus refracted through Irigaray reorients us from within feminism towards the horizon of the human. Any resulting "feminist humanism" would entail no necessary regression to would-be apolitical humanisms of the past. Nor would gender disappear from the equation for as long as women continued both to mark a boundary of the human in philosophical discourse and find themselves precariously and unequally situated on the boundary in political fact.

Notes

1 In this paper, I shall simply bracket the vexed questions of translation that arise both in connection with Irigaray's work and the Greek philosophical texts she cites. See, for example, "Irigaray in English" (Burke 1994a). The question is a large one indeed, since translation in Burke's account means both linguistic and cultural transposition. In the English version of *Speculum*, the extracts from Plotinus's Sixth Tractate are taken from *Plotinus's Enneads* (Plotinus 1956).

2 It should be remarked that Peter Kalkavage (Kalkavage 2001: 1–44) insists that *Timaeus* is already a playful, fanciful, quasi-fictional text.

3 This could be rephrased as the Lacanian question, "What does the Other want of us?" That rephrasing could in turn lead my own discussion in very different directions from the one it takes. Yet to take this Lacanian turn in a paper on Irigaray would be just too incongruous, adding insult to injury, so to speak, and in any case a Lacanian reading of the materials I will discuss does not strike me as urgently needed.

4 My restricted citation and contextualization of Plotinus place the focus exclusively on his theorization of Matter. It is beyond my competence to say how that theorization fits into the larger frame of Plotinus's *Enneads*, or how important it is in the structure of Plotinus's thought. One implication of *Speculum*, which I will accept for the purposes of my argument, is that patriarchal (or just scientifically erroneous) gender-presuppositions at once engender and vitiate Plotinus's project no less than they do Plato's – or the project of Western philosophy in general. For what I take to be a state of the art professional overview of Plotinus, innocent of any gender critique, see Gerson (1994, 1996). I have found no standard account in which gender is treated even as a factor.

5 These are among the elements of *Speculum* that made it a target of virulent anti-essentialist critique, or, as Burke (1994a: 250) puts it, "mired [Irigaray's work] in the anti-essentialism debates of the eighties." See also Schor (1994b: 3–4) on the repressive effect of anti-essentialist arguments in feminism, and, more generally, Chanter (1995).

6 Differently put, the degree to which they are found rigidly oppressive, threatening, or airless will be a highly variable function of different reading practices, personal histories, political convictions, cultural positions, transformative skills and resources, etc. I do

not suggest that Irigaray represents a "collaborationist" as distinct from a "rejectionist" feminism; if anything, *Speculum* enacts the dilemma of that choice.

7   Glossed as follows in the notes *Plato's Timaeus*, (Kalkavage 2001): "receptacle (*hypodoche*) ... any hospitable reception or refuge. It comes from the verb *hypodech-esthai* (literally, receive under), which means receive under one's roof or welcome, undertake, admit or allow, withstand an attack, and conceive or become pregnant" (142). I do not suggest that this thematization of the receptacle is isolated from larger contexts in both Plato and Plotinus. In the *Speculum*, there are clear affinities between the receptacle and the Platonic Cave, of which Irigaray produces a virtuoso reading in "Plato's *Hystera*" (Irigaray 1985g: 243–83).

8   I have stuck to the Jowett translation partly because of its "classic" status and ready availability, and partly to avoid using an English translation that postdates *Speculum*. It says something about the time-warped movement of cultural history that, for the late nineteenth century Jowett, *Timaeus* was only pseudo-science that had been superseded by real science. That fact made it "of all the writings of Plato ... the most obscure and repulsive to the modern reader" (Jowett 1931: 341). Neoplatonism gets equally short shrift: "There is no danger of the modern commentators on *Timaeus* falling into the absurdities of the Neo-Platonists" (343). The extraordinary difference now can be measured simply by consulting the bibliography to Kalkavage's translation of the *Timaeus*, to which Platonic text a great deal of high-powered philosophical attention has been given at least since Heidegger (Kalkavage 2001: 158–61). Kalkavage is not alone in considering the *Timaeus* Plato's single most historically influential dialogue, also the only one that circulated in Europe during the Middle Ages.

9   The difficulties of the "receptacle" are both conceptual and terminological given that it appears to cross between the rich semantic fields of *chora* and *hypodoche*. Commenting on *Timaeus*, however, Butler remarks that "the receptacle (*hypodoche*) is also called *chora*" (152). She importantly adds that "the word matter does not occur in Plato to describe this *chora* or *hypodoche*" (155). She believes this conflation is an Aristotelian inference solidified by Plotinus. Since *chora* and *hypodoche* are not fully interchangeable, I have used both together on occasion. I should simply add here that the basis on which Butler can invoke the human isn't wholly clear to me. Here, it seems more like a humanistic extrapolation from the (dis)figured feminine than like an autonomous term or category. I am far from objecting, however, to Butler's recourse to the term since one of my main points is that keeping open the horizon of the human is ethically and politically desirable.

10 Or even for taking Derridean analysis of the *chora* one step further, as Butler believes Irigaray does (Butler 1994: 154).

11 According to John Sallis, the assimilation of *chora* to matter is strictly neoplatonic and a "distorting assimilation" of Plato. Unusual among Platonic commentators in even mentioning Irigaray, he does so only to object violently to her perpetuation of this alleged distorting assimilation. He further complains that Irigaray "hardly cites Plato at all, and when she does it is screened through Plotinus." John Sallis, *Chorology: On Beginning in Plato's "Timaeus,"* Bloomington: Indiana University Press, 1999: 151. See, however, n. 9.

12 Plotinus's name does not even appear, for example, in the index to Whitford (1991) or to Chanter (1995). I am aware of no feminist commentary in which he features much more prominently than that. See, for example, Gallop (1988); Butler (1994); Hollywood (2002).

13 Notwithstanding, feminist incentives may now exist for considering Plotinus more closely inside the history of philosophy, rather than just as an exponent of ahistorical Platonism. Plotinus claims attention as an important relay between classical philosophy and so-called Christian neoplatonism. This historical sequence is not necessarily without bearing on the French feminists, including the Irigaray of "*La Mystérique*"

(Irigaray 1985g: 191–203), drawn to Christian thematics, often while disclaiming feminism. See also Rist (1996) and Hollywood (2002).

14 If one were seeking evidence that Philosophy remains impervious to feminist critique, or that it still refuses to confront its own gender-presuppositions, one would need to look no further than the standard commentaries on Plotinus. Is it a surprise that Irigaray's name does not appear in the index to the *Cambridge Companion*, published in 1996? Women who contributed were under no more obligation than men to cite Irigaray, but the fact remains that they didn't. Oddly, Irigaray isn't mentioned either in Margaret R. Miles, *Plotinus on Body and Beauty: Society, Philosophy and Religion in Third-Century Rome,* Oxford: Blackwell Publishers, 1999, despite a section titled "Feminism and Plotinus": 167–71. I merely note here that a canonical position within philosophy has increasingly been claimed for Irigaray, partly on the strength of the later works that lie outside my purview. See, for example, Naomi Schor (1994b), "Previous Engagements: The Receptions of Irigaray," *Engaging with Irigaray:* 4–5.

15 That fact, too, notwithstanding, Plotinus belongs to a moment in late antiquity when "classical" gender-constructions and relations are significantly being renegotiated, a process to which Foucault's *History of Sexuality* as well as the work of classical historians and critics has drawn increasing attention. See Michel Foucault, *The Care of the Self,* New York: Random House, 1988 and *The Use of Pleasure,* New York: Vintage Books, 1990; also, Peter Brown, *The Body and Society: Men, Women and Sexual Renunciation in Early Christianity*, New York: Columbia University Press, 1988; David M. Halperin, John J. Winkler, Froma I. Zeitlin, ed., *Before Sexuality: The Construction of Erotic Experience in the Ancient Greek World*, Princeton: Princeton University Press, 1990; James Tatum, ed., *The Search for the Ancient Novel*, Baltimore: Johns Hopkins University Press, 1994; Simon Goldhill, *Foucault's Virginity: Ancient Erotic Fiction and the History of Sexuality,* New York: Cambridge University Press, 1995. These texts open up potentially rich fields of feminist inquiry to which I can do no more than allude here.

16 Perhaps it is worth remarking that appeals to Matter in Materialist arguments do not always precipitate it more unproblematically or productively than do Plato and Plotinus. Quite the reverse in many cases, and often without consciousness of having been anticipated, and remaining indebted. This comment is not intended to be a veiled anti-Marxist one, nor one that underestimates the power of explicit or implicit materialisms at least from the Greek atomists through Francis Bacon to the present. My comment applies, rather, to arbitrary, bullying invocations of the material.

17 This explicit designation seems foreign to the *Timaeus.* It reminds us that Plotinus is writing in the second century CE, at a time when Christian and neoplatonic thought not only interact but are concurrent manifestations of the same forces operating in the culture of late antiquity. It is worth recalling that Plotinus's disciple and editor Porphyry wrote explicit anti-Christian polemic. O'Brien (1996: 171–95) argues that Plotinus's notion of an Evil that must emanate from the One represents a difficult paradox for Plotinians; he also makes the case that Plotinus is responding to Gnosticism.

18 Plotinus's characterization of Matter intersects at moments with Agamben's characterization of the "bare life" of *homo sacer,* beyond the pale of "human rights" or human recognition (Agamben 1998).

19 Plotinus is a distinct historical case too, of course. It is a side issue here, but I do not accept any blanket prohibition decreed in the name of History on discussion of either the human or the human condition. While I accept anti-humanistic caveats at least from Marx onwards, I believe the moment, if ever there was one, for a taboo on the term "human" has passed.

20 There is a sense, of course, in which Woman *is* Inhuman as a reified, exclusive figure. That might contribute to the "reserve" power of the *chora [hypodoche]*, but not without exposing feminism to accusations of hubris and inhumanity.

21 Irigaray argues, of course, that patriarchy turns the fluidity of the feminine – a fluidity that is always also the residue of the One – into a frozen mirror or icy shards (Irigaray

1985g: 237–9). Nothing, however, in the fluid, place-changing economy of the *Speculum* – including a sea of ice – can occupy a fixed position or signify the masculine in fully definitive opposition to the feminine.

22 I do not particularly allude to the conception of the Inhuman found in Lyotard (1988), but I acknowledge that the "human" has a temporal dimension inasmuch as it entails becoming rather than just being human.

23 Although this is practically a commonplace, for a summary see Maclean (1980).

24 It was a specific peculiarity of Roman law that, while legally classified as property, slaves could nevertheless be manumitted, or purchase their own freedom, thus resuming human status. Freemen could also sell themselves into slavery to escape debt, or for other reasons. Without factoring in additional categories including that of citizenship, it would be going too far to say that Romans could thus bear daily witness to the precariousness of the boundary between the human and the material as well as the reversibility of those statuses in the life of any individual. Since, however, slaves have been estimated at 40 percent of the Roman imperial population, Romans did inhabit a radically split world in which the predicament and wishes of "matter" might well be imagined.

4 Coming into the word

Desdemona's story

Barbara L. Estrin

OTHELLO'S CATASTROPHE, DESDEMONA'S ANASTROPHE

Enacting her prescriptive that "discourse has a sex" (1993b: 133) by sexualizing her own discourse, Irigaray maintains that the female "remains unformed as subject of the autonomous word .... [Her] coming or the subjective anastrophe (rather than the catastrophe) ... has not yet taken place." I will use Irigaray's characterization of linguistic subjectivity (the female opening into language through "anastrophe"/the male impulse toward closure or "catastrophe") to describe the trajectories that set Desdemona and Othello on a verbal collision course in Shakespeare's Venetian tragedy. The oppositions Irigaray proposes in *To Speak Is Never Neutral* are, however, complicated by what I think is a deliberate terminological slippage (a subversion of the "imperialism" of all linguistic "paradigm[s]," 2002b: 3) that renders her analysis even more pertinent to an understanding of the gender dynamics of *Othello*.

As she defines the still unrealized potential of female subjectivity, Irigaray points to two very different and not really parallel discursive practices derived from the ancient Greeks. "Anastrophe" is a *rhetorical* tactic, governing a *grammatical* inversion that almost always involves a *temporal reversal*. In her parenthetical allusion to the equally ancient and presumably male "catastrophe," Irigaray refers to the predetermined course leading to the *temporal finality* – the denouement – of a dramatic form.[1] By definition, "anastrophe" includes some sort of turn or retrieval of beginnings; "catastrophe" specifies a point of no return, or a movement toward endings. The parenthetical insertion of "catastrophe" is itself a rhetorical flourish (the French even adds inverted commas around, and a question mark after, catastrophe [Irigaray 1985g: 10]) to indicate that the female "coming" remains open ("turning in a cycle that never resolves in sameness," 1993b: 195) whereas the male direction seems a bit like Groucho Marx's "hello, I must be going." On the run from the start, the male trajectory results in the inevitable climax of its own preordination.

Irigaray front-ends the anastrophic female linguistic approach as a way of avoiding what in her recent work she calls the "growing socio-cultural entropy" – the going nowhere new – that marks the male "form-giving" (2002b: 3) enterprise as inexorably dead-ended. Beholden to the "law of genre" (Goldberg 1985: 121), dramatic form contains an already determined conclusion recognized at the "cat-astrophic" and decisive moment. Contrastingly, "anastrophe" creates transpositions and is therefore open to the unexpected, and always still possible, "coming." Irigaray's terms – "anastrophe" emphasizing transformational rhetori-cal, "catastrophe" stressing fixed dramatic, forms – involve trajectories that are grounded in the space-time continuum governing Irigaray's linguistic theory. In that regard, we can follow Desdemona's progress as she "turns signs over and over in every direction" (Irigaray 2002b: 204) to find, in the boudoir scene of Act 4, "her language, her word, her style" (2002b: 4) and observe Othello's decline in the same act as he loses the prerogative of male narrative control he so confidently asserts in Act 1 when he constructs Desdemona in his own image.

In the first part of this essay, I define the Irigarayan male and female linguistic trajectories and how we might read *Othello* through them; in the second part, I describe what happens when the principal characters collide along those trajecto-ries. Finally, I argue that, when Desdemona finds her voice and releases herself from the cultural imperatives that would leave her "ossified ... frozen in front of what [she] is presumed to be and to become" (Irigaray 2003: 142), she recali-brates the gender dynamics of the play. Her return in Act 4 to a story from her distant past is as important to her characterization as is her initial refutation of Brabantio's hold on her at the beginning. Pulling back from the world of fathers, she breaks the mold that first Brabantio and then Othello prefabricate for her. Desdemona's anastrophic "coming" (Irigaray 2002b: 4) in Act 4 approaches the not-yet-created language that puts her in touch with the "subject that has always been" (2002b: 4), a curious link between a future still unformed and a past still untapped. In terms of the linguistic structure, the two characters move in opposite directions. Othello's downward slide results in the "hysterical collapse" (Smith 1998: 168), "the catastrophe" of Act 4;[2] Desdemona's return facilitates the suc-cessful consolidation of her speaking powers at the end of that same act.

Tracing those divergences, I will treat the Irigarayan time scheme as indivis-ible from the linguistic framework. Intrinsic to each is a spatial dimension: "Living beings, insofar as they are alive, are a becoming ... [and] no becoming is morphologically undifferentiated" (Irigaray 2002b: 3–4). Since the word in both French and English describes bodily and grammatical structure, Irigaray's emphasis on morphology attaches physical and verbal form to the temporality of "becoming." For Irigaray "the story [of that 'becoming'] ... with its projects, its generations, its loops and its repetitions" (2002b: 3) in turn reflects the linear thrust of male "projections and generations" and the reversals of female "loops and repetitions," the gendered language structures that define Othello and Desdemona respectively.

As I will indicate by focusing briefly on Othello's creation of Desdemona in the stories he tells of their courtship in Act 1, Othello's temporality is subject to what Irigaray identifies as a physical rupture that leaves the male in a vacuum: "He must live out the pain and experience the impossibility of being cut off from and in *space* (being born, leaving the mother)," 1993b: 64. In Irigaray's terms, to be *in space* means to be depth-deprived and totally without bodily grounding.

Because he fails to recognize that something solid exists behind "the linearity of the utterance" (Irigaray 2002b: 203) and refuses to acknowledge that there must be a "back side" (2002b: 203) to the projection, Othello hovers between nostalgia and anticipation. Filling in the physical void with the verbal forms he creates to counter the "exile he lives out between the *never more* and *the not yet*" (Irigaray 1993b: 64), he depends for his linguistic presence on the maternal absence that fuels the story he tells the court, "th'imminent deadly breach (1.3.137) ... even from [his] boyish days" (1.3.133). Temporality exists for him as the empty space between memory and desire, the breach he sublimates with language.

Contrastingly, Desdemona's "relation to the cyclical" (1993b: 64) facilitates the anastrophic recovery of a maternal matrix that gives her access to the "reservoir of ... meaning" (Irigaray 2002b: 4) she opens in Act 4. Irigaray defines such a trajectory as a process of "painting" or "*spatial[izing] perception and mak[ing]* time *simultaneous* ... to build bridges, establish perspectives between present-past-future (1993e: 155). In the temporal realm, "painting" changes the ordinary sequence of chronology (past-present-future) by naming the past the middle term and the determinative switch-point. Spatially, it establishes a "depth of field" (1993e: 155) in order to "regestualize the sign" (2002b: 203). More concerned with "refounding than with overcoming" (Irigaray 2001b: 65), Desdemona inverts "the specular operations of projections" (2002b: 203) and folds the "other side of the backside" (2002b: 204) into the structure of utterance. While Desdemona "paints" spatial and temporal bridges, Othello burns them, leaving himself "an outsider, looking in from the outborders, literally ... from [the] outpost" of Cyprus (Little, Jr. 2000: 101).[3] For Othello, suspension – the spatial exile – is all. For Desdemona, the interweaving of past experience into the fabric of her present situation establishes her "specific relational identity" (Irigaray 2002a: 129) in the origin that secures her linguistic destiny.

As I will suggest in the final part of this chapter, Desdemona transforms herself from the woman who, in Act 1, exhibits what Irigaray calls the "mimetic tendencies" that condition her to behave "like the other," (2002b: 4) – "my heart's subdued/Even to the very quality of my lord," 1.3.251–2 – to a woman who discovers a language that constructs her subjectivity. Through her "anastrophe" in Act 4, she recovers a narrative origin based on an actual memory, something that she pulls out of her history and carries into the present with the willow song that will "not go from [her] mind" (4.3.29). Desdemona's reconstruction evokes a long-ago Venice where (like a little Mamillius teasing Hermione's women about matters sexual) she overheard her mother's maid singing. The refrain of the song lives on in Emilia's mind when it dawns on her in Act 5 that her present synchronizes with the betrayals Barbary's lyric describes. Emilia already knows the answer to the question she asks, "what did thy song bode, lady?" (5.2.243). Her "willow, willow, willow" (5.3.247) turns the room in Cyprus into an *echo chamber*, an auditory "painting" that refers back to the original scene in Venice. Barbary haunts the deathbed scene, the devastating revelations of her lyric's "courting and couching" (4.3.46) anticipatory of the final exposure in the "tragic loading of this bed" (5.2.361).

Othello's indictment of Desdemona at the end, "she was false as water" (5.2.132), contrasts to the faithful streams of Barbary's song and defines his "catastrophic" moment as the ultimate shattering of the linguistic empire he constructed at the beginning of the play. In the simile, Othello equates Desdemona with the shifting signifier he himself devised, finding to his horror that "the identity between a thing and its representations holds no assurances" (Irigaray 2002b: 195) and that his "constructions in language merely objectified his own hollow self" (Fineman 1994: 110). His "cold, icy, frozen-freezing" (Irigaray 1993b: 170) mirror melts into the instability of the "false ... water" as Othello loses himself in the narcissistic maze of "the pure signifier that he is" (2002b: 19), his despair suggesting not only that "the thing in the mirror is not the same thing any more," but that "it never was the same thing, and never was actually there" (2002b: 195).

The form Othello can no longer find in Act 5 takes shape in the story he tells the Venetian court in Act 1, where the narrative of his courtship (1.3.129–70) does exactly what Brabantio means when he says, "I had rather to adopt a child than get it" (1.3.202). With that "rather," Brabantio abandons the biological child and her history in favor of one who might more accurately fulfill his patriarchal design. The Othello of the courtship speech "adopts" Desdemona in order to create her as his image, speaking *for* Desdemona (and in her person) of what he "wish[es]" to produce *by* himself (and in his own person): the replication of "such a man" (1.3.164). Othello's fluency early in the play depends on the denial that sets him off on a series of military and romantic exploits, the déjà-vu of the adventures he recounts to the Venetians and the nostalgia for the before-marriage uncertainty, the déjà-woo he rehearses in the history of his courtship.

The linguistic breakdown that ends in the "catastrophic" Act 5 already begins in Act 2 where Othello seems to be denied nothing. In fact, Othello's verbal faultline is established even before Iago systematically provokes him in Act 3. Its principal observer (albeit its unwitting cause) is Desdemona herself. Othello's animus against Desdemona emerges not after the temptation scene, but before it, through the exchanges of 2.1.180–210 and 3.3.35–93. In the first scene, he reacts to Desdemona's contradiction of his assertion that they have attained in Cyprus the perfect climax of, and the total limit to, marital happiness by simply removing her from the field of dispute (2.1.193). In the second round of verbal sparring, where Desdemona refuses to be silenced by him, and when, as projected other, she no longer fits the image he privileges, Othello's response resembles the meanderings of Lear's sputtering invective against his daughters' cruelty ("I will do such things ..." [2.1.277]). Pleading with Othello on behalf of Cassio, Desdemona observes in him the same incoherence we find in Lear: "I wonder in my soul/What you would ask me that I should deny/Or stand so mamm'ring on" (3.3.68–70). Lear's failure to define is caused by what he perceives to be his unyielding daughters. But Othello's similar verbal breakdown is charted by a woman who would "deny" him nothing (3.3.70) and who wants him to engage with her in the playful banter she expects of a partner well versed in Petrarchan foreplay and masculinist war talk.

I think that Othello's "mamm'ring" in Act 3 is caused not by Desdemona's withdrawal but by her proximity, a success that returns him to the mammary access he lost in infancy as well as to the desired breast he sought to reclaim in the wooing stage that before marriage became the source of his linguistic prowess. Desdemona's very word, "mamm'ring," to describe Othello's verbal inadequacy underlines the obverse relationship between his determination to father her through his creative powers and his need to have her mother him through her generative body. Defining Othello's obsession with the maternal, Desdemona performs an Irigarayan analysis *avant la lettre*. "In French," Irigaray writes, "*mamam* means, at least phonetically, that which is kept but which cannot be represented, expressed, mastered, that which suspends consumption but favors respiration, that which covers the whole with a vast blackness expressed by the *m* and potentially matches all colors thanks to the *a*. The name is one of the most perfect words possible" (1993e: 100–1).[4]

Marking Othello's verbal insufficiency in terms of the conjunction of mother and lover, Desdemona's "mamm'ring" links Irigaray's definitions of male temporality to her identification of male verbal subject formation: the appropriative creation produces a faltering articulation. Othello's reaction to his inadequacy at this point is to refuse to confront it. When Desdemona accuses him of the very emptiness his language is supposed to cover over, he simply leaves the scene, disengaging himself from her sight and her words. Alone, he recognizes the connection between her stability as image and his own sense of linguistic control: "But I do love thee! and when I love thee not/Chaos is come again" (3.3.91–2). His temporal trajectory depends on her remaining in the future what he wanted her to be in the past: the projection through which he expressed his cohesiveness. If he retracts the love he imagined he gave her, he will be thrown right back into the "vast unknown blackness" (Irigaray 1993e: 101), the spatial void of maternal absence. It's either all or nothing with him. Later in the play, as she moves totally out of his representational agency, he retrospectively annuls her, his "wouldst thou hadst ne'er/been born" (4.2.69–70), a repetition of Brabantio's "I had rather to adopt a child then get it" (1.3.193). To avoid the possibility of her wavering from the specular place he created for her, the Othello of the early acts seems always to be pushing Desdemona out of sight. In 1.2.200, he hastens, "I have but an hour"; in 3.3.89, he begs her to "grant me this,/To leave me but a little to myself." Locked in the embrace of their first Cyprus kiss (2.1.96), he can neither hear nor see her.

COLLIDING TRAJECTORIES: OTHELLO'S ABSOLUTE, DESDEMONA'S RELATIVE

In the Venice of Act 1, Othello's evocation of the past pressed an anticipatory chain of "not yets" into being; in Cyprus the "wonder" (2.1.181) of the present suggests that this victory will "never again" be duplicated. Nothing can equal the past of the present:

> If it were now to die
> 'Twere now to be most happy, for I fear
> My soul has her content so absolute
> That not another comfort like to this
> Succeeds in unknown fate.

(2.1.187–91)

Othello's "now to die" bears an inverse relationship to the dangers of "th'imminent deadly breach" of 1.3.136. The immanence of love is more threatening than the imminence of death. Succession signifies loss, a secession from the moment of power, measured by the end of metaphor: "not another comfort" can resemble this.

When Desdemona contradicts him and opens to an expansion of love, she envisions both the exact duplication of *even* – an assurance that shall always be equal to theirs now – and the relative equivalent of *as* – a parallel that accommodates the progression of time with a concomitant expansion of space:

> The heavens forbid
> But that our loves and comforts should increase
> Even as our days do grow.

(2.1.191–3)

Desdemona's vision is both exact and unregulated, a mutuality achieved in the doubling of "our." With the permeability of her materiality, simile folds into metonymy.[5] "Even as" allows a "'regrowth' ... in perpetual increase" (Irigaray 1993b: 28).

Attempting to inhibit that amplification, and asserting the divine authority of his control, Othello relegates Desdemona's rebuttal to the decidedly diminutive realm of feminine "sweet powers." In the equation of happiness with restraint, his "content" puts a lid on Desdemona's increase:

> Amen to that, sweet powers!
> I cannot speak enough of this content,
> It stops me here, it is too much of joy
> And this, and this the greatest discords be (*They kiss*)
> That e'er our hearts shall make.

(2.1.193–7)

Joy is excessive ("it is too much") and not enough ("it stops me here") to allow him easy access through the formula of his expressiveness. Their quarrel must be trivialized and reduced to the duration of two stifling kisses (the "this" and "this") which consequently allow him to preserve the language patterns that create Desdemona as his double. But his unease here reveals something deeper, what Irigaray calls the schizophrenic "fear of the excessive ... mother tongue" that poses "the threat of meaning's collapse, disintegration or decomposition" (2002b: 186). Desdemona's "too much" makes Othello feel too little.

The very kiss which brings the argument to a close exposes him to the source of the boundary-crossing Irigarayan "*mucous* of the carnal ... primary in its opening" (Irigaray 1993b: 162) that leaves everything at the brink of "some tactile unfinished in-finite" (2002b: 240). The commanding injunction of Othello's "amen" simply cannot contain Desdemona's corporeality. Stilling the "voice that overflows the 'subject'" (Irigaray 1985d: 112), he finds himself nevertheless stymied by the double female "threshold":

> Two sets of lips that ... cross over each other like the arms of the cross. ... The mouth lips and the genital lips do not point in the same direction. In some way they point in the direction opposite from the one you would expect, with the "lower" ones forming the vertical.
>
> (Irigaray 1993b: 18)

At the entrance of bodily life, the lower lips acquire, in their verticality, the phallic power of linguistic origination, a launching point extended into the open-ended horizontal by the upper lips when women speak. Since merely touching one set of lips subjects him to the other, Othello see-saws between two poles: the gigantism of "the mother's power to give birth, nourish, inhabit, center" (Irigaray 1993e: 14) and the equally threatening specter of the woman as creator of a different language structure. While in Act 2, Othello's pontifical "amen" allows him to retain the illusion of his generative dominion, in the later acts he appears more and more as the sacrificial Christ on the imaginary "cross" of Desdemona's intersecting lips.

When he demonizes Desdemona, Othello fluctuates between the earlier self-promoting aggrandizement that renders him all-controlling father ("I'd whistle her off and let her down the wind/to prey at fortune," [3.3.266–7]) and the belated self-pitying reduction that depicts him as abandoned child: "I am abused" (3.3.272). In Act 3, his two-pronged refutation of Desdemona at first undoes temporality. Still attempting to control Desdemona's expansion, he parallels Brabantio's retrospective annihilation of her as he invents a past and future self he would "rather be":

> I had rather be a toad
> And live upon the vapour of a dungeon
> Than keep a corner in the thing I love
> For others' uses.
>
> (3.3.274–77)

After undoing time with the "rather," he secondarily relegates Desdemona to a space too small to penetrate. With the imagined closure of "a corner," Desdemona is reduced to a nonentity contained by the "thing he loves," the "thing" he projected in Act 1 as the object through which he identifies himself. If she is a corner here, he can remain the reflective source of her being: Desdemona is a miniscule he. Barely noticeable, she is "assigned to be place without occupying a place" (Irigaray 1993b: 52). But, in Act 4, when he finally apprehends how much he has "confused that which [he] projected with [his] identity" (Irigaray 2002b: 203), even that stop-gap ceases to work.

Calling Desdemona "a cistern for foul toads/to knot and gender in" (4.2.62–3), Othello overturns his earlier connection between the discursively primal genital and facial lips to convert the womb into a devouring, rather than projecting, mouth: "a sewer in which anal and urethral waste is poured" (Irigaray 1993e: 16). If what overwhelms him in Act 2 is the undecidability of the half-open lips and if what satisfies him temporarily in Act 3 is the rigid containment of Desdemona's body, in Act 4 he renders her an absolute wasteland, eliminating the upper lips and their linguistic capacity entirely. She is all opening, a snake with its tail shut tight in its mouth rather than the "container [which] is never closed" (Irigaray 1993b: 51). Thus, when he names her "that cunning whore of Venice" (4.2.91), Othello describes Desdemona's falseness of mind in terms of the bodily part that signifies her nothingness. As Daniel Vitkus writes, "her purportedly absent hymen – and the resulting hole, the hymenless orifice – becomes the central imaginary object of Othello's bloody thoughts. ... Desdemona's sexual condition becomes Othello's world" (Irigaray 2002: 352). She is the "cunting" whore of Venice, simultaneously overrun by monsters and marked by her absence both from normative representation and discursive subjectivity.

AB-HORING THE WORD OR DESDEMONA'S "NEW CULTURAL ELABORATION" [6]

Desdemona's question of Iago, "am I that name" (4.2.119), contests the label that Othello assigns her. In parroting him, she asserts her own verbal dexterity:

> I cannot say whore:
> It does abhor me now I speak the word;
> To do the act that might the addition earn
> Not the world's mass of vanity could make me.

> (4.2.163–6)

When she speaks the word apotropaically, Desdemona turns her back to it, in the "ab-hor." But, in the last phrase, she declares a twofold future, annulling the methodology of Othello's original representation and subsequent disfiguration. Her "mass of vanity" indicts the very mirrors through which Othello "fathered" her, dispelling the narcissistic image and defining a different genealogy for the origins of her own speech. She cannot be "made" in the sense of created by any sort of reflective verbal economy and she will not "do" the act of multiplying lovers that would justify the name.

Affirming her female bodily presence, as she has in all her encounters with Othello, Desdemona works out of a double set of memories, one sexual, the other maternal. In the sexual memory, Desdemona thrice asserts what her love involves, each time evoking the constancy of the Irigarayan linguistic space she originally opened. First, with Iago, she calls Othello (as she will at the end) both cruel and out of character. "Unkindness may do much,/And his unkindness may defeat my life/But never taint my love" (4.2.161–3). In the futurity of her phrasing, Desdemona remains faithful to her initial feeling. Functioning as a self-sustaining entity, "[her] love" can neither be removed nor diminished; it exists as a guarantor of an "intentionality" (Irigaray 1996: 110).

In the second confirmation, "my love" acts out its intentionality and becomes the source of something Desdemona brings to Othello through the "creativity difference produces" (Irigaray 1996: 146). Reframing the negative into a positive by using "[her] love," she accepts his changed disposition:

> my love doth so approve him
> That even his stubbornness, his checks, his frowns
> – Prithee unpin me – have grace and favour.

$$\text{(4.3.17–19)}$$

Her insistence this time positions "[her] love" as a stay against Othello's fall from his former self. In Desdemona's "approval," the personification of "my love" accomplishes the revolution around Desdemona that preserves Desdemona's intentionality without "ruminating, sadly and endlessly, over solipsistic questions in a sort of cultural cannibalism" (1996: 110).

If Othello renders Desdemona the all-devouring mouth, Desdemona refuses to eat back her love. To arrive at this point, Desdemona achieves the "growth between the within of an intention and the without of a thing created by the other, a passage from within to without, from without to within" (Irigaray 2002b: 4) that allows her access to the selfhood she is intent on recovering. She has reversed the order. No longer the reflector of Othello (objectified by "the passage from without"), she brings the "within" of her intentionality to the surface, reaching inside to reveal "the subject that has always been" (2002b: 4). At the very moment that she crosses the threshold to enact her intention, she apprehends the "without" of Othello's difference. The movement toward exteriority initiates a "return" (Irigaray 1996: 110) that accepts the other as other. The reproof of Othello's "checks" requires a corresponding new approach, her "approval." At the acoustic center of their different trajectories is the critical "proof" that resonates as a verbal marker throughout the play – Othello's "ocular proof" (3.3.362) and her behavioral "ap-proval." For Othello, "ocular proof" is the static specular object. For Desdemona, "ap-proval" involves an addition, a response to Othello's *reproach* with a corresponding *rapprochement* that assumes an "essentially relational" (Irigaray 2002c: 80) linguistic subjectivity. The process through which Desdemona renders her inner thoughts apparent becomes the condition through which she confirms Othello's separateness, establishing "a chiasmus or double loop in which each can go toward the other and come back to itself" (Irigaray 1993b: 9).

In the last of the defense mechanisms, Desdemona characterizes love as an ongoing restorative she can wield:

Good night, good night. God me such usage send
Not to pick bad from bad, but by bad mend!

(4.3.103–4)

Like Celia at the end of the first act of *As You Like It* ("Now go we in content/To
liberty and not banishment," 1.3.58–9) and Juliet at the end of the balcony scene
("Good night, good night. Parting is such sweet sorrow/That I shall say good
night till it be morrow," 2.2.184–5), Desdemona concludes the act with a couplet
that pronounces her determination.[7] But, unlike Celia and Juliet whose practices
involve fabulations, Desdemona operates through mechanical "usage," weaving
her language into the actual materiality of the experiential. Building from the base
reality of her present situation, she uses it as the métier of a new construction.
With an ambiguous referent to the object of "mending" (will she repair herself or
Othello?), Desdemona accepts the need for change and the responsibility for carrying it out.

If her practice at the end of the boudoir scene depends on reparation, her
preparation begins with the deconstruction of "unpinning" (4.3.19, 33) early on, a
command she twice gives to Emilia, as if, taking off her gown and all the accou-
trements made for "these men" (4.3.52), she assumes an elemental self and a
return to the female discursive matrix. Unadorned, she releases the paralyzing
hold of the male narrative economy and awakens her other – the maternal – set of
memories. In Barbary's song, she reverses the notion that the idealized woman is
made in the image of the ideal man:

If I court moe women, you'll couch with moe men.

(4.3.46)

By taking over the man's voice, the lyric identifies male pluralized courting as the
precondition for female multiple couching.[8] This line, where women ventrilo-
quize men, challenges the handkerchief description, where Othello uses the
sibyl's words against Desdemona. In Othello's story, female slippages are responsible for male unfaithfulness.[9] But in Barbary's song, male incontinence causes
female looseness.[10]

Desdemona's connection between primal memory and subsequent expectation
spurs the willow song into being:

My mother had a maid called Barbary,
She was in love, and he she loved proved mad
And did forsake her.

(4.3.24–6)

Because Barbary and her song will "not go from [her] mind" (4.3.29),
Desdemona is simultaneously shadowed and supported by her past. In the reacti-
vation of Barbary, Desdemona's locution suggests a mutual coherence. Through
the mediation of her "mind," the community of women advances into the present

to form an internal protection just as Desdemona retroactively extends to Barbary the perspective and homage of her current understanding. Inwardly strengthened, Desdemona opens herself to Barbary's commemoration:

> The fresh streams ran by her and murmured her moans,
>   Sing willow, willow, willow:
> Her salt tears fell from her and softened the stones.
>
> (4.3.41–4)

In Barbary's song, the streams "ran *by*" her as she positions herself in conjunction with them and sing *with* her, carrying her sadness as if it were their own. The metonymic closeness of the natural world renders the murmuring stream an echoing song, just as the salt tears soften that world and create an accommodating vessel. Through the motion of her tears, Barbary turns the stones into an extra-uterine holding space, characterized by its changing shape and lack of closure. The welcoming home she sculpts with her watery tears and the sympathetic chorus she enlists in the watery streams offer alternatives to the "nostalgia" of the "male desire to go back toward and into the originary womb" (Irigaray 1993b: 100). The tears keep flowing just as the streams keep running, the operative language suggesting perpetual movement.

When they sing back her song, the waters anticipate what Irigaray says of the woman's voice:

> It speaks "fluid" ... is continuous, compressible, dilatable, viscous, conductible, diffusible ... it exert[s] pressure through the walls of a solid. ... it is already diffuse "in itself," which disconcerts any attempt at static identification.
>
> (Irigaray 1985d: 111)

Resisting the immobility of the Venetian narrative, Desdemona chooses a liquid mutability. The softened stones respond to the tears that, as still other versions of the boundary crossing mucus, penetrate "the walls of the solid" to forge a sustaining base. Enacting what Irigaray calls the "intentionality" of the body: "vertical in genealogy, horizontal in the relation between genders" (2001b: 33), the song illustrates the Irigarayan imperative to allow "speech ... to change levels – vertically and horizontally" (2003: 58). As it converts the downward flow of Barbary's tears into the lateral rush of the streams, the lyric replaces the cold accusations of Barbary's lover with a confirming mutuality. Finally when it inverts all signs "so that one side no longer has the monopoly on its value" (Irigaray 2002b: 203), the very blurring of the teary eyes emphasizes the tactile over the specular just as the lip-like doubling of the lids renders them one of multiple female openings.[11]

The running streams similarly resist containment. Their "murmuring" empathetically repeats and so soothes Barbary's pain. Othello's stuttering and "mamm'ring" signified a disjunction, turning the end of his speech back to the divisional breach of its source. The "murmuring" streams transform the inarticulate "moan" into a melodic counterpart for the tender stones, the rhythm and the space representing a supportive communion. The boundaries between earth and shore, solid and liquid, overflow and "touch against one another while still remaining open" (Irigaray 1993b: 51).

That effusion of diffusion survives into the last act as Desdemona speaks her own valediction and claims ownership of the deed: "Nobody. I myself. Farewell!/Commend me to my kind lord" (5.2.121–2).[12] In the first line, she countermands the simulacrum of Othello's verbal mirroring and identifies the murderer as someone who, annulling the body, refuses to acknowledge the materiality of the flesh. Thus, she calls Othello "nobody" and proclaims her abandonment: "I myself." In the world of no-bodies, she is ultimately alone and responsible for her own fate. But, in the "commend," she defines a measure of success, having restored Othello, by the creativity of her linguistic mending, to the status of her "kind lord." Co-mended, Othello is remanded to the self she remembers.

Exchanging the determining forms of Venetian fathers for a story woven around a community of mothers, Desdemona accepts total responsibility for the life she has chosen to live and the death that, consequently, she is forced to die. Her perseverance, part of what Irigaray characterizes as the unfinished project of human becoming, is revealed in the lines that seem to me the most poignant in the play: "kill me tomorrow, let me live tonight" (5.2.80). The gradually decreasing time she begs for, "but half an hour (5.2.81) … but while I say one prayer" (5.2.83) has already been preempted by Othello's unyieldingness: "thou dost stone my heart" (5.2.63). Even at the last, her wish is phrased as a plea bargain, her prayer an attempt to effect the temporal reversal of "anastrophe." Having moved beyond the "catastrophic" moment, Othello can only respond in terms of the oppositional trajectory I have been tracing.

Finally, however, we are forced to ask what does Desdemona's "refounding" (Irigaray 2001b: 65) avail if it cannot overcome Othello's impenetrable forms? I think Irigaray might answer that question by referring to the "historic gap between the culture that corresponds to female genealogies and the culture produced by the social foundations of patriarchy" (Irigaray 1993a: 165). With regard to any canonized text, she might also contend that "We are dealing with at least two phenomena: the interpretation of a story that is being read after the fact and a period of transition where new meaning has not yet been discovered" (Irigaray 2002b: 6). In the twenty-first century, we're still in that period of "transition," living in the after-life of the "historic gap" and still struggling to find ways "for the [female] subject to come back to itself" (2002b: 4). If we read only for Othello's trajectory, there is nothing but "catastrophe." But if we recognize that the "linearity of the utterance … is no longer sufficient" (2002b: 203), we might understand that the "anastrophe" of Desdemona's story rekindles "the memory of a culture of life which we have erased" (Irigaray 2001b: 65) even as her rhetorical practices augur a generic sea change, "necessitat[ing] the passage to another order" (2002a: 135).

Notes

1 Patricia Parker's analysis of a parallel to rhetorical anastrophe, "hysteron proteron," in *Love's Labor's Lost* concentrates on "reversals of gender, class, and other forms of ordering" (1993: 446) which involve transferring existing terms rather than what Irigaray proposes, "another discourse, one that is put together differently" (1993e: 177).
2 Ian Smith stresses the relationship between "cultural incivility and linguistic barbarity" which, he maintains, Iago exploits in designating Othello as a cultural alien. In arguing that Othello is an insider, I follow Irigaray's contention that "race is in fact a secondary problem" (1996: 47) as well as her belief that "the most universal and irreducible difference … is the one that exists between the genders" (2002a: 98).
3 In Little, Jr.'s reading (2000), Venice redefines Othello until Othello fits its actual expectations of him. Such a reading renders Othello the object of preconceived Venetian notions. Two recent critics also provide compelling arguments for casting Othello as the target of a racist, rather than the generator of a sexuate power structure. Peter Erickson reasons that "racial issues shape the marital conflict" (2002: 138). Janet Adelman's thesis about Iago's Kleinian envy (1997) specifically links misogyny and racism in the play by centralizing Iago as the necessary first cause of a domino effect that renders Othello the victim, as Emily Bartels writes, "by unfortunate chance" (1990: 454). But the view of Desdemona as the inheritor of Othello's feelings of inadequacy still supports the equation made by Patricia Parker (1994) and Karen Newman (1987) that Othello and Desdemona are caught together in the web of socially determined notions of monstrous difference. All these readings (mine included) are halted by Dympna Callaghan's admonition: "There are indeed, no authentic 'others' – raced or gendered of any kind, only their representations. But if Othello was a white man so was Desdemona" (2000: 76).
4 Writing that Othello "describes not his heroic sufferings among men but his sufferings in the strange and desolate landscape of female deprivation" (1992: 66), Janet Adelman theorizes Othello's rage as both a need for and a fear of female generativity. But an Irigarayan reading of *Othello* allows us to find another source for language formation even as it establishes the difference between Othello's dependence on separation from the maternal for his linguistic presence and Desdemona's return to the mother for the recovery of the female "reservoir of the meaning … of discourse" (2002b: 4).
5 Irigaray stresses the male "privilege granted to metaphor (a quasi-solid) over metonymy (which is more closely allied to fluids)," 1985a: 110.
6 Irigaray 2002a: 139.
7 Linking Desdemona to the heroines of Shakespearean comedy, Carol Thomas Neely also comments on Desdemona's final couplet as a response that "would be more active than acceptance yet more loving than retaliation" (1994: 75).
8 On the willow song as a traditional ballad, see Fineman 1994: 105.
9 Susan Frye writes "the point of this tale is not to charm but to situate the handkerchief in a narrative that parallels the suspicion and domestic violence through which Othello is now narrating his life" (2000: 223).
10 Barbary's ventriloquizing the male voice in Desdemona's song enacts what Elizabeth D. Harvey calls Irigaray's idea of "subversively employing a traditionally patriarchal definition of women" (1992: 157).
11 Irigaray suggests that the eye-lids are like the lips (1993e: 49).
12 Harry Berger, Jr. reasons that Desdemona's alliance here could be read simultaneously as a total victimization, a reduction of herself to poor Barbary, and a preparation for her final at least partial retaliation. Desdemona's "saintlike forgiveness of her tormentor vibrates through her last words and solicits a different reading: he will discover too late what a jewel he has thrown away" (1996: 240).

5 "Mutuall elements"

Irigaray's Donne

Elizabeth D. Harvey

In her lecture, "Divine Women," later published in *Sexes and Genealogies*, Luce Irigaray explained her recurrent preoccupation with the four elements and the design of the tetralogy she constructed around them: *Marine Lover* focused on the water imagery that Nietzsche eschewed, *The Forgetting of Air in Martin Heidegger* anatomized the essential place of air in Heidegger's thought, *Elemental Passions* was made up of lyrical love letters that explored the relationship of man and woman in sensory and elemental terms, and the fourth book, still unwritten, was to be a meditation on Marx and fire.[1] Irigaray argued that "we still pass our daily lives in a universe that is composed of and is known to be composed of four elements: air, water, fire, and earth. We are made up of these elements and we live in them. They determine, more or less freely, our attractions, our affects, our passions, our limits, our aspirations" (Irigaray 1993c: 57). Her reflexive comments in "Divine Women," which were contextualized by the occasion (the Women's Center's interdisciplinary study of *Melusine*) and delivered in Venice, a city whose watery setting insistently evokes its elemental foundations (and their erosion), yield instructive insights into Irigarary's methodology and intellectual proclivities. She characterizes her interest in the elements as a return to "the origins of our bodies," a "deep, dark, and necessary intuition" designed to plumb the cultural imaginary and reveal "the flesh of our passions" (Irigaray 1993c: 57). Her project, an uncanny mimicking of Freud's own archaeological method, seeks simultaneously to uncover the individual subject's forgotten material origins and to reveal the elemental foundations of our encrypted cultural history, beginnings which, while palimpsested in myth, recalled by poetry, and defined by science, nevertheless remain buried in the cultural unconscious (Irigaray 1993c: 57–8). *Melusine* represents for Irigaray a coded text, a narrative whose fourteenth-century origins provide keys to lost material aspects of our gendered and erotic humanity through its focus on hybrid bodies, love between human and divine beings, marriage, maternity, and genealogy, and the passions figured by the elements. The motivation for Irigaray's desire to retrieve the elements, which she sees as obscured by the very language that should name them, is parallel to and intertwined with her imperative to recover tactility, the sense that underlies the other four sensory faculties. Closely linked to ideas of materiality and incarnation in Irigaray's writing, tactility's importance is also evident in the vestigial linguistic traces of its nature: it is the "feeling" sense, a word that shuttles continually between the physical and the psychic. Touch is not only an instrument for knowing the world and defining the body's boundaries, but in addition to supplying receptors for pleasure and pain, it is also the sense that first joins mother to infant through a touch suffused with affect.[2] It is for Irigaray the sense that is foundational to subjectivity in its suturing of the elements and materiality to emotion, and this formulation of the centrality of *pathos* lies at the heart of her ethics.

Where Margaret Whitford attributes Irigaray's use of the elements as a structuring principle partly to Gaston Bachelard's influence, Elizabeth Grosz suggests that Irigaray drew on the pre-Socratic philosophers, especially Empedocles (Grosz 1989: 168–72). I will extend Grosz's insight by arguing that Irigaray's engagement with the pre-Socratics replicates Heidegger's own fascination with Heraclites, Parmenides, and others, and that her recovery of Empedocles via Heidegger is central to *The Forgetting of Air* and pivotal in her formulation of a gendered ethics. Indeed, not only does Empedocles's materialist philosophy help to explain the presence of the elements in Irigaray's writing, but his linkage of the elements to emotion enables Irigaray's exposure of the passions as the "repressed conditions of philosophical, scientific, and speculative theory" (Grosz 1989: 182). The mechanisms that animate the universe for both philosophers are thus predominately and primordially affective, and this linkage furnishes, among other things, resonant connections between cosmic geography and human physiology. My aim here is to investigate this elemental–emotional bond; to do so, I will examine how the Empedoclean legacy passed into classical and early modern medicine and saturated Renaissance poetry. As I will attempt to demonstrate in an analysis that moves between her critique of philosophy and science and John Donne's engagement with erotic poetry, elemental philosophy, and medicine, Irigaray's theoretical roots join her to an early modern culture to which she is indebted and on which, given her professed desire to be read in rigorously philosophical rather than literary terms, she is a surprisingly articulate commentator.[3]

Irigaray remarks in her chapter on Descartes and *The Passions of the Soul* in *An Ethics of Sexual Difference* that philosophers, except for the most recent ones, have tended to be physicists and "have always supported or accompanied their metaphysical research with cosmological research, whether it concerns the macrocosm or the microcosm" (Irigaray 1993h: 72). This claim echoes and inverts Heidegger's belief that the greatness of sixteenth- and seventeenth-century natural science was that all the scientists were philosophers (Heidegger 1977: 247); the value of these disciplinary couplings is the etymological and historical connections they activate among and between intellectual speculation, emotion, and science. If classical and early modern physics involved natural science and cosmology, the knowledge of the phenomenal world, for the early moderns, "physic" also described the science dedicated to the workings of the human body in the arts of healing and medicine. For Donne, the two forms of natural philosophy are intimately related, especially in poems like the *Anniversaries*. Donne's interest in physic and physics was matched by his fascination with metaphysics, which the sixteenth-century French encyclopedist Pierre de la Primaudaye defined in his anatomization of the kinds of knowledge in *The French Academie* this way: "Physike ... is the studie of naturall things: Metaphysike ... of supernaturall things" (de la Primaudaye 1594: 72).[4] This formulation nests one definition inside the other, suggesting both the way physic and metaphysic are implicated in each other for the early moderns and also presaging Irigaray's desire to recover the "physical" in the male metaphysical tradition. "Metaphysical" may be more familiar in this context, however, as the term inaugurated almost casually by John Dryden, subsequently elaborated by Samuel Johnson, and rendered pivotal by T. S. Eliot because it came to define not only Donne's writing and a poetic category, but also proposed an implicit theory about the relationship between intellection and feeling.[5] T. S. Eliot's categorization of Donne as writing before the dissociation of sensibility divided thought and affect evokes a profound nostalgia for a lost form of subjectivity. Indeed, Sir Herbert Grierson and T. S. Eliot's recuperation of a sensible and passional seventeenth-century subject has strong correlations to the Heideggerean and Irigarayan privileging of the pre-Socratics, for both versions of this historical recovery look to the past in order to imagine different relationships between body and soul, human and divine, subjects and their environments, and men and women. Heidegger's attraction to the pre-Socratics grew out of his sense of a rupture in early Greek philosophy between thought and its objects, a break that gradually resulted in modern technological intervention (Hodge 1994: 205). Irigaray reproduces Heidegger's idea of a rupture in the philosophical tradition, but for her, what has been lost is sexual difference, the mother, the trace of the feminine. Both, however, seek to mobilize the "presystematic thought of the pre-Socratics against the rigidities of philosophical categories" (Hodge 1994: 199). Irigaray's desire to uncover the affective infrastructures of science and philosophy has an affinity with Donne's emotional responses to the epistemological and scientific change he witnessed. His conceptions of seventeenth-century medicine and science, particularly with respect to the elements, can help us to excavate the physic in metaphysical and ponder its relationship to the passions.[6]

Although T. S. Eliot does not explicitly name Descartes in his discussion of the dissociation of sensibility, philosophers and theorists of culture locate the early modern origins of the mind–body split and the development of a notion of inwardness in Cartesian philosophy.[7] Michael Schoenfeldt, for instance, in his recent study, *Bodies and Selves in Early Modern England*, explicitly ties Eliot and Descartes together in his analysis of the Cartesian inheritance: " ... the force of the famous 'Je pense, donc je suis' – produced a pronounced dissociation of essential self from body, a dissociation from which we are still trying to recover" (Schoenfeldt 1999: 11). While he does not pursue the implications of this yoking, his more optimistic echo of Eliot's famous formulation, "In the seventeenth century a dissociation of sensibility set in, from which we have never recovered" (Eliot in Clements 1966: 128), effectively glosses the Eliotic term through the Cartesian *cogito*.[8] But it is really Irigaray's two sustained interpretations of Descartes that illuminate the affective dimension of Eliot's phrase.[9] Her first analysis in *Speculum of the Other Woman* is a scathingly critical reading of Descartes's treatise on telescopes and refraction, *La Dioptrique*. "Speculum," the central section of the book, engages by turns and in chronological order Plato, Aristotle, Plotinus, Descartes, Kant, and Hegel and is thus a reversed image of *Speculum*'s inverted history, which begins with Freud and ends with Plato. The Descartes chapter is the fulcrum in this miniature account of the philosophical tradition. It is set at the exact center of "Speculum," and in it Irigaray deconstructs the mind–body split through Descartes's theory of optics. The chapter title suspends the quotation from Descartes's Fifth Discourse, with the disembodied eye at its center, between ellipses, " ... And If, Taking the Eye of a Man Recently Dead, ...," thus enacting her critique of the Cartesian autonomy of cognition. Adopting the perspective of Descartes's (dead) eye, she surveys the world from inside his discourse, using his own skepticism, which is marked by the frequency of her interrogatives, to expose the philosophical problems produced by his privileging of vision, his jettisoning of the body, and its reproductive processes, and his severing of copulation from the copula: " – the 'I' will confer existence upon itself. Being without any copulation? The 'I' therefore 'copulates' without copulation in/of its ancestors: major or minor" (1985g: 184). The mother is the mirror that secures the autonomy of the thinking, reasoning Cartesian subject but who remains invisible, without access to her own reflection, and Irigaray's recuperative tactic is to borrow Descartes's own optical theories in order to investigate the tain of the mirror, the space behind the eyeball, this "blind spot" in the history of philosophical speculation (1985g: 181–3). This feminist reading, which questions "the ascetic ellipsis of the body," a thinking or being purged of corporeality, gives way to a radically different treatment of Descartes in *An Ethics of Sexual Difference*, where Irigaray makes his theorization of wonder as the first passion in *The Passions of the Soul* foundational to her "carnal" ethics (1985g: 185).[10]

Wonder, according to Irigaray, is the passion of "encounter between the most material and the most metaphysical, of their possible conception and fecundation one by the other (1993h: 82). This is a version of her idea of the sensible transcendental (1993e: 129), and she seeks continually in her *Ethics* and elsewhere to re-embody philosophy, science, and language, to infuse these formal structures with blood, flesh, and material elements (1993e: 127). The language of the passions, which she absorbs from Descartes, provides a rich historical discourse that carries with it notions of mediation between the somatic and the psychic, the human and divine. If ancient and early modern natural philosophers and physicians distinguished between the body and what animates it – spirit, soul, mind – many saw the passions as intermediaries in this dualism.[11] Pierre de la Primaudaye, for instance, vividly described the divine nature of the soul being fastened to the body "with the naile of pleasure" and grief (1594: 30). Whereas, as we shall see, early modern thinkers saw the passions as originating in corporeal perturbations of the humors, Irigaray follows Descartes in defining wonder as the inaugural passion, not as somatically invested as the other passions, and notable in its ability to preserve difference: "Neither one nor the other. Which is not to say neutral or neuter. The forgotten ground of our condition between mortal and immortal, men and gods, creatures and creators" (Irigaray 1993e: 82). Despite the initial privileged place that wonder occupies, Irigaray aligns Descartes's description of the passions in general, which he articulates in the "language of the physiologist," with Freud's theory of the drives (Irigaray 1993h: 80). Her use of Descartes's *Passions of the Soul* turns philosophy, psychoanalysis, and science on themselves, not as in *Speculum*, in order to reveal their deficiencies, but in order to search within their own histories for a cure, a kind of philosophical homeopathy.[12] The remedy she finds in Descartes – wonder – is the bridge or remediation not only between the body and soul, but also "between physics and metaphysics, corporeal impressions and movements toward an object, whether empirical or transcendental" (Irigaray 1993h: 80). This is cognate with the healing project she envisions in *To Speak Is Never Neutral*, where she advocates questioning the language of science and scrutinizing the sexualization of language, a double process that entails reimporting the elements, material particles charged with affect, and bodies back into the neutrality of a scientific language emptied of emotion (Irigarary 2002b: 1, 5). She asks "How does the subject come back to itself after having exiled itself within a discourse?" (Irigaray 2002b: 4). One answer she seems to offer in different guises and through her own example is a return, although not in any nostalgic sense, to the cultural and philosophical sources that underpin Western culture, a rereading of the historical matrix or imaginary for the traces of a lost pathos.

PERTURBATIONS OF KNOWING

In *The Second Anniversary*, Donne encapsulates the seventeenth-century epistemological and medical crisis surrounding the elements:

> Have not all soules thought
> For many ages, that our body'is wrought
> Of Ayre, and Fire, and other Elements?
> And now they thinke of new ingredients.
> And one Soule thinkes one, and another way
> Another thinkes, and ty's an even lay.
>
> (Donne 2: ll.263–8)

Donne's reference is, of course, to the disruption by Paracelsus in particular of a tradition inaugurated in the fifth century BCE by Empedocles. Heir to the Monists and especially to Parmenides, Empedocles sought to explicate the complexity of phenomena by positing the existence of four essential elements. His innovation, which was to be foundational for future chemical, physical, and medical science, was to suggest that all creation and dissolution was produced by the mixture of these four components in different proportions (Bailey 1928: 28–9).[13] Love and strife propelled combinations of the elements to create sensible matter, but matter was not reducible beyond these four essential elements, which, he believed, formed the building blocks of the universe. Hippocrates, Empedocles's younger contemporary, made elemental theory integral to medicine by linking the elements to corresponding bodily fluids, the humors (blood, phlegm, black and yellow bile). Health for Hippocrates and his followers was the equilibrium among the four humors, and disease caused by humoral imbalances could be measured in various ways by the evidence of the senses. But it was really Galen, some six centuries later, who, following Aristotle's endorsement of the primacy of the elements and their qualities, consolidated the humoral system into a theory of temperament whose precipitate is still evident in our use of such terms as "good humored," "sanguine," "temperate" (Paster 1993: 6), and which was to serve as the basis for a nineteenth-century psychoanalytic classification of personality types. It was as if the Empedoclean elements with their affective motivations had been transposed into the human body, where the love and strife among the humors produced configurations of personality stamped with the imprint of dominant feeling.

The question of exactly how the elements and humors interacted with the passions was, of course, the subject of constant debate in early modern culture. The Dutch physician Levinus Lemnius said in his late sixteenth-century compendium of humoral temperaments, *The Touchstone of Complexions*, "All the complexion and temperament of mans body proceedeth from the power of the Elements and not the Humours: and of them is the whole body tempered and compounded" (Lemnius 1633: 40). According to many physicians inspired by Galen, the elements were transmuted into the quarternary humoral system with its nine dispositions of character, from which was derived a theory of the passions; the mingling of elements and qualities made up crasis or complexion, and temperament was thus a register of temperature, with the "temperate" personality forming the ideal type (Lemnius 1633: 52). Thomas Wright tells us in *The Passions of the Mind* that:

> there is no Passion very vehement, but that it alters extreamely some of the foure humors of the bodie, and all Physitians commonly agree, that among divers other extrinsecall causes of diseases, one and not the least, is the excesse of some inordinate Passion: for although it busieth their braines, as also the naturall Philosophers, to explicate the manner how an operation that lodgeth in the soule can alter the bodie, and moove the humors from one place to another (as for example, recall most of the bloud in the face, or other parts, to the heart, as we see by daily experience to chance in feare and anger) yet they consent that it may proceede from a certain sympathie of nature, a subordination of one part to another, and that the spirits and humors wait upon the Passions, as their Lords and Masters.
>
> (Wright 1620: 4)

That Donne was intimately familiar with theories of the elemental and humoral body we know from his mocking of them in *Devotions Upon Emergent Occasions*. There he chastised "mere" philosophers who think that the soul "is nothing but the temperament and harmony, and just and equal composition of the elements in the body, which produces all those faculties which we ascribe to the soul; and so itself is nothing, no separable substance that outlives the body" (Donne 1959: 114). Far from being a disavowal of a belief in the connection between the elements and the passions, Donne argues strenuously in this meditation for the existence of an immortal soul that is separable from the body and the vegetative and sensitive souls. The force of his claim is less epistemological, then, than spiritual. Indeed, Donne here jettisons all explanations advanced by philosophers, philosophical divines, whole bodies of thought and whole churches until only belief and faith are left. Just as he rhetorically discards the body in his passionate preparation for death, so too does he dispense with all the systems of knowledge he has accumulated, although his rejection of knowledge is paradoxically also a record of what he describes in a letter to Henry Goodere in 1608 as the "hydroptique immoderate desire" of learning that everywhere infuses his writing (Donne 2001: 388).

Donne was well aware of the Paracelsian challenges to Galenic theory, as we saw in *The Second Anniversary*, and even though he may have lamented the replacement of the traditional elements by the Paracelsian principles of mercury, sulphur, and salt, he was elsewhere enraptured by the possibilities these new theories offered. It was not so much that Paracelsus proposed new principles to replace the Galenic quaternion, but rather that his theories of disease and infection constituted a new model. If disease according to Galenic theory was produced by the imbalance of humors, for Paracelsus, pathogens had their own ontology. Paracelsus did not think disease was endogenous, as Jonathan Gil Harris notes, but rather that it originated outside the body and attacked by infiltrating pores or orifices (1998: 23–4). The conception of the humoral body as an ecology responsive to its surroundings and to its internal balances thus began to be intermittently displaced by the Paracelsian structure that ultimately sought to fortify the body against the incursion of foreign elements. Despite these differences, what Galenic humoral medicine had in common with Paracelsian theory is that both systems implicated emotion or imagination, and physiology was thus bound up with psychological or mental states (Debus 1965: 30; Weeks 1997: 67, 138–40; Fletcher 2003). Scholars have heatedly debated the nature and the extent of Donne's learning and whether his medical knowledge was Paracelsian or Galenic. There is certainly ample evidence that he knew both, and we hardly need the record of Donne's signature and motto on the title page of Paracelsus's *Chirurgia Magna* (1573) (Keynes 1958: 218) in his library or the dramatic appearance of Paracelsus in *Ignatius His Conclave* to know this (Donne 1969: 19–25).[14] What interests me more is the use he makes of these competing systems. As we know, epistemological change happens slowly, and it is characterized by the co-existence of apparently contradictory systems of knowledge. As Donne himself recognized, "Almost all knowledge is rather like a child that is embalmed to make Mummy," conserved, in other words, in an early, arrested state rather than progressing to maturity (Donne 2001: 524). The palimpsesting of medical knowledge systems is illustrated in the figure of the mummy, an idea that Donne reiterates in many contexts, and one that draws on Paracelsus's own ideas about embalming and yet is used paradoxically here to describe the inert longevity of such scientific and medical theories as the Galenic tradition. New forms of knowledge do not, as he implies, ensure acceptance either in part or as whole systems, nor do they erase older knowledge which, while contested, may nevertheless be integral to cultural structures of belief. In this sense, perhaps especially with knowledge that impinges on bodies and subjectivity, acceptance is as concerned with emotional as scientific truth.

In a sermon preached at the funeral of William Cokayne in December of 1626, Donne laments the state of epistemological uncertainty:

> How imperfect is all our knowledge! What one thing doe we know perfectly? Whether wee consider Arts, or Sciences, the servant knows but according to the proportion of his Masters knowledge in that Art, and the Scholar knows but according to the proportion of his Masters knowledge in that Science; Young men mend not their sight by using old mens Spectacles; and yet we looke upon Nature, but with *Aristotles* Spectacles, and upon the body of man, but with *Galens*, and upon the frame of the world, but with *Ptolomies* Spectacles.
>
> (Donne 2001: 524)

Knowledge for Donne occupies a position that is analogous to the role played by the body. Just as bodies provide a mediated access to the world and enable the imperfect sensory gathering that constitutes human life, peering through the "lattices of eies" or hearing "through the Laberinths of eares," so do theories of knowledge make understanding, however deficient, possible (Donne 1985: 2: ll. 296–7). Where spectacles represent a scientific improvement on natural vision, an advance in optical knowledge that is also figured in such seventeenth-century writing on optics as the Cartesian treatise that Irigaray cites, they also furnish a metaphor for structures of knowledge. Even though epistemological models may be superseded, they supply frameworks of perception, spectacles through which to view the world. Donne's epistemology hinges on unanswerable questions:

> Knowst thou but how the stone doth enter in
> The bladders Cave, and never breake the skin?
> Knowst thou how blood, which to the hart doth flow,
> Doth from one ventricle to th'other go?"
>
> (Donne 1985: 2: ll.269–72)

These puzzles of nature are "mysteries" that no seventeenth-century subject could then understand, and as if to confirm the futility of the search for scientific or medical truth, the speaker chastises the "poore soule" he addresses: "When wilt thou shake off this Pedantery,/Of being taught by sense, and Fantasy?" To inquire into wordly knowledge is to look "through spectacles," where "small things seem great," which is to be contrasted with the view from the "watch-towre," where one can see all things "despoyld of fallacies" (Donne 1985: 2: ll. 291–5). And yet, as Donne demonstrates in his "Elegie on Lady Marckham," the passions themselves are the spectacles that illuminate or disfigure perception: "Teares are false Spectacles, we cannot see/Through passions mist, what wee are, or what shee" (Donne 1985: ll.15–16). While grief may cloud the vision of eternity's expanse, tears also enable the purgative and poetic responses to death that ultimately provide consolation. Tears, false spectacles though they may be, are also the generative medium of expression, as "A Valediction of Weeping" with its impregnated globes of sorrow and its display of the new knowledge of cartography, memorably shows.

Despite the subsequent destabilization of epistemological certainty, Donne's response is nevertheless conditioned by an inherited worldview that shaped even his melancholic awareness of change. In the same funeral sermon, for instance, he uses the elements to metaphorize his sense of loss associated with changing knowledge systems:

> I need not call in new Philosophy ... to prove this, That nothing upon Earth is permanent; The Assertion will stand of it selfe, till some man assigne me some instance, something that a man may relie upon, and find permanent ... In the Elements themselves, of which all sub-elementary things are composed, there is no acquiescence, but a vicissitudinary transmutation into one another; Ayre condensed becomes water, a more solid body, And Ayre rarified becomes fire, a body more disputable, and in-apparent.
>
> (Donne 2001: 526)

Far from offering consolation as stable entities, the elements themselves are ceaselessly transforming, and the perpetual metamorphosis of the world thus requires responses that draw on other registers, faith or emotion, for instance, modes that respond to the mutation of knowledge. Donne uses the elements not only to talk about the loss of stable knowledge systems, but the passional Empedoclean charge they carry informs his own affective response. Far from embracing a Cartesian detachment, his response to metaphysical anguish is Irigarayan, articulated, even in its vistas of heaven, from the perspective of a gendered corporeality.

ELEMENTAL EMOTION

Margaret Whitford reminds us that Irigaray's "recourse to the elemental provides a vocabulary for talking about the passions, including the erotic passions, without depending on the erotic vocabulary currently available" (Whitford 1991: 62). This elemental lexicon allows Irigaray to avoid:

> the dominant sexual metaphoricity which is scopic and organized around the male gaze: she can speak of it instead in terms of space and thresholds and fluids, fire and water, air and earth, without objectifying, hypostasizing, or essentializing it. These terms are not so easily reduced to the body

of one sex or the other. They are more pliable, accessible to the imagination of others and available for their private mental landscapes.

(Whitford 1991: 62)

The desire to recast sexual relations in a new language helps to explain not only Irigaray's attraction to the elements but also Donne's, for although Donne is frequently charged with misogyny, I will argue that his representation of women and eroticism is both more complicated and more flexible than is customarily acknowledged.[15] Indeed, Donne's love poems rarely describe and objectify female bodies (the obvious exception, "Elegie XIX" images the mistress's body through a metonymic description of the articles of clothing the speaker would have her discard), and his poetic occupation of feminine subject positions coincides with a sympathy for and self-consciousness about the place women occupy in early modern culture. Poems such as "Breake of day," "Sappho to Philaenis," and "Holy Sonnet XIV" represent only the more formal experiments with gender crossing, and they are supplemented by a pervasive sympathetic inhabitation of female-gendered perspective in the valedictory poems, the *Elegies*, the *Anniversaries*, and in some of the verse letters to female patrons. Although Dryden long ago presciently objected to Donne's use of metaphysical speculation in amorous contexts, Donne's mixture of intellection and passion, his metaphorization of the elements, and his constant preoccupation with corporeality as a condition shared by the sexes anticipate some features of Irigaray's radical reconceptualization of sexual relations.

Donne's preoccupation with the erotic is matched by and overlaps with his ubiquitous interest in the ligature between the body and the soul. He frequently represents liminal states – parting, death, illness, birth – in order to explore the in-between, the middle term, the nature of the tie that joins spiritual and bodily natures. In Elaine Scarry's illuminating analysis of the lovers' return to their bodies in "The Extasie," she asserts that Donne needs "a set of metaphors that define with ever-greater precision the exact relationship between body and soul" in order "to prolong the moment of standing outside the body, and hence dramatize the deliberateness and deliberation with which the body is reembraced" (Scarry 1988: 72). While this suspension is created and sustained syntactically through the repetition of "but," "though," and "but Yet," as Scarry remarks, it is worth noticing that the language of return is medical. Early modern natural philosophy provided a way of thinking about this middle state, for it understood the passions to be intermediaries between corporeal and psychic states. Levinus Lemnius, for instance, details the mechanism that transmutes the elements into emotion: " … the spirits exhaled by the humours, doe participate with other qualities, and thereby distemper the braine, [and] it commonly hapneth that such persons become thereby wayward, testy, and very easily carried into sundry other affections of the mind" (Lemnius 1633: 20). The interaction between the elements, their exhalations, and emotion is even more complex than this explanation would suggest, however, for not only does it involve both bodily organs and incorporeal or spiritual faculties, but the causes and origins of strong emotion are also various.

Thomas Wright claims in *The Passions of the Minde* that the passions are the acts of the sensitive power or faculty of the soul, which are produced by "sensual motion of our appetitive faculty, through imagination of some good or il thing, because when these affections are stirring in our minds they alter the humour of our bodies, causing some passion or alteration in them" (Wright 1620: 8). Donne uses his knowledge of the passions in medicine and natural philosophy in "The Extasie" to describe the disembodied lovers' descent to their corporeal shells:

> As our blood labours to beget
> Spirits, as like soules as it can,
> Because such fingers need to knit
> That subtile knot, which makes us man:
> So must pure lovers soules descend
> T'affections, and to faculties,
> Which sense may reach and apprehend.

> (Donne 1985: ll. 61–7)

The knitting together of soma and psyche is accomplished through the intermediary union of spirits, which are begotten of blood and constitutive of affection, but also partake of the incorporeal.

The universe in Donne's poetry and prose, especially when he imagines threshold states – just before death, just after death, or the passage into heaven – is typically understood through somatic spectacles. Knowledge of other conditions of being is absorbed into a bodily awareness that subordinates cosmic to corporeal understanding, a phenomenon that is enacted in "Holy Sonnet V":

> I am a little world made cunningly
> Of Elements, and an Angelike spright,
> But black sinne hath betraid to endless night
> My worlds both parts, and (oh) both parts must die.
> You which beyond heaven which was most high
> Have found new sphears, and of new lands can write,
> Powre new seas in mine eyes, that so I might
> Drowne my world with my weeping earnestly,
> Or wash it if it be drown'd no more:
> But oh it must be burnt; alas the fire
> Of lust and envie have burnt it heretofore,
> And made it fouler; Let their flames retire,
> And burn me ô Lord, with a fiery zeale
> Of thee and thy house, which doth in eating heale.

> (Donne 1985)

The intricate suturing of body and soul through the operation of the passions can be glimpsed in the image of connection that Lemnius furnishes. If the passions derive from amorphous vapours exhaled by the humors that rise into the brain, Lemnius gives them form as spirits, which, he tells us, were called genii or tutelary gods by the ancients. He prefers to name them "good and ill Angels, which being entermingled with the humours and spirits, cause sundry changes and mutations in mens mindes" (Lemnius 1633: 31). Although Lemnius's description begins as medical and physiological, it quickly moves into psychological and even theological territory. Donne's "Angelike spright" in this sonnet is cognate with Lemnius's description of the good angel, and the "black sinne" that invades the speaker's little world evokes not only the properties of Lemnius's devil or bad angel, but it carries with it the distempering of melancholy associated with the tyranny of this dark genius, who incites those with an abundance of black bile to "sorrow, heavinesse, desperation, distrust, and last of all, to a lamentable and shamefull end" (Lemnius 1633: 37). The speaker's despair at this betrayal to "endless night" isolates in the final line of the first quatrain what has been lost: "My worlds both parts, and (oh) both parts must die." Conventionally glossed as the separation of body and soul, the division is dramatized through the repetition of "parts," which is severed by the medial caesura and further punctuated by the parenthetical "(oh)," the linguistic figuring of a breath, a sigh, a bodily exhalation of the emotion that joins the two aspects of the human subject.

Like breath, Lemnius's bodiless "ayrie spirits" can glide "slily and secretly" into bodies, just as air is drawn in (1633: 36, 34–5), and the capacity of these intermediary spirits to transgress bodily thresholds, to move between earth and heaven or between corporeal and incorporeal realms, makes them potent figures both for Lemnius's theory of affect, for Donne's sense of his spiritual nature, and for Irigaray's ethics. In "Belief Itself" and *An Ethics of Sexual Difference*, angels are mediators, an idea that draws on the Greek and Hebrew etymology of angel as messenger, and they function as gestures of passage between opposite states. Whereas Irigaray sees Western culture as a history of the "dissociation of body and soul, of sexuality and spirituality, of the lack of passage for the spirit, for the god, between the inside and the outside, the outside and the inside, and of their distribution between the sexes of the sexual act" (Irigaray 1993e: 15), angels are the restorative intermediaries, harbingers of a new, ethical world order. They "move – or stir up? – the paralysis or *apatheia* of the body, or the soul, or the world" (Irigaray 1993e: 16). "*Apatheia*," a word that means literally without pathos or feeling, was a state cultivated in Stoic philosophy, but emotion and sensation are, in contradistinction, crucial aspects of Irigaray's sensible transcendental, a carnal ethics that attempts to bring together the divine and human, the immanent and transcendent (Irigaray 1993e: 32, 129). Angels in Irigaray's *Ethics* "stir up" emotion, disrupting the affective paralysis that limits, divides, and defines human experience. For the early moderns, of course, passion was useful only insofar as it was constrained in its operations (usually by rationality), a vision that governs the Platonic and Neoplatonic representations of eros, but for Donne and Irigaray, extreme emotion allows the subject to step outside the boundaries of sexual identity, to partake of an imaginary consciousness, to become "ecstatic."[16]

Gail Kern Paster has written eloquently about the permeability of the humoral body, its openness to the world around it, and its susceptibility to climate, bad air, and contagion, what Helkiah Crooke called its *"Transpirable"* and *"Trans-fluxible"* nature (Paster 1993: 9, 9–16). The fungibility of elements and rhetorical and poetic modes defines the rest of Donne's sonnet. The speaker entreats a God who has enabled cosmological and geographical exploration to remake the seas of his eyes, so that he can "Drowne my world with my weeping earnestly" (8). Petrarchan tropes of hyperbolic emotion are recast within an expanded world, one that is defamiliarized cosmologically by Galileo's discoveries and augmented by geographical explorations of the New World.[17] This refashioned world is even more radically recreated here through emotion, reduced to its constituent elements through the action of the passions. Human emotion is, finally, however, inadequate to the affective razing that the speaker so ardently desires, and he must exhort God in his "fiery zeal," words that join element and emotion, to consume him. The elements provide for Donne a tropological vocabulary for imagining an intersubjective or human–divine union that is at once intimate in its mingling and cosmologically sweeping, implicating the whole universe. If early modern bodies are permeable not only to their environments and climates, so that cold regions produce "grosse blood," which in turn engenders fierceness, rudeness, courage, and boldness (Lemnius 1633: 20), they also create a porosity between subjects, which is often figured as an elemental fusion. In her essay on Donne's humoral body, Nancy Selleck suggests that Donne's emphasis on the "fluid body figures not just change, but exchange – not just *personal* flux, but *inter*personal flux" (Selleck 2001: 157), and we can see this erotic reciprocity in Donne's love poems. In Donne's epigram on Hero and Leander, for example, the lovers are paradoxically dissolved into their elemental components: "Both rob'd of aire, we lye in one ground,/Both whom one fire had burnt, one water drownd" (Donne 1985: 127). Punctuated into four parts, one for each element, the couplet unites the lovers in their mutual deprivation of the life-sustaining element air, in their common destruction by fire and water, and by their burial in "one ground." Although ostensibly separated by death, they are joined in an erotic bond that simultaneously depends on their corporeality and also transcends it by substituting the eternity of the elements, which are drenched with the lovers' passion and which organize death's chaos into poetic and elementally balanced parts. It is in "The Dissolution" that we see the precise operations of this intersubjective fusion. If bodies and selves are permeable to the environment, with its pestilential miasmas, and to other human beings, with all the attendant perils of being subsumed or taking on the characteristics of the other, a contagion of habits, this danger is also the source of the most profound erotic interanimation.

The scientific interpenetration of elements furnishes Donne with a witty conceit for depicting a union of subjectivities in "The Dissolution" more complete than the inherited lexicons of love could furnish.

> Shee'is dead; And all which die
>   To their first Elements resolve;

And wee were mutuall Elements to us,
    And made of one another.
  My body then doth hers involve,
And those things whereof I consist, hereby
In me abundant grow, and burdenous,
    And nourish not, but smother.
  My fire of Passion, sighes of ayre,
Water of teares, and earthly sad despaire,
    Which my materialls bee,
But ne'r worne out by love's securitie,
Shee, to my losse, doth by her death repaire,
    And I might live long wretched so
But that my fire doth with my fuell grow.

                             (Donne 1985: ll. 1–15)

The ambiguity of the title's referent shapes the poem. The dissolving alludes simultaneously to death's separation of the lovers and to the departed lover's resolution into four constituent elements. Although mortality loosens the connections between the elemental components, they seem still to retain their affective force, and that the elements replicate the properties of the speaker's body joins the lovers in spite of death, as if the echo of the universe's essences could continue a conversation begun in life. The poem's wit is Galenic. If health is a balance of the humoral proportions, the surfeit of any of the four unsettles the harmony. The lover's death, then, is a legacy of superfluous elements, which in the speaker "abundant grow, and burdenous." "Burden," a word whose etymology is intertwined with birth, and the line, "My body then doth hers involve," suggest a kind of bodily "rolling up" or incorporation, as if death had bequeathed a kind of elemental pregnancy, as if the male speaker inhabited, however briefly, the position of a pregnant woman. The speaker, whose body is infiltrated and occupied by parasitic grief, is less nourished by this posthumous residue than "smother[ed]," a word that simultaneously bears and suppresses the "mother" within it. "Burden" is also a reference to a musical term, of course, a "bourdon," the undersong or accompaniment to a melody (the musical version of the element of "air," which is also, of course, a musical reference). The lovers are thus acoustically bound together, incorporated within a song or poem whose scattered rhymes combine and recombine in elemental coupling. The affective charge of the unleashed elements feeds the speaker's passions, which take on the excessive force of a Petrarchan cliché: "My fire of Passion, sighes of ayre,/Water of teares, and earthly sad despaire." His store and expenditure of emotion is increased by this affective legacy to the explosive proportions of the last image of a bullet: "my soule more earnestly releas'd,/Will outstrip hers; As bullets flowen before/A latter bullet may o'rtake, the pouder being more" (Donne 1985: ll. 22–4). Donne also uses the figure of the bullet to figure the release of soul from the body in *The Second Anniversarie* (Donne 1985: 2:179–83), but here his emotional impulses are motivated by an erotically competitive yearning for union and elemental recombination.

The elaborate conceit of an elemental nurturing of the passions may offer in "The Dissolution" an amorous exercise in Galenic theory, but it also provides the scientific basis for Donne's fundamental and recurrent grappling with the problem of separation. If, as Empedocles asserted, there is no beginning or end but only a ceaseless recombination of elements, then the division between body and soul cannot be as decisive or as isolating as it threatens to be.[18] There can be no breach between souls, but only an "expansion," or diffusion, "Like gold to ayery thinnesse beate," as the speaker assures his beloved in "A Valediction forbidding mourning" (Donne 1985: ll. 97–8). Indeed, all four valedictory poems feature the elements, initially as potentially divisive or destructive forces, but ultimately – most notably in "A Valediction of weeping" – as transmuted into an elemental passion that joins the lovers across space and death. We can witness this belief at work in "Aire and Angels," where the beloved is brought into being by passion, constituted from a state of elemental dispersion:

> Twice or thrice had I loved thee,
> Before I knew thy face or name;
> So in a voice, so in a shapelesse flame
> *Angells* affect us oft, and worship'd bee,
>   Still when, to where thou wert, I came,
> Some lovely glorious nothing I did see,
>
> (Donne 1985: ll. 1–6)

"Love," Irigaray says in her Heideggerean reading of Empedocles, "draws things together in a mixture that brings about birth" (Irigaray 1999: 76), and in Donne, too, the affective force of the elements works towards recombination and creation:

> But since, my soule, whose child love is,
> Takes limmes of flesh, and else could nothing doe,
>   More subtile than the parent is,
> Love must not be, but take a body too,
>   And therefore what thou wert, and who
>   I did Love aske, and now
> That it assume thy body, I allow,
> And fixe it selfe in thy lip, eye, and brow.
>
> (Donne 1985: ll. 7–14)

Desire and passion here become a kind of creation, a parenting or begetting that summons a body into existence in all the specificity and complications of its individual parts, its lips and eyes and brow. The speaker occupies the position of the generative parent, and he shares poetically the physiology of the pregnant woman whose powerfully generative imagination can shape the being inside her. The structure of the poem, with its two inverted Petrarchan sonnets (Wiggins 2000: 120), begins to suggest the difficulties of gender relations in the post-elemental stage where affect must assume a body and linguistic expression. Peter DeSa Wiggins

suggests that the poem has affinities both with the *dolce stil novo* and Latin elegiac traditions, "as if Donne were assuming the roles of Dante and Ovid
simultaneously" (Wiggins 2000: 130), but the poem testifies to Donne's willing-
ness to imagine a passion or a desire that predates and outlasts the social and
poetic conventions that structure gender relations.[19]

Eschewing the blazon itself, he speaks instead of that anterior process through
which passion invokes a body in the first place. The second 14 lines of the poem
address the difficulty of crafting a language adequate to wonder: "Whilst thus to
ballast love, I thought,/and so more steddily to have gone,/With wares which
would sinke admiration,/I saw, I had loves pinnace overfraught." The mercantil-
ism of his metaphor suggests the commercialization of the available languages of
love (accentuated by the numismatic meaning of angel), and the speaker retreats
to a recognition that love "inheres" "nor in nothing, nor in things," but rather in
the intermediary, Irigaray's interval of desire (Irigaray 1993e: 28), Donne's
"Angell, face, and wings/Of aire." The pun on male and female genitalia ("nothing" and "thing") is a bawdy subtext to the philosophical argument: love
"inheres" neither in one nor the other sexual organ, but only in their union.[20] The
enigmatic gloss the speaker offers in the poem's last lines is that "Just such dis-
paritie/As is twixt Aire and Angells puritie,/T'wixt womens love, and mens will
ever bee." The force of the analogy, ultimately derived from Aquinas, seems to be
that angels are visible only to the extent that the thickness of air allows their
shapes to manifest themselves to vision, as Henry Lawrence's 1646 treatise on
angels reminds us.[21] Just as air is "grosser" than the subtle angelic nature to
which it lends appearance (Lawrence 1646: 9), so, too, does human love take a
body, "limmes of flesh," which is less rarified than love in its idealized (and
therefore invisible) state. The "disparity" between the purity of angels and air
weighs these alternatives: what angels (or love) lose in diminished purity is com-
pensated by their acquisition of a visible body. The relation between the sexes
struggles similarly with the contest between an idealized love that inheres in
"nothing" and its corporealization in sex and sexed language, and this is the subject of amorous controversy in poems like "The Flea" and "The Extasie."[22]
Though Donne here and elsewhere stages the controversy between the sexes and
between spiritual and carnal love, his practice demonstrates that he, like Irigaray,
sees transcendence as taking place through – not in spite of – the body and its
fleshly passions.

THE COLOR OF FLESH

Donne's phrase in "Aire and Angels," where the speaker's soul takes on "limmes
of flesh," is a punning, paradoxical reference to bodily members and to color
(limning), for "limn" comes from the L. *lumen*, light, and thus the fleshly
appendages are themselves composed of luminosity, more like angels than
flesh. Limning meant to illuminate, especially with color, a practice that
Nicholas Hilliard described in detail in his treatise the *Arte of Limning* (1598).[23]

As Irigaray reminds us in her essay, "Flesh Colors," Aristotle said that flesh is diaphanous, "but it is always taking on and giving colors" (Irigaray 1993d: 159). Irigaray's interest in color is apparent in much of her work, particularly the repeated use of red and white blood, where the homonym *sang blanc* and *semblant*, positions white, the absence of color, as sameness, and red becomes the sign of color or difference (Whitford 1991: 118–9). "Flesh Colors" offers a more sustained sense of her preoccupation with the chromatic, or what she calls the "chroma-soma," the color-body that figures sexuality, fleshly matter, and female genealogy (Irigaray 1993d: 156–8). She argues that color, like rhythm, has been repressed in cultures that privilege symbolic structures (letters, abstract forms, numbers, laws, non-figurative writing), and that color returns us to the body, passion, blood, the incarnation of the divine (Irigaray 1993d: 159). Irigaray's ideas about color emerge primarily from psychoanalytic theory and practice, but as with much of her writing, they derive from the same cultural and historical matrix that feeds psychoanalysis, in this case, the conjunction of elemental and passional theory that I have been exploring in this essay.

Indeed, one of the analogies Empedocles offers for his theory of elemental mingling is the artist's mixing of primary pigments to produce other hues: "As when painters adorn votive offerings,/... they take in their hands many-coloured pigments,/mixing them in harmony, some more, others less,/from them they prepare forms resembling all things" (Empedocles 2001:231). Painting's ability to mimic cosmic creation derives from its method of blending different hues, and color, perhaps the most visible expression of elemental combination, articulated both artistic excellence through the harmonious blending of pigment and the beauty of natural creation through its balancing of elemental composition. Color became integral to the humoral tradition as a visible indicator of the balance of proportions, evident in the color of the complexion, and to the theory of the emotions that emerged from the Empedoclean legacy, apparent in movements of the blood that manifest themselves in the hue of the skin.[24]

Donne draws on these traditions in his lament for Elizabeth Drury's death in the *First Anniversary*; if she was the form of harmonious combination – "Both Elements, and Passions liv'd at peace/In her, who caus'd all Civill warre to cease" (Donne 1985: 1:321–2) – her death infects the world, producing a diseased complexion that is sapped of color:

> But beauties other second Element,
> Colour, and lustre now, is as neere spent.
> And had the world his just proportion,
> Were it a ring still, yet the stone is gone.
> As a compassionate Turcoyse which doth tell
> By looking pale, the wearer is not well,
> As gold fals sicke being stung with Mercury,
> All the worlds parts of such complexion bee.

(Donne 1985: 1:339–46)

The turquoise was renowned in classical and early modern natural histories for its magically sympathetic character. It had, according to Thomas Nicols and other writers on gems, the capacity for compassion, literally to "feel with" its wearer, to grow pale in concert with its sick owner.[25] Just as color drained from the complexion is a sign of illness, so does the world's blanched complexion betoken its disharmony. The *Anniversaries* are shaped by an analogous sympathetic linkage – between Elizabeth Drury and the world, between Donne and the Drurys – a connection that is forged by affect, com-passion. If the *Anniversaries* mourn not only the girl's death but also the epistemological convulsion that disrupts coherence and correspondence, the consolations they give derive from the new imaginative connections Donne constructs in these elegiac poems. The hyperbolic praise and mourning that so outraged Ben Jonson dramatize a world in which emotion and imagination replace a rationally ordered universe, allowing Donne to explore the traffic between heaven and earth and the connection between body and soul through the "middle nature" of verse, an intermediary position that is, as we have seen, also occupied by angels and the passions (Donne 1985: 1:473).

When she was alive, Elizabeth Drury was distinguished not only by her beauty but also by her color: in her "all white, and redde, and blue/(Beauties ingredients) voluntary grew." She was a kind of chromatic generative source: "Being all colour, all Diaphanous," she lent "verdure" and "lustre" to the world (Donne 1985: 1:361–2, 364–6). As Irigaray reminds us, Aristotle says in *On Sense and Sensible Objects* that transparency is a quality that resides in all bodies to a greater or lesser extent, and it is color that defines the boundary of the body (Irigaray 1993d: 159). The Pythagoreans, he says, "called the surface of the body its colour," and while color is thus linked for Irigaray to flesh and an erotics of surface, Aristotle suggests that we understand the nature of the bodily interior by means of the color exhibited outside (Aristotle 1957: 439a). Deprived of color, as the world is in the wake of Elizabeth Drury's death, the senses grow wan, the blood retreating to the interior of the body in the inverse of a blush:

> Yet sight hath only color to feed on,
> And color is decayd: summers robe growes
> Duskie, and like an oft dyed garment showes.
> Our blushing redde, which us'd in cheekes to spred,
> Is inward sunke, and onely our soules are redde.
>
> (Donne 1985 1:353–8)

The body and its fluids, especially blood, thus become a language inscribed on the "outward skin" of the soul that Donne translates for us: "her pure and eloquent blood/Spoke in her cheeks, and so distinckly wrought,/That one might almost say her bodie thought" (Donne 1985 2:505, 244–6). This chromatic vocabulary joins the early modern discourse of the passions, implicated as they are in the body and its humors, to the radical feminist psychoanalysis that Irigaray describes in "Flesh Colors." The new analysis Irigaray envisions would be attentive to rhythm and color, to non-figurative writing, which includes the various languages of the body and

hysteria, and to "building new linguistic structures – by poetry in the etymological sense of the word" (Irigaray 1993d: 157). Rhythm and color are aspects of
pre-discursive experience, components that evoke Irigaray's imaginary, and it is
fitting that she sees the conclusion of a successful analysis as giving the
analysand the "power of his or her imagination" (Irigaray 1993d: 161). For her,
the imaginary is both phenomenological and psychoanalytic, bound up with the
Bachelardian elements and with knowledge, more primordial than the Lacanian
imaginary and also socially constructed (Whitford 1991: 53–7). For Irigaray,
"affect finds a haven within and by means of the imagination" (Irigaray 1993d:
162), thus offering the possibility of re-making the masculine imaginary in order
to allow true sexual diversity and "the flesh of our passions" to flourish.[26]

Notes

1   Philippa Berry suggests that *Speculum*, as a study that both anticipates and concludes
    the tetralogy, may be the missing "fire book" (Berry 1994: 231). See also Margaret
    Whitford's discussion of Gaston Bachelard's unacknowledged influence on Irigaray
    (Whitford 1991: 55–6; 61–2). Theresa Krier's superb essay (2003) on Irigaray and the
    elements in Spenser and Shakespeare is the best and most extensive treatment of this
    subject. She focuses in particular on fluidity and mutability as properties of daemonic
    allegory, on Irigaray's use of "fluxional materialism" and the interval as disruptions of
    the binarisms that structure Western philosophy, and on the elements in relation to
    ideas of cosmic justice.
2   For a more extensive treatment of this topic, see *Sensible Flesh: On Touch in Early
    Modern Culture*, especially my introduction, "The 'Sense of All Senses'" (Harvey
    2003: 1–21, 255–9).
3   Irigaray assigns a privileged place to philosophy because of its capacity to shape cul-
    ture, and she designates literature as a more traditionally acceptable site of intervention
    for women. She is thus insistent about her desire to have her texts read as philosophy.
    See Irigaray 1995b for her statements on this position.
4   I have silently modernized i/j and u/v and expanded abbreviations in the early modern
    texts I cite (with the exception of the Donne texts, where I defer to practice of the
    respective editors).
5   John Dryden's famous criticism of Donne was that he "affect[ed] the metaphysics" (*A
    Discourse Concerning the Original and Progress of Satire* [1693], Clements 1966:
    106), that is, that in his amorous verse he invoked philosophically abstract principles,
    instead of engaging, as he properly should have, the hearts of the "fair sex." Samuel
    Johnson echoed Dryden's division between the intellect and emotion, arguing that the
    Metaphysical poets were "beholders" rather than "partakers" of human nature, looking
    on like "Epicurean deities" "without emotion" (*Lives of the Poets*, [1779–81] qtd.
    Clements 1966: 108). It was really Herbert Grierson who heralded a change in this
    conception of Donne. Grierson saw him as "a creature of feeling and imagination …
    whose acute and subtle intellect was the servant, if sometimes the unruly servant, of
    passion and imagination" ("Donne and Metaphysical Poetry" [1921], qtd. in Clements
    1966: 122). T. S. Eliot's subsequent pronouncement about the dissociation of sensibil-
    ity provided an understanding of a unity of thought and feeling in Donne's poetry that
    has shaped our understanding of metaphysical poetry and that furthermore saw poetic
    inspiration as originating in the "cerebral cortex, the nervous system, and the digestive
    tracts" (Clements 1966: 130).
6   My discussion of Irigaray's two readings of Descartes is indebted to Naomi Schor's
    perceptive essay, "This Essentialism Which Is Not One." She argues that Irigaray's goal

is not so much to put physics back into metaphysics, but to "ruin" metaphysics by substituting a physics of fluidity for the patriarchal metaphysics of solidity, Heidegger's "crust" of the earth (Schora 1994: 71). While I also cite Heidegger's and Irigaray's use of the metaphysics/physics conjunction, my recovery of "physic" as the early modern term for medical science foregrounds the body as figure and philosophical problem central to Donne's thought and to Irigaray's theoretical projects.

7   The somatic and cerebral/psychic relationship and the question of interiority are, of course, overlapping although distinct problems. Recent discussions include Rorty (1979) and Bordo (1987). Schoenfeldt (1999) and Maus (1995) both trace the notion of inwardness in early modern literature. Teresa Brennan offers a provocative variation on this theme in her book, *Exhausting Modernity*. She develops a theory of what she calls "energetics," an idea that draws on Spinoza among others and that studies affective connections between individuals, other people, and the environment (2000: 10). She argues that the exhaustion of late capitalism, environmental collapse, and depleted psychic lives ultimately stems from the early modern development of an inner consciousness that cordoned the self off from the world. The partitioning of the subject and the consolidation of the subject/object perspective diminished the circulation of affect, and the psychical, affective, and imaginative interactions that we witness so frequently in early modern thinkers migrated to a cultural unconscious to which modern subjects have little access.

8   F. W. Bateson (1951) provides a brief history of Eliot's coinage of the "dissociation of sensibility" from its initial appearance (1921) in an anonymous review of Grierson's *Metaphysical Lyrics* to Eliot's own disclaimers about its usefulness in a Milton lecture in 1947 ("All we can say is, that something like this did happen; that it had something to do with the Civil War" [qtd in Bateson 1951: 63]). He argues that Eliot's source for the term is Remy de Gourmont's *Problème du Style* (1922), and that the concept had more to do with the Anglo-American *avant-garde* than with the seventeenth century. Bateson also claims that when Eliot spoke about "feeling," he was referring not to emotion but to sensation (1951: 50), but this idea comes out of Bateson's interest in Imagism, and it belies the invocation of emotion as a category by Dryden, Johnson, and Grierson and the subsequent interpretation of most critics, who assume that Eliot's use of "feeling" involved the emotions. The "dissociation of sensibility" was both immediately adopted into our critical vocabulary and relentlessly criticized and rejected for its imprecision. Frank Kermode, for instance, declared in 1957 that the concept was "absolutely useless historically" (Kermode 1957: 76), although he conceded that the power of this "historical myth" derived paradoxically from its vagueness (1957: 82). My interest in Eliot's use of the term is not as a category that is useful as a stylistic concept to distinguish Donne from, say, Milton, or as a moment of historical rupture, but rather as it points to a profoundly different sensibility about the body and the physiology of the emotions.

9   Her reading of Descartes situates Irigaray in a long tradition of women who engage with and contest Cartesian thought, beginning with Descartes's patron, Queen Christina of Sweden and his correspondent, Elisabeth of Bohemia, and including Margaret Cavendish and Anne Conway. For a survey of recent scholarship on seventeenth-century women and Cartesian philosophy, see Findlen (2002).

10   Naomi Schor discusses the two representations of Descartes (1994a: 71), and Susan James complicates the mind/body split in her analysis of the emotions in seventeenth-century philosophy (James 1997: 17–19, 85–108). See also Gail Kern Paster's consideration of Descartes and the passions in Shakespeare's plays (Paster 2001).

11   For an excellent survey of this tradition, see *Psyche and Soma*, ed. Wright and Potter (2000). Beate Gundert's chapter, "Soma and Psyche in Hippocratic Medicine," Heinrich von Staden's "Body, Soul, and Nerves: Epicurus, Herophilus, Erasistratus, the Stoics, and Galen," and Emily Michael's "Renaissance Theories of Body, Soul, and Mind" are especially illuminating.

12 Elizabeth Weed relates Irigaray's "homeopathic" approach to her cultivation of a mimetic reading strategy, a repetition that preempts her implication in the system of logic that she attempts to disrupt (Weed 1994: 83–4).

13 David Hirsch (1991) provides an instructive history of the revival of atomic theory in the seventeenth century. Associated principally with Lucretius by the early moderns, atomism incorporates and supersedes Empedoclean elemental theory by claiming that the elements themselves are composed of smaller, atomic particles (Hirsch 1991: 71). Whereas Hirsch believes that Donne discarded elemental theory in favor of atomism (Hirsch 1991: 77–8), I argue that there is ample evidence for Donne's use of and belief in multiple and incompatible theories. As I suggest in my discussion of Paracelsian and Galenic theory, Donne ultimately understands the epistemological claims of all scientific theories to be ineffective in combating fears about dissolution and decay.

14 Donne's self-consciousness about humoral theory in relation to Paracelsian innovation is reflected in his humoral joke in *Ignatius His Conclave*: when Lucifer listens to Paracelsus, both Ignatius and Lucifer experience strong emotions, imaged as complementary temperamental perturbations: "By this time *Ignatius* had observed a tempest risen in *Lucifers* countenance: for he was just of he same temper as *Lucifer*, and herefore suffered with him in every thing and felt al his alterations" (Donne 1969: 21).

15 Heather Meakin (1998) supplies a useful summary of the debate around Donne's putative misogyny. See also Mueller's position, which has become increasingly sympathetic to Donne's treatment of women (1989, 1993).

16 Although Irigaray invokes angels in "Divine Women" and *Ethics*, the idea of emotion or desire as constituting the interval or the in-between is also the animating idea in "Sorcerer Love," her reading of Diotima's speech in Plato's *Symposium*, where the *daimon* is eros (Irigaray 1993g). See Krier's essay in this volume for an excellent discussion of the daimonic and elemental in Irigaray and in ancient and early modern literature.

17 William Empson's remarkable essay, "Donne the Space Man," investigates Donne's interest in the idea of other worlds and their possible inhabitation. His positioning of Donne's "new sphears" in the context of astronomical discovery opens "Holy Sonnet V" to these currents of new scientific thought and suggests the ease with which Donne and his contemporaries moved among apparently incompatible theological, scientific, and medical theories.

18 Victor Harris (1949) provides an intellectual history for the idea of world decay and disintegration in the sixteenth and seventeenth centuries. See also Hirsch (1991) on the revival of atomism as antidote to early modern anxiety about degeneration.

19 The *John Donne Journal* devoted a special issue to "Aire and Angels," and the essays there, especially John R. Roberts's "'Just such disparitee': The Critical Debate about 'Aire and Angels,'" provide an instructive sampling of approaches.

20 Shakespeare uses similar wordplay in Sonnet 20. See also Ronald Corthell's citation of Irigaray for a glossing of these lines: "Woman's castration is defined as her having nothing you can see … nothing penile, in seeing that she has No Thing" (Corthell 1997: 78). See also Labriola (1990) for an interpretation of the sexual innuendo in the image of the pinnace.

21 "The Angells assumed bodies for the manifesting themselves … if you aske of what those bodies consisted? It is like ordinarily of some of the Elements, as of the ayre. And if you object that the ayre is improper to take figure or colour, because it is so thin and transparent? The answer is, that although the ayre remaining in its rarity doth not reteyne figure or colour, yet when it is condenced and thickened, it will doe both as appears in the clouds" (Lawrence 1646: 14–15).

22 Many critics understand this analogy as a direct correspondence between "aire" (less pure) and women's love and between "angels" (purer) and men's love, and they thus see these lines as evidence of Donne's misogyny. Empson refers to and then refutes this assumption, arguing that Donne's joke targets not the woman, but the concept of

"purity" (Empson 1993: 114–18). He supports this reading with reference to alchemy and the emergent chemistry's precoccupations with distillation and essence, an interpretation that accords well with my own focus on the elemental. Although Achsah Guibbory concurs with the traditional reading of the lines, her conclusion is Irigarayan: "The poem invites us to ask whether we can think of man's love and women's love, of men and women, as being different without necessarily invoking the hierarchical discriminations involved in conventional distinctions between body and soul, air and angel. The poem also makes clear how difficult it is to love someone else for her(him)self, as (s)he is, rather than as a reflection or mirror of the lover's needs and desires" (Guibbory 1990b: 111).

23 Donne mentions Hilliard by name in "The Storme," his verse letter to Christopher Brooke (Donne 1985: 4). For an excellent discussion of Donne's knowledge of visual art and miniatures and the chance that Donne himself may have sat for Hilliard, see Wiggins (2000: 64–70).

24 Early Modern treatises on the humors are full of descriptions of color, perhaps nowhere quite so "purple" as in Thomas Walkington's description of the sanguine temperament: "The purple Rose, whose high Encomium that witty Poetess *Sappho* in a sweet ode once sang, did not merit to be adorn'd with such beauteous titles of words, to be lim'd out in so lively colours of Rhetorick nor to be invested with such a gorgeous and gallant suit of Poetry as this golden *crasis*, this happy Temperature, and choice complexion, this Sanguine humour, is worthy of a *Panegryrical* tongue, to be limn'd out with the hand of Art it self" (1607: 110). There is, of course, a close historical link between humoral medicine and painting, because Apelles, the most celebrated Greek painter of antiquity, was a younger contemporary of Hippocrates, and we know from Pliny's *Natural History* that many of the best classical painters used a palette of four colors (Gage 1993: 29). But it is really not until Galen that color theory was fully extended to include complexion, and the portrait painting and encaustic mummy-effigies of Roman Egypt employed a palette for flesh that seems to correspond closely to Galenic doctrine (Gage 1993: 29).

25 "Rueus saith that ... [the turquoise] doth change, grow pale and destitute of its native colour, if he that weareth it do at any time grow infirm or weak; and again upon the recovery of its master, that it doth recover its own lovely beauty which ariseth of the temperament of its own naturall heat, and becometh ceruleous like the serene heaven" (Nicols 1659: 149).

26 I am grateful to the Toronto Renaissance and Reformation Colloquium for the opportunity to present this material in an earlier version, to the students in my graduate seminar on Donne in 2002–03 who first listened to some of these ideas in inchoate form, to Georgianna Ziegler for an elusive reference, and especially to Theresa Krier for her intellectual generosity and editorial acumen.

6 Spenser's coastal unconscious

Elizabeth Jane Bellamy

THE COASTAL GOD

The concluding section of Irigaray's *Marine Lover of Friedrich Nietzsche*, entitled "When the Gods Are Born," meditates on the incarnation of the child-god. Embedded within and distanced from Nietzsche's contrast of Apollo and Dionysos, this section continues her book's preoccupation with the sea's "fluid depths," and the child who "lives in the wet":

> The element of the child-god is still women or sea goddesses. Much beloved nurses of his cradle and growth. ... *The god is born on an island. The smallest, most barren, least prosperous of islands. ... No land wanted any part of him. A foreigner in all parts. ... Of uncertain genealogy.* ... In order to define and affirm himself, the god holds back, in suspension, impassive. Reining in his passion, he gazes upon himself and admires himself. ... And if he prefers jousting to passion, isn't this necessary for the establishment of his power?
>
> (Irigaray 1991: 137–9, 156; italics mine)

This spliced excerpt italicizes certain lines that I will repeatedly revisit in my attempt to trace Spenser's coastal unconscious. But first, I wish to focus on the unitalicized lines. Calling attention to the child-god as self-admiring, Irigaray demonstrates her familiarity with the mythic topos of the narcissistic, maternally overprotected child-god such as Adonis or Achilles, pampered by his sea-nymph mother Thetis. Her description of the child-god can also remind us of *The Faerie Queene*'s watery hero Marinell, son of the mortal Dumarin and the immortal sea-nymph Cymoent, who secludes her son on the isolated Faerie seacoast "strond." When Irigaray describes the narcissistic child-god as "preferr[ing] jousting to passion," again we are uncannily reminded of Marinell aggressively charging Britomart on the Faerie coast (3.4.25). Though wounded, he suffers no shortage of nurturing sea-goddesses (in Irigaray's words, "much beloved nurses of his cradle and growth"): all of Cymoent's sisters minister to him, pouring balm into his wound while the "lilly handed" Liagore tenderly feels his pulse (3.4.40–1).[1]

Irigaray's pampered child-god is impassive, enveloped within an amniotic marine plenitude, suspended at the threshold of a marine unconscious. At first glance, Irigaray's marine unconscious appears to be a kind of Jungian, oceanic unconsciousness. But closer scrutiny of the italicized lines in my essay's opening excerpt reveals a disalignment in her marine child-god that undermines any Jungian plenitude. To echo Irigaray, *the god is born on an island* – for *no land wants any part of him. A foreigner in all parts.* Though surrounded by sea-goddesses, Irigaray's child-god – as a "hybrid infant" (123) – neither dwells in the sea, nor finds a home on land. The marine child-god is, of necessity, a *coastal* god. But there is a crucial distinction between the coastal dwelling of Irigaray's child-god and the fluid economy she customarily privileges: the coast of the child-god is a void where land and sea are presumed to "meet."

More precisely, Irigaray's marine unconscious is a *coastal* unconscious, alerting us that the pampered plenitude of the child-god's marine birth will be followed by life on the coast, where not-land and not-sea (fail to) merge with his uncertain status as not-human and not-deity, *a foreigner in all parts.* Her coastal child-god is born on the *least prosperous of islands.* Thus, Irigaray implicitly encourages us to tease out a play on words between the noun "strand" as a coastline, and the verb "strand," i.e. to be (literally) driven ashore, and also to be (figuratively) rendered helpless. Spenser's Marinell is surely pampered – but more often, he is "luckelesse" (4.12.53). The coastal unconscious, then, emerges as a stranding on a strand where one becomes, like the unconscious itself, *a foreigner in all parts.*[2]

Irigaray's coastal child-god motivates a return to Spenser's Faerie "strond," birthplace of Marinell, *stranded* on the "strond" – in her words, "[a]lways already exiled from the place that gives him place" (123). My essay proposes *The Faerie Queene's* seacoast, the liminal dwelling of the child-god Marinell, as the locus of Spenser's coastal unconscious. Much has been written about Spenser's riverine imagination, his fascination with English and Irish rivers as cataloged in Book 4's marriage of the Thames and Medway, where he reveals a particular fondness for his own Irish river, "Mulla mine," flowing through Kilcolman (4.11.41). But Spenser's Faerie seacoast has been less scrutinized – and, in light of Irigaray's "When the Gods Are Born," perhaps undertheorized, as well.

Nowhere in *The Faerie Queene* does the poet declare a *heimlich*, Mulla-like "seacoast mine," least of all the boundaries of his unlocatable Faerie strand. To echo Irigaray, the child-god is not just island-born: he is also born on *the least prosperous of islands.* Thus, my effort to trace Spenser's coastal unconscious begins by foregrounding the sheer ugliness of his Faerie strand. In contrast to, say, the eminently poetic "pleasant floods" of England's tributarial Sture or the quaint "stony bancke" of the Tyne (4.11.33, 36), the Faerie seacoast is battered by:

> the surges hore,
> That gainst the craggy clifts did loudly rore,
> And in their raging surquedry disdaynd,
> That the fast earth affronted them so sore,
> And their deuouring couetize restrained.

> (3.4.7)

Marinell's domain is a treacherous zone where land and sea violently clash, where thunderous breakers smash against defiant rocks.[3] So hyperbolically dire is Spenser's strand that it's as if he refuses to take the seacoast seriously. One might provisionally (if anachronistically) label his style "seacoast gothic," befitting Book 3 as a legend of psychosexual angst as much as a legend of chastity: the turbulence of the strand is a melodramatic projection of the psychic turbulence of Book 3's many characters struggling with their adolescent sexual fears and desires.[4]

But Spenser's pseudo-comic "gothicness," his sophisticated distance from this angst, should not distract us from a more sustained analysis of the bleak Faerie strand as a mirror of his *own* coastal unconscious. His river-catalog savors the provinciality of English and Irish rivers, described in loving, geographic detail, as he all but invents the genre of the river marriage as inherently English (Roche 1964: 167–76). But this topographical poetics does not extend to his *unheimlich* seacoast. British coastlines seemingly have no special pull on him – as if *their* provinciality lacks any charm or poetic potential. Thus, my analysis of Spenser's coastal unconscious centers on his stranding of poetic ugliness on his "strond," displaced into a Faerie *non*-Britain. I identify this coastal exile on a Faerie strand as a Spenserian moment of "acting out." If the provinciality of English and Irish rivers afforded Spenser an opportunity to shape a new river genre, it was too late for the seacoast: the venerable, extensive reach of literary history from the continent had already, as it were, passed judgment on British (and Irish and Scottish) coasts, branding them as comically isolated in the *not*-Mediterranean.

As my essay's central claim, this observation requires careful unpacking. Spenser famously challenges the alert reader to search for Faerie land by detecting "certaine signes here set in sundry place" (2.Proem.4). Reading intertextually, focusing on "sundry place[s]" within literary history, I reveal his gothic "craggy clifts" as the same British coasts that literary history has coded as isolated. Ironically, Spenser's *unheimlich* seacoast is more "homey" than he may have bargained for. I argue that the Faerie strand is a British (or Irish or Scottish) coast – the repressed but traceable result of how a "strand" (pun intended) in literary history has "stranded" certain ugly, remote coasts precisely in the British isles.

To read Spenser's Faerie strand against the grain of Irigaray's "When the Gods Are Born" is to peel back the layers of literary history that are the substrate of Spenser's coastal unconscious. Irigaray's emphasis on the child-god's birthplace as *the least prosperous of islands* invites us to ponder other menacing coastlines in literary history to uncover what Spenser may have disavowed when he fashioned his stranding, stranded "strond." Such a coastal literary history necessarily begins with a consideration of manifestly *beautiful* coasts and, thus, with Sannazaro's marine eclogues as *the* definitive genre of the seacoast. I then turn to manifestly treacherous coastlines, namely the rugged Brittany coast of Chaucer's "Franklin's Tale" and the Ebudan coast of Ariosto's *Orlando Furioso* as prototypes for the ugliness of Spenser's seacoast.[5]

This literary history fully involves the question of genre. Enabling my conception of a coastal unconscious as generically determined is the political unconscious (Jameson 1981), briefly summarized as a repression of ideological contradictions occurring as certain genres are neglected or are remotivated by newly emergent genres – a repression offering clues that Spenser's Faerie seacoast is located in Britain, after all. I argue that even as Spenser deploys the seacoast "gothic" style of Ariosto's Ebudan coast, he excludes (misreads? represses?) Ariosto's tightly controlled expulsion of the Mediterranean coasts of the Sannazaran marine eclogue. Somewhere between Sannazaro and Ariosto, the Neo-Latin beauty of the Mediterranean becomes effaced amidst the harsh, craggy – and eminently vernacular – coastlines of Ireland and Scotland. In the coastal *translatio* from the *Furioso* to *The Faerie Queene*, Spenser fails to acknowledge Ariosto's ironically encrypted Sannazaro. Thus, Spenser's Faerie "strond" becomes the Irigarayan child-god's *least prosperous of islands*; and Marinell uncannily anticipates her disaligned coastal child-god as *a foreigner in all parts*.[6] Dispersed – *stranded* – as it is amidst the generic seams of the Chaucerian Breton lay, the Sannazaran marine eclogue, and Ariostan epic romance, Spenser's seacoast represses the possibility that it might be as displaced as the unconscious itself, displaced, that is, somewhere in the coastlines of the British isles as, poetically speaking, the provincial, isolated *not*-Mediterranean, the dwelling of *a foreigner in all parts*. What Spenser's coastal unconscious hides is that his Faerie seacoast may be as inherently British as his beloved genre of the river marriage.

HYDROPHOBIC MARINELL

Reading Marinell in depth – reading him *in his depths* – resonates with Irigaray's claim that *no land wants any part of the sea-god*. No poetic genre from the European continent may want any part of him either. This dislocated Marinell is a generically neglected Marinell.

No land wants any part of the sea-god. But does Spenser's Faerie coast want any part of Marinell? Irigaray's meditation on the uncertainties of marine genealogy sheds light on what has been, for me at least, one of *The Faerie Queene*'s oddities – i.e. why Marinell never seems as comfortable around water as his name implies. Though "halfe mortall" (4.12.4), Marinell strikes the reader as somehow different from, say, Sannazaro's Glaucus, a mortal fisherman turned sea-deity – as if the dalliance between Dumarin and Cymoent were not endorsed by Nereus, Neptune, and her other sea-chaperones. Of Marinell's mortal father Dumarin we know nothing – except that his name signifies a life of marine fulfillment. Dumarin is "of the sea," and Marinell's sea-nymph mother is a "wave-tamer." The happy result of this (etymological) union should have been a water-baby at home on land or sea, a child ordained to enjoy a life of marine plenitude. But Marinell, as Dumarin and Cymoent's "halfe mortall" son (Irigaray's marine child *of uncertain genealogy*) is neither secure in the waves of Cymoent's ocean nor at home at the battering, battered Faerie seacoast – in Marinell's own words, "this forbidden way" (3.4.14).

Raised in a dreary coastal "rocky caue as wighte forlorne" (3.4.20), he does not swim in the ocean; and even on the coast, he seems eminently susceptible to drowning – a very real danger at odds with the topos of the Achillean, protected youth.[7]

Marinell's marine limitations are evident in Book 4, where he accompanies his mother to the wedding festivities for the Thames and Medway "to learne and see/The manner of the Gods when they at banquet be" (4.12.3). The renowned sea-gods in attendance include Neptune, who "rules the seas," Eurypulus, who "calmes the waters wroth," and Alebius, who "know'th/The waters depth, and doth their bottome tread" (3.11.11–14): all three sea-gods dwell happily – literally – "in their element." But Marinell is unable to join his mother at the banquet:

> He might not with immortal food be fed,
> Ne with th'eternall Gods to bancket come;
> But walkt abrode, and round about did rome,
> To view the building of that vncouth place.

> (4.12.4)

In Virgil's fourth *Georgic*, Aristaeus, son of the sea-nymph Cyrene, is conveyed by a mountain-wave beneath the ocean to visit the source of all the rivers. But Marinell – also at the confluence of the world's seas – is strangely hydrophobic: readers are told that Cymoent "of his father Marinell did name" (3.4.20), but the *marin* of Du-*marin* has not been fully enfolded into the *marin* of *Marin*-ell. Or, it may be the case that as Mari-*nell*, Dumarin and Cymoent's son is seemingly the *negation* of the sea, fated to dwell in the grievous "margent" – the *not*-sea (and certainly not land) of the Faerie strand.

Marinell's marine limitations extend beyond his role as overprotected son to his other role as the lamenting coastal lover of Florimell, imprisoned in Proteus's bower. Precariously positioned "[v]nder the hanging of an hideous clieffe," Marinell hears Florimell crying for help (4.12.5). Proteus's bower is Spenser's pseudo-comic "gothic" seacoast at its most terrifying, located as it is:

> Vnder a mightie rocke, gainst which do raue
> The roaring billowes in their proud disdaine,
> That with the angry working of the waue,
> Therein is eaten out a hollow caue
> That seems rough Masons hand with engines keene
> Had long while laboured it to engraue.

> (3.8.37)

His dungeon is assaulted by waves, as if "they the cliffe in peeces would haue cleft" (4.11.3–4). Anticipating Marinell's childhood "rocky caue," this sea-cave dungeon constitutes a churning zone of precipitous dropoffs and high tides disguising roiling turbulences – a grim boundary where land and sea grudgingly fight to establish dominance. As the waves smack the rocks, walls of water shatter. But with each absorption of the waves' impact, the sea-rock loses more of its mass, resulting in caves "engraue[d]" by the "Masons hand" of erosion. As Marinell hears Florimell shrieking for help, the cliff-cleaving waves "[d]oe pearce the rockes, and hardest marble weares" (4.12.7).

Despite the promise of his watery name, Marinell cannot approach Proteus's grievous "hollow caue" to rescue Florimell: "… he found no way/To enter in, or issue forth below:/For all about that rocke the sea did flow" (4.12.15). Unlike the sea-god Alebius, whose marine athleticism gives him knowledge of "[t]he waters depth," Marinell is imprisoned amidst his own coastal rocks, on the brink of being dashed to bits should he seek to "issue forth below." Unable to swim, dive, or hold his breath while submerged, "[i]n this sad plight he walked here and there,/And romed round about the rocke in vaine,/As he had lost him selfe, he wist not where" (4.12.17). Even when he is "at home" (either on the coast or accompanying his sea-nymph mother), Marinell is in exile – a "walker abrode" amidst "vncouth" marine realms, a lonely coastal roamer "round about" the dangerous breakers. "Lost … he wist not where," Marinell is truly Irigaray's marine child-god – *a foreigner in all parts, exiled from the place that gives him place*, stranded on *the least prosperous of islands*.

FAERIE'S COASTAL "MARGENT"

The harshness of Spenser's Faerie strand is particularly evident when contrasted with the idyllic ocean depths of Marinell's mother Cymoent. As a sea-nymph, Cymoent, "deuoyd of mortall slime," dwells in a protected realm of marine plenitude (3.4.35). As Nereus's daughter, Cymoent – like all the Nereids – possesses mysterious marine powers: "with her least word [she] can assuage/The surging seas, when they do sorest rage" (4.11.52). Cymoent also enjoys a life of marine-pastoral bliss. Prior to hearing of Marinell's wounding, she and her sister-nymphs play by a pond, gathering "sweet daffadillyes" to shade their "forheads faire" from the sun (3.4.29). When she hears of her son's wounding, she does not grieve alone, as each of her nymphs "did teare her girlond from her crowne" in sympathetic unison (3.4.30). In Book 4, Cymoent gives Marinell's healer-god Tryphon a whistle "[t]hat of a fishes shell was wrought with rare delight" (4.11.6). While Marinell copes in a world of "craggy clifts," Cymoent enjoys a marine dream-world of balmy seas and finely wrought seashell-treasures.

The Latinate charm of Cymoent's domain is never so cloying as when she and her sisters summon sea-chariots to take them to the wounded Marinell. Neptune responds to the crisis by calming his "roaring billowes" for the train of chariots:

> Great *Neptune* stood amazd at their sight,
> Whiles on his broad round back they softly slid
> And eke himselfe mournd at their mournfull plight …
> For great compassion of their sorrow, bid
> His mightie waters to them buxome bee.

> (3.4.32)

A school of graceful dolphins, "raunged in array," draws Cymoent's chariot, described in some of *The Faerie Queene*'s most self-consciously mannered poetry:

> As swift as swallowes, on the waues they went,
> That their broad flaggie finnes no fome did reare,
> Ne bubbling roundell they behind them sent,
> The rest of other fishes drawen weare,
> Which with their finny oars the swelling sea did sheare.

(3.4.33)

Cymoent's chariot sliding softly on Neptune's back, her broad-finned dolphins gracefully leaving "ne bubbling roundell" in their wakes, the other chariot-drawing fish "shear[ing]" the sea-swells with their "finny oars," etc., are all images so precious in their piscatory perfection that, at this moment, the reader altogether forgets Marinell "inglorious[ly]" smeared in "cruddy bloud" (3.4.34). For six carefully crafted stanzas, the focus is not on Marinell's abjection, but rather on the extravagance of Cymoent's grief as the poetic occasion for a synchronized marine ballet.

The passage describing the sea-nymphs' arrival at the Faerie coast gives us pause, for at this turbulent "margent" we can begin to tease out Spenser's coastal unconscious. In the exquisite poetry that typically describes Cymoent's world, as the nymphs dismount their chariots they assure themselves that:

> their temed fishes softly swim
> Along the margent of the fomy shore,
> Least they their finnes should bruze, and surbate sore
> Their tender feet vpon the stony ground.

(3.4.34)

Even as Marinell wallows in gore, the poet (like Cymoent?) seems more preoccupied with the safety of the sea-nymphs' dolphins and other "temed" fish as they deftly avoid "the fomy shore," protecting their delicate fins and "tender feet" from the battering, "bruzing," "surbat[ing]" perils of Spenser's gothic seacoast.

To digress, we can contrast the poet's churning "margent of the fomy shore" with his mythopoeic description of the ocean-born Venus that concludes Book 4: "*Venus* of the fomy seas was bred;/For that the seas by her are most augmented./Witnesse th'exceeding fry, which there are fed" (4.12.2). Here, the "fomy seas" signify fertility and abundance as the venerean sea-spume nurtures the ocean's "exceeding fry." These same "fomy seas" constitute Cymoent's idyllic domain. But the "fomy," wave-battered Faerie strand is a far cry from this venerean "fome." No longer the obedient waters of Cymoent's depths, Marinell's seacoast is a gothic terrain of raging "surges hore," where the "fomy" ocean waters do not nurture but rather "bruze" and "surbate." Here exist no exquisitely intact "fishes shells wrought with rare delight" – only smashed shell fragments.

Here flourish no "exceeding fry" – only whatever primitive marine life (barnacles? algae?) are able to survive the waves that continually rake over the rocks.

The "margent" of Spenser's seacoast is a liminal threshold where the plenitude of Cymoent's marine realm ends and the very real violence of the jagged, rocky coast begins. To pose a question: why must Marinell dwell amidst the churning, body-battering turbulence of the Faerie seacoast, while Cymoent's pampered fish keep a safe distance from the "craggy clifts" lest they "bruze" their delicate fins against the half-submerged rocks? Animal lovers can respond to the charm of Cymoent's pampering priorities. But there is no denying this Faerie "margent" as a coastal black hole in her marine plenitude. Neither the land's border nor the sea's edge, this "margent" is both where Marinell is unable to "issue forth" amidst the battering waves, and where Cymoent's sea-creatures prudently halt their progress toward "the fomy shore."

SANNAZARAN BEAUTY-COASTS

Why is Spenser's seacoast so persistently *gothic*? What currents (literally and figuratively) in literary history created this black hole, this terror-*margent* of raking, racking coastal rocks? As a barrier between poetic beauty and ugliness, the Faerie "margent" might also be viewed as a barrier between Neo-Latin and vernacular coasts. Earlier I suggested that Marinell cannot find his proper place in any genre from the Continent: the inhospitable Faerie seacoast offers him no recognizably generic "home." This section further probes Marinell's generic exile by considering the beautiful Neo-Latin coasts of the Sannazaran marine eclogue as the *not*-Faerie strand.

There are not one but two largely unrelated Marinells in *The Faerie Queene*: Book 3's maternally overprotected adolescent, and Book 4's pining lover of Florimell. Despite the unrelatedness of the two Marinells, their ongoing association with the Faerie seacoast is constant, prompting a consideration of Marinell's coastal prototypes within literary history. Of Book 3's overprotected Marinell, we recognize two key classical antecedents, Achilles and Adonis. And it should be emphasized that both figures are, at times, also explicitly *coastal* precursors for Marinell (Nohrnberg 1976: 587). *The Faerie Queene*'s second Marinell (Florimell's pining coastal lover) also has a literary history directly traceable to the seacoast.

If the seacoast has a genre, it is surely Sannazaro's Neo-Latin piscatory eclogues, a richly intertextual genre of stylized laments for dead or absent lovers amidst a coastal backdrop of erotic *pietàs*. The piscatory eclogue originates with Theocritus's *Idylls*, their loving descriptions of shepherds glimpsing the sea amidst the distant poundings of the surf, or of forsaken lovers singing for their lost beloveds while waves sparkle beneath the moon. Almost a century ago, Henry Hall captured the picturesque charm of the Theocritean pastoral of the shore thus: "In a land of islets, sounds and promontories many a youth drove his flock afield on hillsides whence he could look down on the blue shield of the sea, rimmed with white surf, seething and thundering on rock-ribbed coasts ..." (Hall 1914: 1). Theocritus's idylls were imitated by Virgil, whose celebrated fourth *Georgic* features such delights as Proteus sheltered in a coastal cave on a hot day, while his companion sea-creatures gambol in the waves. The marine eclogue became fully constituted as a genre in Renaissance Italy with the 1526 publication of Sannazaro's five *Eclogae piscatoriae*, continuing the Theocritean and Virgilian traditions of idealizing the seacoast. Though not as widely read as his vernacular *Arcadia*, these Neo-Latin eclogues inspired a significant vogue.[8] Among other carefully-cultivated charms, Sannazaro's eclogues intimately reflect his fondness for his native Bay of Naples and his villa's views of the Mediterranean. If Spenser had his riverine "Mulla mine," Sannazaro surely had his Neapolitan Bay "mine."

We can read Cymoent's coastal lament for Marinell, as well as Marinell's own later coastal pining for his beloved Florimell, in the context of Sannazaro's first eclogue ("Phyllis"), a poem that revels in the allures of coastal life. Here, the rocky shores of the Mediterranean resound with the plaints of sea-birds, mourning the anniversary of the death of the fisher-girl Phyllis. Her grieving lover Lycidas visits her coastal grave, lying "stretched upon the seaweed of the shore" (54), eventually reconciling himself to "journey through the vasty deep/Through stormy waves that surge to heaven's steep,/Past monsters of the sea, past Triton-throngs" (70–2) – an exile more topographically exotic than sad.[9] In Sannazaro's second eclogue ("Galatea"), the fisher-youth Lycon's lament for his absent beloved Galatea reflects his compulsion to give voice to his melancholia through coastal tropes: "Your pride rejects my words as rocks the wave" (9). In vain he offers her robes that are "softer than the ocean's spray" (41). Although the sea-loving Lycon chides the ungrateful Galatea for also spurning the seacoast's bounty, what lingers with the reader is Sannazaro's eye for the special charms of the coast:

> Misenum's hanging rocks have yielded scores
> Of oysters, gifts for you; Euploea's shores
> A thousand keep; her sister-island saves
> As great a store beneath the glassy waves.
> So Nesis' isle, in never-ending store,
> Of spiny urchins keeps a thousand more.
>
> (27–32)

Loyal to Lycon (where are Marinell's friends?) is the mythic Glaucus, once a simple fisherman but later transformed into a sea-deity of "swelling wave and pleasing shore."

The piscatory eclogue, as *the* poetic genre of the seacoast, caresses the coastline, proffered as a gently erotic backdrop for dying youths and/or lamenting lovers – replete with gorgeous place-names: "Misenum's hanging rocks," "Euploea's shores," and "Nesis' isle," etc. Lycon's noting the sea-rocks' cornucopia of "scores of oysters" and thousands of "spiny urchins" is an intriguing mix of naïveté and sophistication. Sannazaro's crying shore-birds, seaweed-draped lovers' graves, and robes "softer than the ocean's spray" are all highly erotic images. Even granting an elegant rusticity as intrinsic to the pastoral genre, the images of the piscatory eclogue offer the seacoast as perhaps nature's most profound mirror of the psychic unrest of bereaved lovers. So in tune with the genre's plaintive melancholia are the wave-resounding waters of the piscatory eclogue (i.e. Glaucus as "a watcher of the watery strand" [54]) that the clash between rocky coast and ocean wave is more seductive than threatening. The piscatory eclogue's "vasty deep" rhythmically *merges* with the laments of the shore-lovers: the breakers' pounding energy erotically intensifies in direct relationship to the lover's sadness.

In *The Faerie Queene*, the preciousness of Cymoent's marine world can now strike us as largely indebted to the marine motifs of the Mediterranean piscatory eclogue. But Marinell's Faerie "strond" cannot be so easily inserted within this genre. Marinell is not easily located within the topos of the overprotected son (Achilles, Adonis, etc.); nor is the coast the kind of sequestering haven for him that it is for Sannazaro's Lycon or Lycidas.

As we have seen, the rocky seacoast of Marinell's domain is explicitly threatening. Cymoent has the power to assuage the seas; but, oddly, it does not extend to her own son's coastline, where she needs assurance that her beloved dolphins will steer clear of the breakers, protecting their delicate fins from the rocky shore. The "margent" of the Faerie coast affords Marinell no opportunity for erotic solipsism – only bleak coastal exile. The Faerie seacoast's "surges hore" are "bruzing" and "surbating." Its angry, cliff-cleaving breakers are "disdainful," "sorely raging," and "couetizely deuouring." Its "hideous clieffes" are "vncouth," carved out "by rough Masons hand." It is ugly, baleful, migrainous, and unforgiving – as perilous as the beaches of the piscatory eclogue are seductive. Hence, Marinell is truly the Irigarayan coastal child-god, *born on the least prosperous of islands. A foreigner in all parts.*

Spenser's "gothic" seacoast erases any memory of Sannazaro's picturesque coastlines. If Marinell were a Sannazaran Lycidas or Lycon, the wave-resounding surf would sympathetically reflect his grief. But Spenser's inaccessible coastal rocks – not reflective, but actively *deflective* – form a barrier that cannot be penetrated: Marinell cannot "enter in" to its rocky caves or "issue forth below." If, in the Sannazaran eclogue, the melancholia of the marine lover induces the actions of the surf to increase in sympathetic intensity, on the Faerie coast it is the cruel surf that intensifies the lover's terror and physical danger.

TERROR COASTS: FROM EBUDA TO THE FAERIE "STROND"

On Spenser's Faerie seacoast no Theocritean shepherds catch seductive glimpses of the sea, no Sannazaran Lycons count "spiny urchins." The Faerie strand, then, prompts a simple question: where *is* this gothic seacoast? To pursue this question is to tease out a coastal intertextuality between Sannazaro and Ariosto as one of Sannazaro's better-known admirers and, in turn, greatly admired by Spenser.

Generically speaking, Spenser's gothic seacoast can be found in Ariosto's *Orlando Furioso*. Spenser's portrait of Marinell's beloved, the imperiled Florimell – chaste, but always "chased" – has long been identified by critics as indebted to Ariosto's romance heroine Angelica. Thus, any perception of Spenser's seacoast as "gothic" must first pass through the *Furioso*, whose elusive Angelica is also terrorized on a sadistic coastline (8.30–50). To briefly rehearse her coastal trauma, Angelica, fleeing Europe, is pursued by a lecherous hermit who conjures a demon that impels Angelica's horse to bolt out to sea, eventually carrying her to a remote island. On this harsh and lonely (*aspro et ermo*) coast, Angelica is trapped among dark rocks (*scuri sassi*) and frightening sea-caves (*spaventose grotte*), praying that she will drown amidst its protruding rocks (*rilevato sasso*) and horrid reefs (*scoglio*) (8.37–49).[10] The inhabitants of the even more remote island of Ebuda, scouring the coastal waters in search of women to sacrifice to the vengeful sea-god Proteus's monstrous orc, capture her and chain her helplessly to Ebuda's coastal rocks. (By contrast, in Sannazaro's "Galatea," coastal orcs do not devour victims, but rather slumber in sympathy with the grieving Lycon.) Awaiting sacrifice to the orc, Angelica is rescued by Ruggiero, riding on his hippogriff.

I argue that Ebuda, as an earlier version of Spenser's "gothic" seacoast, is all the more gothic because of its remoteness. As if the towering coastal rocks where Angelica's horse strands her are not inhospitable enough, Ariosto's narrative sweeps his heroine further westward to the Ebudan coast. And at this point, readers cannot be certain exactly where, on the map, Ariosto's narrative is. Ebuda is in the Hebrides; but where is *Ariosto's* Hebrides? The poet narrates that Ruggiero, meandering across Europe on his uncontrollable hippogriff, spots Angelica while flying beyond the straits of Hercules, beyond the "*ultima terra*" (the "distant land") of England, arriving at Ebuda, "nel mar di tramontana inver l'occaso,/oltre l'Irlanda" ("in the great northern sea, toward the west,/Green Ireland past" [8.51]). Ariosto has pointedly (dis)located Ebuda *beyond* Ireland in the extreme northwest. Douglas Biow usefully historicizes this odd location of Ebuda beyond Ireland by turning to an early Ptolemaic map that Ariosto himself had studied: "In the codex acquired by Borso d'Este in 1466 ... , one may pinpoint Ebuda situated in the top left corner, precisely where Ptolemy indicated the island should be" (Biow 1996: 108).

So remotely northwest is Ariosto's (and Ptolemy's) Ebuda that it is scarcely discernible in the top left corner of the late fifteenth-century maps acquired by the Estensi. If, for Ariosto, England is already an *ultima terra*, then Ebuda, "oltre l'Irlanda," is even more *ultima* – a cartographical *extremity*, stranded in "the top left corner" of the map. Albert Ascoli, commenting on Ruggiero's inability to control the hippogriff, helps us imagine the sheer remoteness of Ebuda, observing that Ruggiero is carried "westward beyond the long-established limits of human experience" (Ascoli 1987: 136). Even more to the point, Ariosto, however inadvertently, equates coastal remoteness with gothic terror. Ebuda's hostile, orc-patrolled strand is not only remote but also sadistic: where the shorelines of an *ultima terra* become the site of *ultimate terror*.

To place the remote ugliness of Ebuda in perspective, one can juxtapose it with the *Furioso*'s best-known shoreline, the exotic coast of Alcina's isle, where Ariosto's enchantress charms the coastal dolphins, seals, and sperm whales (6.20–3). Though presumably located on the other side of the world, Alcina's isle seems far less remote than Ebuda: for all its isolation, the exoticism of Alcina's false paradise familiarly doubles back on the storied shores of the Mediterranean basin, i.e. Circe's Aeaea, Calypso's Ogygia, or Dido's Carthaginian shores. For that matter, it also recalls the many charms of Sannazaro's "Euploean shores" or "Nesis' isle." This is the moment, then, to emphasize that Ariosto had closely read Sannazaro's piscatory eclogues, enthusiastically praising their elegance and declaring them a new poetic genre (Hall 1914: 54). In fact, in the *Furioso*'s final canto, Ariosto singles out Sannazaro for praise as the poet who "lures/The Muses from the mountains to the shores" (*ch'alle Camene/lasciar fa i monti et abitar l'arene*) (xlvi.17.7–8).

But on the treacherous Ebudan seacoast, Ariosto's high regard for the elegant melancholia of Sannazaro's new coastal genre cedes place to the *Furioso*'s notorious comic – often sadistic – irony. Ariosto seemed more interested in fashioning his gothic Ebudan coast as a patently *anti*-Mediterranean terror coast. Put another way, the sado-comedy of Angelica's adventures increases proportionately with the eighth canto's increasingly *unheimlich* distance from the Mediterranean.

In *The Faerie Queene*, Ariosto's Ebudan terror-coast, not Sannazaro's exotic shores, is the model for Spenser's Faerie seacoast, where female terror is also fetishized. Florimell's imprisonment in Proteus's sea-walled dungeon closely imitates Angelica's imprisonment among the dark rocks of Ariosto's Ebuda (Alpers 1967: 195; Roche 1964: 11–14). So extensive were Spenser's borrowings from Ebuda that Florimell is almost exclusively a *coastal* heroine – with significant portions of Books 3 and 4 becoming coastal episodes. As critics have often noted, Florimell is *The Faerie Queene*'s paradigmatic "fearefull damzell," all the more desirable for being perpetually in flight. Coming to *The Faerie Queene* from Ebuda, we should not be surprised that it is on Spenser's gothic Faerie seacoast that Florimell becomes allegorized as fear itself.

As Florimell flees the witch's hyena-monster that "feeds on womens flesh" (3.7.22), the poet depicts her escape route topographically: she is "compeld to chaunge/The land for sea, at randon there to raunge" (3.8.20). Though wandering "at randon" is the romance trajectory *par excellence*, Florimell's wandering impels her specifically to the seacoast. When Spenser narrates that "now she gan approach to the sea shore" (3.7.25), he might just as well have alerted readers that Florimell "now gan approach" the sado-comic narrative impulses he inherited from Ebuda. The poet compares her to Ovid's Daphne fleeing Apollo "on th'*Aegean* strond" (3.7.26). But if Daphne is saved by Peneus, Florimell must undertake a lonely struggle for survival on the Faerie "strond," immediately established as a terror-coast for her, as it is where her horse is disemboweled by the witch's hyena-monster. The exoticism of Daphne's "*Aegean* strond" cedes place to Florimell's arrival at the gothic "roring shore" (3.7.27), where roving hyenas devour defenseless horses – all the more distant from the mythic shores of an Ovidian Mediterranean as the site of wondrous metamorphoses.

Florimell's coastal terror intensifies when she seeks refuge in a fishing boat, where a lecherous fisherman attempts to rape her (3.8.21–2). (Here Spenser, on his Faerie strand, seems particularly intent on deploying an Ariostan mix of debased sexuality and terrorized beauty.) His response to her pleas to return to shore is to throw her down, "ne car'd to spill/Her garments gay with scales of fish that all did fill" (3.8.26). Spenser's image of Florimell smeared with slimy fish scales borders on the pornographic (3.8.29). At the very least, these displaced fish scales are absurdly distant from any Sannazaran celebration of marine bounty, such as Lycon's delicate "spiny urchins."

The sea-god Proteus saves Florimell from the fisherman, only to imprison her in his coastal dungeon when she spurns his own attempts to seduce her. Thus, Florimell is not rescued, but rather "chaung'd from one to other feare" (3.8.33), i.e. from peril in the coastal fishing waters to even greater peril amidst Proteus's coastal "roaring billowes," raging as if "they the cliffe in peeces would haue cleft" (4.11.3–4). Prior to his rescue of Florimell, Proteus "abroad did roue,/Along the fomy waues driuing his finny droue" (3.8.29). Here, the sea-god is the Virgilian Proteus of the fourth *Georgic*, surrounded by his gamboling sea-companions. But as Florimell's would-be seducer, Spenser's Proteus exits the idyllic world of the marine eclogue and enters Ariosto's realm of coastal terror. This Proteus is both an eminently poetic, Sannazaran presider over "finny droues" – described by Spenser as the "Shepherd of the seas of yore" (3.8.30) – and a terrifying Ariostan custodian of a sadistic coastline. Put another way, Proteus straddles both the Neo-Latin of the Sannazaran marine eclogue and the vernacular of Ariosto's epic romance.

I now turn to the question of Ebuda's location and how it provides clues to the location of Spenser's Faerie strand. Throughout his epic romance, Ariosto does not hesitate to be geographically explicit, and his eighth canto is no exception. At the time Angelica's demon-driven horse bolts into the ocean, the poet informs us that she rides along a seacoast road in Gascony, in southwest France. Angelica's trajectory, then, is traceable not just from one seacoast to another, but also from an explicitly locatable *Continental* seacoast to a distant coast in an extreme north-westerly, west-of-Ireland Hebrides. It is as if the *Furioso*'s urbane westering of empire goes momentarily berserk – like Ruggiero's uncontrollable hippogriff. Ariosto's narrative momentarily speeds *too* far west, warped into the remote, improbable Hebrides, far removed from the more serious epic (and Continental) "matter" of Charlemagne. If Ariosto, as one of Sannazaro's most well-known admirers, did deploy the Mediterranean eclogue as a kind of shadow-genre for his Ebudan coast, then we can unpack the humor of his eighth canto thus: momentarily stranded in the Hebrides (virtually off the map of western Europe), the *translatio imperii* has, in effect, abandoned the Mediterranean – or, more particularly, the lovely "Euploea's shores" of Sannazaro's idyllic blue Mediterranean – and stranded itself on Irish/Scottish coastlines, implicitly depicted as the harsher, grayer, utterly distant "other" of Continental coastlines. The eighth canto sweeps its readers away from Sannazaro's Mediterranean culturo-geographic axis to a confrontation with the harsh, rugged outpost-coastlines of the British isles.

In his Marinell–Florimell sub-plot, as we have seen, Spenser preserves Ariosto's sado-comedic terror coast virtually intact. But unlike Ariosto, he offers no precise location for his Faerie seacoast – and in this refusal we can begin to tease out his coastal unconscious as the aftermath of genres falling into neglect. Spenser reactivates the sado-comic potential of Ariosto's Ebudan coast, but forecloses on Ariosto's high regard for the Sannazaran marine eclogue and his subsequent ironic gesture to expose the Hebrides as the *not*-Mediterranean. Though the Mediterranean (at the very least, France's Gascony coast) is the implicit shadow-coast of Ariosto's Ebuda, the coastal unconscious of Spenser's Faerie coast, as the epic inheritor of Ebuda, has inadvertently located the "strond" in the harsh Hebrides that was barely perceptible in the "top left corner" of the maps of the Estensi. Hence, the battered, battering Faerie seacoast becomes Spenser's (repressed) *not*-Mediterranean as he fails to discern the gradual process by which certain hostile, remote coasts become coded, within literary history, as British/Scottish/Irish coastlines. Angelica is eventually freed from Ebuda; but, in Irigarayan terms, the Faerie strand becomes the permanent home of the child-god Marinell as *a foreigner in all parts*, exiled on *the least prosperous of islands*.

FROM CHAUCER TO SPENSER: BRITAYNE, BRITEYNE, OR BRITAINE?

Britomart's coastal lament on the Faerie strand is well-known to readers of *The Faerie Queene*. Eagerly searching for Arthegall, she is also tormented by adolescent sexual anxieties, "ghastly feares" and "anguish rife" (3.2.31–2) that – hardly coincidentally – impel her to the Faerie seacoast and its gothic turbulence: "Why do thy cruell billowes beat so strong,/And thy moyst mountains each others throng,/Threatning to swallow vp my fearfull life?" (3.4.7). Britomart's insistence that the "cruell billowes" pose a physical threat traces the psychic contours of *her* coastal unconscious – almost as if she desires being "swallow[ed] vp" by the hydraulic energy of waves and rock. Asking if her heart must "be wrackt/On the rough rocks … ," her fear of being wrecked, raked, racked, "wrackt" on the Faerie terror-coast is both a source of dread and a consummation devoutly to be wished (3.4.9).[11]

A literary history of a coastal unconscious should read this episode against the grain of Spenser's beloved Chaucer – specifically the prominence of the coastal topography of "The Franklin's Tale" as both an intriguing example of the gendering of gothic terror-coasts, and as yet another indispensable clue to the location of the Faerie coast. Because it predates Sannazaro (because there is no generic inmixing with the Neo-Latin marine eclogue), "The Franklin's Tale" is perhaps the most unmediated source for an ugly coastline in all of the medieval vernacular English literature that Spenser would have read. In this tale, Dorigen, longing for Arveragus's safe return from England, obsesses over the craggy rocks of the Brittany coast: daily, she roams the cliffs, "cast[ing] hir eyen downward fro the brynke," staring at "the grisly rokkes blake" at whose sight "[f]or verray feere so wolde hir herte quake" (859–60).[12] At once revolted and compelled by the rocks as a "foul confusion/Of werke" (869–70), Dorigen despairs: "Se ye nat, Lord, how mankynde it destroyeth?/An hundred thousand bodyes of mankynde/Han rokkes slayn."

If the marine eclogue, as we have seen, offers such charms as weary shepherds catching seductive glimpses of the sea from their promontories, Chaucer's "gothic" Brittany coast, threatening to smash bodies into oblivion, presents a heroine not so much lamenting for her absent husband as obsessing about the coastal rocks from a precarious "brynke." Chaucer's "grisly rokkes blake" jutting angrily into the sea are conspicuous in their threatening ugliness. The rocks of the Brittany coast – not simply nature's passive backdrop for coastal love-laments – *are* the psychic landscape of Dorigen's unconscious: the coastal rocks *themselves* become her daily obsession. No Mediterranean *pietàs* here – only the threatening presence of the "grisly rokkes blake" that render Dorigen not so much melancholic as trapped in a state of fear and dread. Though the jagged rocks make her "herte quake" and though she yearns for their disappearance, Dorigen, anticipating Britomart at the Faerie strand, remains enthralled by the sheer destructiveness of their "foul confusion," their menacing ability to rip apart "an hundred thousand bodyes."[13]

In "The Franklin's Tale," situated as it is on the harsh Brittany coast, as well as on the hippogriff's aerial route to Ariosto's dislocated Hebrides, we are at a distant remove from the picturesque coasts of the Mediterranean eclogue. The poet pointedly tells us that Arveragus and Dorigen reside in "Armorik, that called is Britayne" (729), and that Arveragus eventually sails away to "Engelond, that cleped was eek Briteyne" (810). The marine expanse between "Britayne" and "Briteyne" traces the borders of the English Channel to the north and the Bay of Biscay to the south, an area notorious for its rugged coastline. But "The Franklin's Tale" sets up a geographically obscure interchangeability between "Britayne/Briteyne." One way of further tracing the literary historical relationship between Chaucer and Spenser is to ponder the extent to which the rocky coast of "The Franklin's Tale" has made its way into Books 3 and 4 of *The Faerie Queene*. Any attempt to locate Spenser's otherwise unmappable Faerie seacoast could do worse than to pass through the "looking glass" of the orthographic slippages of Chaucer's "Britayne/Briteyne." To move from "The Franklin's Tale" (as well as from Ariosto's Ebudan coast) to the middle books of *The Faerie Queene* is to discover Spenser's coastal unconscious, where the westering of empire takes us further away from Mediterranean coastlines and closer to "Britayne/Briteyne" – and further westward to Ariosto's even more provincial Hebrides.

We are reminded that Britomart begins her search for Arthegall by leaving "Britaine." It is at the (*not*-"Britaine") seacoast where Britomart, like Dorigen, encounters a mirror of her own unconscious. Or is it at the "Britayne/Briteyne" seacoast? It is tempting to imagine that even as Britomart was leaving "Britaine" for the coast, she might have crossed paths with Chaucer's Arveragus, leaving "Britayne" to seek adventure in "Briteyne." It is also tempting to imagine that had

Ariosto's Ruggiero gazed down on the Brittany coastline at precisely the right moment, he might have spotted Dorigen obsessing over the "grisly rokkes blake." Or perhaps he happened near Dorigen when, having rescued Angelica from Ebuda, he carries her away on his hippogriff back to the jagged Brittany coastline where he attempts to rape her. Rather than tediously sorting out the geographical distinctions among "Britayne/Briteyne/Britaine," I suggest that the Brittany coastline is further evidence that the result of one "strand" in literary history has been to leave the coastlines of "Britayne/Briteyne/(not)Britaine" stranded as provincial, sado-comic terror coasts.

Though England was becoming an increasingly powerful marine presence within an expanding late sixteenth-century imperialism, what can nonetheless be deduced from Spenser's coastal unconscious is his repressed concern that continental literary history will have judged *The Faerie Queene* itself to have been written on an Irigarayan *least prosperous of islands*. At the moment Cymoent hears of her son's wounding, she plays "[a]mongst her watry sisters by a pond." Prior to summoning sea-chariots to take her to her son, Spenser narrates that, in her grief, "[s]he threw her selfe downe on the Continent" (3.4.30). Because the sea-nymph Cymoent is never far from the shoreline, I think it safe to imagine that this Continental "pond" is near Mediterranean coastlines. It is as if her sea-chariot, bearing her from continental "pond" to Faerie "strond," transports her from the "buxome" plenitude of Neo-Latin Mediterranean beauty-coasts to the vernacular terror-"margent" of Faerie's "craggy clifts." Cymoent is at home at or near continental coasts, but her disaligned coastal child-god Marinell must dwell on *the least prosperous of islands*. Searching for Florimell, Marinell is an Irigarayan *foreigner in all parts*, wandering "[l]ost ... he wist not where." But with the help of an Irigarayan coastal unconscious, *we* now know where, in all likelihood he is, i.e. stranded in the provincial terror-coasts of "Britayne/Briteyne/Britain."

Notes

1 All references to *The Faerie Queene* are from Hamilton 1977. For a recent positive assessment of Cymoent's maternal bond with Marinell, see Krier 2001: 230–1.

2 Here, Irigaray participates in a powerful trend in French intellectual thought in the past forty years or so to experiment with the many resonances of specular "otherness," i.e. the tropes of *l'altérité, déracinement, l'étrangeté*. One benefits from reading her chapter in conjunction with, among others, Jabès 1963, and Kristeva 1988.

3 This is not to ignore what readers generally view as the most memorable description of Marinell's strand as "bestrowed all with rich aray/Of pearles and pretious stones of great assay" (3.4.18). The "pretious stones" – cast ashore by Nereus as the lost treasures of shipwrecks – do not so much beautify the coast as render it a junkyard for the plundered "spoyle of all the world" (3.4.23).

4 Though I deploy the term "gothic" differently, I should mention Margreta de Grazia's 6 July 2001 keynote address to the Spenser Cambridge Conference, "Spenser's Antic Disposition," which ponders the nature of the Gothic in Spenser's verse (i.e. the "studied barbarity" of *The Shepheardes Calender*).

5 My coastal focus does not extend to shipwreck narratives where stranded victims either die or await rescue, thus excluding works such as Shakespeare's *The Tempest* and

The Winter's Tale, or Milton's "Lycidas." My concern is with works that foreground the coast as an original, not accidental, dwelling.

6 Of possible relevance here is the poet's description of the Britain of "antique times" as a desolate "saluage wildernesse,/vnpeopled, vnmanurd, vnprou'd, vnpraysd" (2.10.5).

7 In this regard, Marinell can be contrasted to Arthegall who, though armored, "in swimming skilful was" (5.2.16).

8 For more on the *Piscatoriae* as "reviv[ing] the Latin language at the root of ancient pastoral," see William J. Kennedy, *Jacopo Sannazaro and the Uses of Pastoral*, Hanover and London: University Press of New England, 1983: 149.

9 The English verse translations are by W. Leonard Grant in his *Neo-Latin Literature and the Pastoral*, Chapel Hill: University of North Carolina Press, 1965.

10 All references to the *Orlando Furioso* are taken from Caretti 1954. The English translations are from Reynolds 1977.

11 Susanne Lindgren Wofford (1987), reading Britomart's lament on the Faerie strand as the boundary between narrative and allegory, argues that here Britomart becomes aware that "inner and outer are hard to distinguish in her world" (53).

12 All references to "The Franklin's Tale" are from Robinson 1957.

13 Ellen Martin (1992) traces an intriguing psychoanalytic relationship between the "grisly rokkes blake" and Dorigen's marital anxiety. She argues that Dorigen, fearing the sexual and emotional commitments of marriage to Arveragus, displaces her marital anxiety onto the rocky coast of Brittany (thus a major motive for her impossible appeal to her would-be suitor Aurelius to make the rocks disappear). Dorigen's "verray feere" – the fear that her husband, in danger of being dashed against the rocks, will not return – is also a "feere" that he *will* return and (metaphorically) dash her to bits.

7 "That glorious slit"

Irigaray and the medieval devotion to Christ's side wound

Amy Hollywood

Readers of Luce Irigaray agree that one of her philosophical projects is to valorize the female sex in the service of a feminine imaginary and symbolic.[1] Just as the image of the penis serves as the basis for male claims to plenitude and mastery within a phallic imaginary and symbolic, so Irigaray argues that the vulva and vagina might become the partial basis for an imaginary register supportive of women's subjectivity (and one not dependent on problematic claims to wholeness).[2] What is less often recognized is that one of Irigaray's first attempts to valorize the female sex occurs in a reading of Christ's side wound as vaginal.[3] Although she will later contest her earlier reading of Christ and his woundedness, in *Speculum of the Other Woman* Irigaray finds within premodern Christian mystical and devotional traditions the beginnings of a feminine imaginary.[4]

Encountering Christ, the miming voice of *Speculum*'s "*La Mystérique*" asks: "Could it be true that not every wound need remain secret, that not every laceration was shameful? Could a sore be *holy*? Ecstasy is there in that glorious slit where she curls up in her nest, where she rests as if she had found her home — and He is also in her. She bathes in a blood that flows over her, hot and purifying."[5] As I will show, Irigaray here mimes central passages from Angela of Foligno's (c.1248–1309) *Memorial*, which itself draws on a long tradition of devotion to Christ's side wound. Entry into Christ's wound, in that tradition as in Irigaray's text, marks the shattering of vision into affect, an experience of wounding laceration that is simultaneously the site of an ineffable ecstatic jouissance.

Irigaray, in the voice of the mystic, goes on to explain the cause of her pleasure:

> if in the sight of the nails and the spear piercing the body of the Son I drink in a joy concerning which it is impossible for me to speak a single word, let no one conclude too hastily that I take pleasure in his sufferings. But that the Word thus and to this extent was made flesh, this could only be so that I might become God in my finally recognized jouissance.
>
> (Irigaray 1985g: 200, translation modified)

Yet as Irigaray also notes, the mystic *does* speak, a speech and a writing enabled by her divinization. Irigaray turns to Christian devotional and mystical traditions because they are the sites "within a still theological onto-logical perspective" where:

"she" speaks – and in some cases he, if he follows "her" lead – speaks about the dazzling glare which comes from the source of light that has been logically repressed, about "subject" and "Other" flowing out into an embrace of fire that mingles one term into another, about contempt for form as such, about mistrust for understanding as an obstacle along the path of jouissance and mistrust for the dry desolation of reason. Also about a "burning glass" ["*miroir ardent*"].

(Irigaray 1985g: 191)

Despite Irigaray's insistence throughout *Speculum* that every theory of the subject has "always already been appropriated by the 'masculine'" (Irigaray 1985g: 133), the Christian mystical tradition offers a glimpse of another possibility, one that will become crucial to Irigaray's later projects.

Yet even as Irigaray's work after *Speculum* returns to and augments the claim that through a rigorous process of miming and subversion new possibilities for genuinely other forms of subjectivity are possible, she rejects *Speculum*'s reading of Christ's wound as the site of a feminine imaginary and the potential base for a feminine symbolic. As I will show, in rejecting the devotional–mystical interpretation of Christ's wound as vaginal, Irigaray explicitly rejects an understanding of the female sex as wound-like. Also salient is Irigaray's turn from an understanding of human (sexual) relations in terms of penetration and penetrability to what Judith Butler refers to as a "rigorously anti-penetrative eros of surfaces" (Butler 1993: 45). Before questioning this turn in Irigaray's thought and its potentially essentializing and heterosexist connotations, however, I need first to provide an account of the interlocking scriptural, devotional, and mystical texts and images embedded within *Speculum*'s highly evocative appeal to Christ's side wound.

***

Irigaray's description of a glorious slit into which the mystic enters, there to be covered in "hot and purifying" blood, sounds startling – even grotesque – to modern ears. So too might the words of the Umbrian mystic, Angela of Foligno, whom Irigaray mimes.[6] Two passages in her *Memorial*, dictated by Angela to a Franciscan friar, make reference to Christ's side wound.[7] In describing the stages toward union with God, Angela writes:

In the fourteenth step, while I was standing in prayer, Christ on the cross appeared … to me. … He then called me to place my mouth to the wound on his side. It seemed to me that I saw and drank the blood, which was freshly flowing from his side. His intention was to make me understand that by this blood he would cleanse me.

(Angela of Foligno 1993: 128)[8]

As in Irigaray's text, the blood flowing from Christ's side is purifying. Within the theological context of the Christian Middle Ages, Christ's blood renders humans clean from sin, for his suffering and death on the cross atone for human sinfulness. Angela's words echo a host of devotional texts and images that show a human being drinking from Christ's side wound in a moment of exculpation (see Figure 7.1 overleaf). Angela is particularly adamant about the extent of her own iniquity and the necessity of Christ's saving action – and cleansing blood – to render her worthy of standing before and with him.

Later in the *Memorial*, Angela takes the image of the side wound to more dramatic heights, writing that "at times it seems to my soul that it enters into Christ's side, and this is a source of great joy and delight" (Angela of Foligno 1993: 176).[9] Like a host of medieval devotional texts to be discussed further below, for Angela entry into Christ's side wound serves as an image of her unification with Christ.[10] Now no longer simply cleansed, purified, and saved by Christ's blood, Angela here understands herself as united with him. A graphically physical image becomes the means of rendering vivid this moment of spiritual identification, one that will lead Angela to assert her own share in Christ's salvific role. Irigaray's words in *Speculum* bring together these two sets of images (and the many others like them in medieval devotional and mystical texts) in an even more intensely physical, eroticized, and explicitly homosexuated account of the relationship between the mystic and Christ.

In describing herself as drinking the blood flowing from Christ's side and becoming unified with him through entry into that wound, Angela encapsulates at least two of the primary themes found in the late medieval devotion to Christ's wounds. As Douglas Gray shows, within this devotional tradition, Christ's wounds are "(i) a place of refuge, (ii) openings from which the faithful can drink, and (iii) openings which reveal the way to the Sacred Heart of Christ (*arcanum cordis*)" (Gray 1963: 86). (This final meaning only attains its official form in the modern era, yet in that Angela understands Christ's side wound not only as a place of refuge, but also of union with Christ, her text anticipates the complex theology of the Sacred Heart [see Jonas 2000].) The meanings are not arbitrary but converge around Christ's side wound through a series of metaphorical and metonymic links between what appear to be unrelated Biblical texts.

Latin narrative accounts of Christ's suffering and death play a key role in the development of devotion to Christ's wounds. A host of recent scholars demonstrates the centrality of meditative practice to medieval Christian religious life, first in the monastic setting and, increasingly, in the latter Middle Ages among the mendicant orders and the laity (see Despres 1989; Bestul 1996; Carruthers 1998; Hamburger 1990; Hamburger 1997; Hamburger 1998; and Fulton 2002). Narrative accounts of Christ's life and death – first in Latin and later in the vernaculars – serve as tools for meditation and the imaginative recreation of events key to salvation history. These texts were designed to evoke heightened emotional responses in the reader (or perhaps better practitioner), who is called on by the often hortatory authorial voice to participate actively in the events as a spectator or active participant in them. (The line between the two is often difficult to discern. Mary is the model of compassionate suffering with Christ on whom the reader is often called to model him or herself. Yet ultimately Mary's suffering with

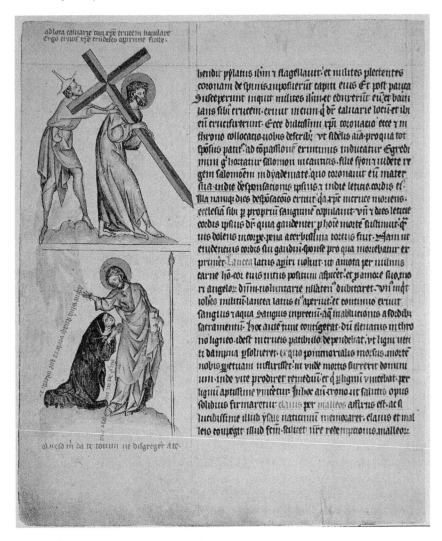

Figure 7.1 Passional of Abbess Kunigunde, Prague, National and University Library, MS
XIV A 17, fol. 7V.

Christ is so great as to render her Christ-like. Hence through a series of intense identifications, the reader as compassionate spectator becomes a participant in Christ's saving actions [Fulton 2002].) Meditation, as Mary Carruthers brilliantly shows with regard to medieval monastic culture, is an art of memory and imagination. Meditative practice is a type of memory work that generates emotion, which in turn facilitates the act of memorialization (Carruthers 1998). By calling forth the events of Christ's death with compassion and identification, the person meditating both commemorates and participates in the redemptive power of that moment.

In his study of the Latin Passion narratives, Thomas Bestul demonstrates that narrative rewritings of the Passion make use of a variety of traditional texts. First, of course, are the gospels themselves. The New Testament texts are sparse in detail, yet, as Bestul explains, they "contain in rudimentary form what proves to be a very productive method for embellishing the Passion story in a way that ... carried the highest theological sanction" (Bestul 1996: 27). Each of the gospel narratives attempts to demonstrate that Jesus' suffering was a fulfillment of the messianic prophecies of the Hebrew Bible. Hence the gospel writers apply verses from these prophecies to Jesus in his suffering and death. Subsequent exegetes take this as:

> a justification for applying almost any verse of the Hebrew Bible to the events of Christ's life, especially those of the Passion. In this way, the Hebrew Bible offered what was taken to be a divinely authorized way of filling out the details of Christ's life where the gospels were silent.
>
> (Bestul 1996: 27)

Other key sources for Latin Passion narratives are 1) the liturgy, particularly the conjunction of Biblical texts used to commemorate Christ's Passion; 2) the apocryphal gospels;[11] 3) the tradition of biblical exegesis that precedes the development of the specifically Passion-centered narratives; and 4) two key high medieval texts, Peter Comestor's (d. 1179) *Historia scholastica* and Jacobus de Voragine's (d. 1298) *Legenda aurea* (Bestul 1996: 26–33). (The former is an encyclopedic historical narrative, including Christ's life and death. The latter is a compendium of hagiographical texts, also including an account of Christ's Passion.) Writers of high and late medieval Passion narratives make use of these various sources in order imaginatively to evoke the intensity of Christ's suffering.

The liturgy for Holy Week is particularly important for the development of extended narratives of Christ's Passion. The conjunction of texts and images heard and seen within the yearly ritual plays a decisive role in high and late medieval devotional practices and images. For example, following the New Testament tradition of citing the Hebrew prophets in conjunction with the figure of Christ, passages from Isaiah play a key role in the Holy Week liturgy. As befits the tenor of Isaiah's prophetic vision, these passages emphasize Christ's role as redeemer of the just and scourge of the evil.

Figure 7.2 Crucifixion, Cologne, Schnütgen Museum Inv. Nr. M340.

Who is this that cometh from Edom, with dyed garments from Bosra, this beautiful one in his robe, walking in the greatness of his strength? I, that speak justice, and am a defender to save. Why then is thy apparel red, and thy garments like theirs that tread in the winepress? I have trodden the winepress alone, and of the Gentiles there is not a man with me: I have trampled on them in my indignation, and have trodden them down in my wrath, and their blood is sprinkled upon my garments, and I have stained all my apparel.[12]

The liturgical use of Isaiah typologically identifies the man with garments dyed red from the blood of the Gentiles with Christ, bloody with the wounds of the Passion.[13] Images of Christ literally drenched in blood may reflect this liturgical tradition; Christ's blood becomes a garment in which he is fully covered, like Isaiah's man from Edom (see Figure 7.2).[14]

Similarly, Christian exegetes often interpret the Hebrew Bible in terms of Christ's life and death. Probably the single most important source for the cluster of images conjoined in Latin Passion narratives and then in Angela's meditation on Christ's side wound is a Passion-centered reading of Song of Songs 2:14, "My dove in the clefts of the rock, in the crannies of the wall, show me your face, let your voice sound in my ears."[15] Bernard of Clairvaux (d. 1153), in his sixty-first sermon on the Song of Songs, follows Gregory the Great (d. 604) in interpreting the clefts of the rock as Christ's wounds (Bernard of Clairvaux 1979: 142; and Bernard of Clairvaux 1957–77: Vol. 2, Sermon 61, 149).[16] The clefts in the rock are then read by Bernard as a place of refuge for the soul; "And really where is there safe rest for the weak except in the Savior's wounds? There the security of my dwelling depends on the greatness of his saving power" (Bernard of Clairvaux 1979: 142–3).[17] Moreover, from the wounds, Bernard writes, "I can suck honey from the rock and oil from the flinty stone – I can taste and see that the Lord is good" (Bernard of Clairvaux 1979: 143).[18] Finally, through the clefts in Christ's body "the secret of his heart is laid open ... that mighty mystery of loving is laid open, laid open too the tender mercies of our God, in which the morning sun from on high has risen upon us. Surely his heart is laid open through his wounds!" (Bernard of Clairvaux 1979: 145).[19] In Bernard, then, we see all three of the aspects of the wound image laid out by Gray.

Bernard refers to the wound gored in Christ's side by a lance (John 19:34) in close proximity to the claim that one can drink from Christ's wound; similarly, revelation of the secrets of Christ's heart is premised on "the iron" that "pierced his soul" (Psalms 104:18, here presumably read typologically with reference to the spear with which Christ's side is pierced in John 19:34). Yet Bernard attends equally throughout the sermon to the clefts created by the nails in Christ's feet and hands. The singular focus on Christ's side wound appears in the work of Bernard's fellow Cistercian, Aelred of Rievaulx (d. 1167), in a text probably written shortly after Bernard's death.

The *Rule of Life for a Recluse*, written for Aelred's sister, ends with meditations on Christ's life and death. One highly compressed passage brings together many of the themes found in Bernard's Sermon 61 – and later to be found throughout the more fully developed narrative accounts of Christ's Passion. In the midst of a visually and viscerally vibrant description of Christ's suffering and death, Aelred elaborates on the Gospel of John's account of Christ's side, pierced by a Roman soldier.

> Then one of the soldiers opened his side with a lance and there came forth blood and water. Hasten, linger not, eat the honeycomb with your honey, drink your wine with your milk. The blood is changed into wine to gladden you, the water into milk to nourish you. From the rock streams have flowed for you, wounds have been made in his limbs, holes in the wall of his body, in which, like a dove, you may hide while you kiss them one by one. Your lips, stained with his blood, will become like a scarlet ribbon and your word sweet.
>
> (Aelred of Rievaulx 1971a: 90–91)[20]

Here it is explicitly the side wound that is understood as the cleft in which the dove of the Song of Songs finds refuge. From hence too flows the blood and water – reminiscent of the blood and water into which wine is transubstantiated in the eucharistic sacrament – that will purify and save those who imbibe it.[21]

The Latin Passion narratives often exhort the one meditating on Christ's passion to drink from the blood pouring from Christ's side wound and to enter into that wound. The theme continues to play a crucial role in the Franciscan tradition of Passion narratives, both in Latin and the vernacular (see Fleming 1977; and Despres 1989). In the *Tree of Life*, Bonaventure (d. 1274) follows Bernard and Aelred in comparing the hole in Christ's side to the dove's refuge in the Song of Songs and the reader or listener is enjoined to "draw waters out of the Savior's fountains" (Bonaventure 1960: 128).[22] (Here Bonaventure follows Isaiah 12: 3, "haurietis aquas in gaudio de fontibus salvatoris.") Bonaventure's *The Mystical Vine* calls for even more vivid representations of Christ's suffering flesh. Central to these representations are Christ's wounds and blood. The text calls on the readers or listeners to contemplate Christ's wounds and to penetrate them, coming finally to rest in Christ's heart (see Bestul 1996: 47–8).[23]

Bonaventure's devotional works and others falsely attributed to him were widely disseminated throughout Europe in the later Middle Ages. Even more popular was a book of meditations attributed to the Franciscan James of Milan and known in its first English translation, prepared by the Augustinian canon and mystic, Walter Hilton (d. 1396), as *The Goad of Love*. *The Goad of Love*'s central image for meditative union is the soul's immersion in Christ's wounds (Bestul 1996: 56; and Lewis 1996: 214).[24] No longer is the side wound simply a place of refuge for sinners – although it always remains that – but entry into the wound also signifies the union between the soul and Christ. Similar language is then found throughout late medieval devotional literature. In Angela we see a devout woman enacting that to which the devotional texts enjoin her.[25]

The correlation between Christ's side wound and the vagina suggested by Irigaray becomes most apparent in devotional images produced in the later Middle Ages. Clearly related to the tradition of meditation on Christ's Passion, visual representations of Christ's side wound are startling, not only in their vulvic/vaginal resonances, but also in their iconographic starkness and intensity. Images of the side wound are generally life size (or claimed to be so).[26] David S. Areford argues compellingly, in fact, that the side wound stands in for Christ's body, a form of visual synecdoche in which the wound represents the Passion in its entirety (Areford 1998: 220).[27] (The wound most often appears surrounded by disproportionately smaller representations of the instruments of Christ's passion – the cross, the whip, the lance, the nails, and other implements by means of which his suffering was accomplished. Hence the synecdoche depends, in part, on a related set of associations between the instruments of the passion and the wounds engendered by them. [On the association of the instruments of torture with the tortured body and its pain, see Scarry 1985: 13–19].)

Two of the earliest images of Christ's side wound are found in a famous early fourteenth-century Bohemian devotional collection made by Benes, a canon, for Kunigunde, abbess of St George's Benedictine nunnery in Prague castle. In one of these images, Christ appears as the Man of Sorrows surrounded by the instruments of his torture (the *Arma Christi*), including a life-sized wound (Lewis 1996: 204–6). Karma Lochrie reproduces a similar image that dates from the late fourteenth-century (Figure 7.3). Here again Christ appears as the Man of Sorrows; to the left is his side wound, enlarged to life-size (just above two inches) (Lochrie 1997: 190–1).

Related images are found in a miscellany now in Brussels. The manuscript was compiled in 1320 by nuns from the Cistercian convent of Vrouwenpark, under the supervision of the Cistercian monk, John of St Trond, who was responsible for their spiritual care. Most of the manuscript consists of the lives of holy women associated with the Cistercian order (Hamburger 1998: 305). Hence the miscellany is a devotional work, centered on the lives of holy women dedicated to the imitation of Christ. Included in the miscellany are drawings both of the *Arma Christi* and of Christ's side wound surrounded by the *Arma Christi* (Hamburger 1998: 305–6; and Lewis 1996: 206).

The devotion to Christ's side wound appears not only in texts produced for nuns, but also for the laity. The earliest images appear in manuscripts produced in France, also in the 1320s (Lewis 1996: 206–7). Among the most arresting is an image in the mid-fourteenth-century Psalter and Hours of Bonne of Luxembourg, a wealthy lay woman, later to become the mother of Charles V (Lewis 1996: 206; and Lochrie 1997: 190). Once again, the wound appears life-size, surrounded by disproportionately smaller representations of the *Arma Christi*.

Instructed in religious literature to taste, touch, suck, kiss, and enter into Christ's side wound, those who saw and held these images seem to have made them the object of intense affective response, both imaginatively and physically (Lochrie 1997: 190). Areford studies a woodcut from the late fifteenth century, now in the National Gallery of Art in Washington, DC, in which what Areford describes as a "mandorla-shaped wound" stands in for Christ's body (see Figure 7.4). To the left of the wound appears an inscription, clarifying one way in which such images were treated: "This is the length and width of Christ's wound which was pierced

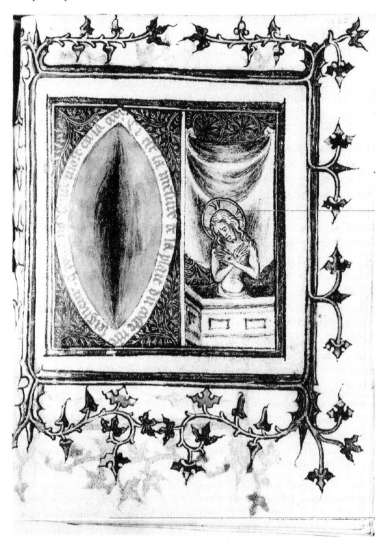

Figure 7.3 Man of Sorrows and Wound (c.1375), New York, The Pierpont Morgan Library, New York, M. 90, fol. 130.

Figure 7.4 Psalter of Bonne Luxembourgh, New York, Cloisters Museum, MS 69.86, fol. 331r.

Figure 7.5 The Wounds of Christ with the Symbols of the Passion, woodcut (c.1490), Washington, DC, National Gallery of Art.

in his side on the Cross. Whoever kisses this wound with remorse and sorrow, also with devotion, will have as often as he does this, seven years indulgence from Pope Innocent" (Areford 1998: 223).[28] Some manuscripts represent the wound solely with a slit in the parchment, one now so often touched, handled, and kissed as to render the manuscript itself fragile, worn, and opaque. These images and physical remnants suggest a homoerotic relationship between the female reader and a feminized representation of Christ's wound (Lochrie 1997:190–1). (Although not all readers and devotees would have been women, raising the issue of what this form of devotion might have meant to men [see Lochrie 1997: 181–6; and Lewis 1996: 204].)

Karma Lochrie, who reads the images of Christ's wounds as potentially homoerotic, situates her interpretation in relationship to Caroline Walker Bynum's groundbreaking work on medieval women's spirituality. As Lochrie shows, Bynum both argues against making too marked a distinction between sexuality and affectivity within mystical texts and devotional images[29] and also insists, particularly in *Holy Feast and Holy Fast: On the Religious Significance of Food to Medieval Women* (1987) and *Fragmentation and Redemption: Essays on Gender and the Human Body in Medieval Religion* (1991), that medieval attitudes toward the body have "less to do with sexuality than with fertility and decay" (Bynum 1991: 182; cited by Lochrie 1997: 183). As Lochrie rightly notes, Bynum is motivated by what she views as an overemphasis on sex and sexuality in the reading of medieval women's writings and writings about them and a concomitant overvaluation (or alternatively denigration) of sexuality that ignores other salient aspects of bodily experience (see Bynum 1995). Bynum thereby brilliantly expands our recognition of the meanings ascribed to corporeality in late medieval texts, images, and practices. At the same time, she suggests that these other aspects of bodily existence – food, drink, fertility, disease, decay, and death – play a larger role in medieval mystical texts than does sexuality (see Bynum 1995).

Yet as Lochrie and Richard Rambuss convincingly show, Bynum "herself can be quick to delimit the erotic – and especially the homoerotic – potentialities of her own devotional polysemy of the medieval body" (Rambuss 1998: 48; and see also Lochrie 1997: 187–8). When Catherine of Siena (1327–80) writes of "putting on the nuptial garment," Bynum explains, "the phrase means suffering" and so is "extremely unerotic." As portrayed by her confessor and hagiographer, Raymond of Capua, Catherine, like Angela of Foligno, follows the injunctions of the meditative treatises I have described. Raymond says that Christ:

> put his right hand on [Catherine's] neck and drew her towards the wound on his side. "Drink, daughter, from my side," he said, "and by that draught your soul shall become enraptured with such delight that your very body, which for my sake you have denied, shall be inundated with its overflowing goodness." Drawn close in this way to the outlet of the Fountain of her Life, she fastened her lips upon that sacred wound, and still more eagerly the mouth of her soul, and there she slaked her thirst.
>
> (Cited by Bynum 1987: 172)

Having cited this and similar passages, Bynum argues that in Catherine's:

> repeated descriptions of climbing Christ's body from foot to side to mouth, the body is either a female body that nurses or a piece of flesh that one puts on oneself or sinks into ... Catherine understood union with Christ not as an erotic fusing with a male figure but as a taking in and taking on – a becoming – of Christ's flesh itself.
>
> (Bynum 1987: 178)

Bynum operates here with a number of contentious assumptions about sexuality and erotic desire – most crucially, that erotic desire can be clearly distinguished from suffering, the maternal, and identification. In addition, as Rambuss and Lochrie argue, Bynum implicitly denies that same-sex desire can be sexual.

Lochrie shows that the mystical texts Bynum discusses are full of a violent, painful, ecstatic eroticism – one that undermines the distinction between pain, suffering, decay, death, and sexuality Bynum is often at pains to make. As Lochrie shows, when Bynum discusses eroticism in *Holy Feast and Holy Fast* it is always "linked with specific images of fertility and decay." The result is that Bynum comes very close to saying "that eroticism and sex in the religious experience of medieval women were constructed in terms of violence, suffering, and decay" (Lochrie 1997: 183). Bynum thereby usefully deromanticizes the image of bridal or nuptial mysticism found in many accounts of medieval women's religiosity. Yet as the passage I cite above suggests, and as Lochrie herself argues, Bynum also insists that suffering is not erotic and so attempts to take sexuality out of the complex matrix in which she simultaneously embeds it.

Just as Bynum separates suffering from sex and eroticism, she similarly denies the possibility of same-sex desire. Following Rambuss's and Lochrie's arguments, we can see that for Bynum if Christ's body is feminized (and so becomes a point of identification for women), it cannot also be the locus of female sexual desire (or even of a desire for the divine *analogous* to sexual desire). Bynum's insistence on the feminization of Christ, one in which the side wound is interpreted as a breast and the blood from that wound as life-giving milk, serves two functions, both providing a locus for female identification with the divine and protecting the divine–human relationship from even metaphorical sexualization.

But given Bynum's own injunction that we recognize the fluidity between male and female, masculine and feminine, affective and erotic within medieval texts and images, why must we be forced to make a choice between reading the feminized Christ as maternal or erotic? As Lochrie cogently argues, "the mystical maternal body of Christ does not enact such repudiation of the sexual but 'opens a mesh of possibilities' for the queering of categories – of mystical devotion, the body of Christ, female desire, and the medieval construction of maternity" (Lochrie 1997: 188). Christ's wound, as we have seen, has a multiplicity of meanings within medieval texts and images, and at least some of them are explicitly erotic.

Bynum, in reading Christ's side wound as homologous to Mary's breast and hence Christ's blood as like breast milk in its nurturing and salvific nature, explicitly rejects a sexualized reading of the wound and its blood. Lochrie insists that the maternal does not exclude the sexual. Medieval medical discourses further underline the polysemy of the wound and its blood. Hence a much commented on treatise dealing with human reproduction and women's bodies, *Women's Secrets* (long falsely attributed to Albert the Great), argues that breast milk is created from surplus menses not released during childbirth (Lemay 1992: 71, 109, 126, 142; and see also Wood 1981). Not only are blood and breast milk tied together within medieval medical theory, then, but that blood is explicitly menstrual blood. (Although many medical and religious texts insist on the polluting quality of menstrual blood, suggesting that its transmutation to breast milk requires a process of purification [L'Hermite-Leclercq 1999].) The association of blood with Christ's side wound ties the wound both to the vagina and to the breast, thereby enabling the threefold association of wound, vagina, and breast for which Lochrie – and Irigaray – argue.

Medieval devotional and mystical texts and images, when brought together with salient medical and philosophical literature from the period, suggest that Lochrie and Irigaray are amply justified in associating wounds, vaginas, and breasts. Woundedness and fecundity, maternity and sexuality, masculinity and femininity – all of these categories are interlocked in complex and fungible ways within medieval Christian discourse and practice. As Irigaray demonstrates in *Speculum*'s *"La mystérique"*, the Christian Middle Ages offer rich resources for thinking about sex, sexuality, and divinity in ways that radically destabilize traditional distinctions and hierarchies.

Yet Irigaray very quickly rejects *Speculum*'s valorization of Christ's wounds as the site of a new feminine imaginary.[30] *Speculum* was published in 1974. Already in 1975, an essay devoted to psychoanalyst Jacques Lacan's account of femininity demonstrates Irigaray's growing discomfort with any image or metaphor that associates the female sex with woundedness (Irigaray 1985b: 86–105). Irigaray's later revisionary reading of Christ's wounded body and self-sacrifice, most clearly articulated in *Marine Lover of Friedrich Nietzsche* (1980) (Irigaray 1991: 164–90), rests on this rejection of the valorization of woundedness. Irigaray argues – correctly, I think – that Lacan understands femininity as a figure for human nature in its lack, woundedness, and castration (in terms of the Christian theological tradition, one might argue, its sinfulness) (see Lacan 1998). According to Irigaray, Lacan's move ineluctably implicates women in a rhetoric of impotence that any new feminine imaginary must challenge. "The problem," as she puts it, "is that they [Lacan and Lacanian psychoanalysts] claim to make a law of this impotence itself, and continue to subject women to it" (Irigaray 1985a: 105).

The female sex can only be understood as a wound, Irigaray suggests, if it is read according to the logic of castration. Within psychoanalytic discourse the bleeding fissure is the site of a lack – the lack of a penis. Only within these terms does the association of sex with woundedness make sense. To read woman as emblematic of human nature in its woundedness, then, is to participate in a logic that insistently reads femininity in terms of masculinity – precisely the logic

Irigaray's work unremittingly challenges. Christianity, insofar as it substitutes the bleeding body of the son for that of the mother, participates both in the association of femininity with castration, impotence, and self-sacrifice *and* in the reduction of femininity to masculinity (in the figure of the feminized man on the cross) (Irigaray 1991: 164–90).

By rejecting the association of femininity with woundedness, however, Irigaray also forecloses the possibility of a female-to-female penetrative and interpenetrative eroticism. Judith Butler's critique of Irigaray's "eros of surfaces" closely parallels, then, Lochrie's critique of Bynum on medieval devotion to Christ's wounds. (There are crucial differences, of course. Most importantly, Irigaray attempts to reconfigure sexuality or eros in non-penetrative ways, whereas Bynum desexualizes penetration and penetrability, reading them in terms of eating, drinking, decay, and fertility rather than in terms of sexuality. The ramifications of the two moves for sexual identity and sexuality, however, are very similar.) Already in *Speculum*, Butler argues, Irigaray's reading of Plato posits masculinity and femininity in terms of penetration and penetrability. Although Butler misses the moment – "*La mystérique*" – in which Irigaray challenges the dominant philosophical tradition's account of sexual (in)difference, Butler is correct that throughout much of *Speculum* Irigaray is in danger of allowing that tradition to determine her own use of terms. (Butler suggests this may be an inevitable danger of Irigaray's mimetic procedure.)

As Butler argues, in Irigaray's reading of Plato, the masculine "he":

> is the impenetrable penetrator, and she, the invariably penetrated. And "he" would not be differentiated from her were it not for this prohibition on resemblance which establishes their positions as mutually exclusive and yet complementary. In fact, if she were to penetrate in return, or penetrate elsewhere, it is unclear whether she could remain a "she" and whether "he" could preserve his own differentially established identity. For the logic of non-contradiction that conditions the distribution of pronouns is one which establishes the "he" through this exclusive position as penetrator and the "she" through this exclusive position as penetrated. As a consequence, then, without this heterosexual *matrix*, as it were, it appears that the stability of these gendered positions would be called into question.
>
> (Butler 1993: 50–1)

In a telling reversal of Butler's formulation, the instability of gendered positions within medieval devotional and mystical images and practices works to destabilize precisely this heterosexual matrix. Only if it is taken as a given that penetration is masculine and penetrability feminine does the heterosexual matrix hold sway (just as it is the heterosexual matrix that renders these oppositions stable). Yet these presumptions – ones also operative within medieval medical and philosophical literature (see, for example, Elliott 1997; and Caciola 2000) – are continually undermined by the devotional texts and images Irigaray mimes in "*La mystérique*."

Both Bynum and Irigaray (at least after *Speculum*) miss the radicality of medieval devotional practices, which refuse any absolute identification between masculinity and penetration or between femininity and penetrability. The very mode of reading implied by medieval devotional texts and images, with their constantly interpenetrating biblical, extrabiblical, and liturgical citations, suggests the ubiquity of an erotics of penetration within medieval spiritual traditions. (Butler demonstrates that Irigaray's *Speculum* also participates in an erotics of interpenetrative reading, despite Irigaray's explicit claims to the contrary [Butler 1993: 45–6].) The fluidity of sexual difference may be, at least in part, an outcome of such reading practices.

The soul in Bernard of Clairvaux's *Sermons on the Song of Songs* is described as a female beloved sucking honey from the hard rock that is Christ, even as Christ, the male Lover, is laid open to penetration through his bodily wounds. In Aelred's *The Rule of Life for a Recluse*, Christ's body is an impenetrable rock and a body full of holes – and both at the same time. Honey, wine, milk, and blood (interchangeable substances within Aelred's imaginary) stream from Christ and penetrate the body of the beloved (as food and drink, although not only as food and drink), even as the beloved hides in Christ's wounds like a dove in the cleft of a rock. Although the image of Angela with her mouth pressed to Christ's side wound evokes female-to-female sexuality, it also displaces any simplistic sexual referentiality, for Christ's body is both masculine and penetrable, both rock and feminized.

Finally, medieval texts and images suggest that the analogy between the wound and the vulva/vagina operates not only to associate women with lack and castration, but also to associate men – preeminently, of course, one man – with fertility, nurturance, and healing. Christ's wounds save, heal, and solace. Their association with the breast and the vulva enables these multiple understandings. By rejecting a masculinist logic of penetration and penetrability, wholeness and lack, containment and seepage – a logic endemic to and unchallenged by the psychoanalytic tradition about and out of which Irigaray writes – Irigaray too quickly forecloses alternative imaginative possibilities available within the Christian Middle Ages.

Notes

1 This is not, of course, to posit a so-called essentialist reading of Irigaray, for Irigaray posits imaginary and symbolic configurations of the female sex as sites of potential philosophical and cultural meaning rather than valorizing the female sex in and of itself. For Irigaray's explicit critique of biological (and psychological or cultural) essentialism, see Irigaray 1991: 86.

2 Ewa Ziarek argues that Irigaray insists on "the discontinuous temporality of the body" and so "theorizes the interminable becoming of women's bodies" in ways that work against phallic claims to mastery and totality – and arguably also against the kinds of representative claims Irigaray appears to make in *Speculum* (although I believe that the two issues can be separated). Patricia Huntington also argues for a temporal dimension to Irigaray's conception of the imaginary, the symbolic, and their relationship. At the same time, Huntington maintains that Irigaray's conception of "woman" is not as empty as some of her commentators claim. (Drucilla Cornell, to whom Huntington refers, more recently discusses the problematic nature of Irigaray's insistence on the

primacy of sexual difference.) Although I agree with Ziarek's reading of Irigaray, Irigaray's continued dependence on sexual difference as the privileged site of futural difference (however impossible that future difference may be) works to efface other conceptions of difference in problematic ways. See Ziarek 1998: 64; Huntington 1998: 134–40, 246–6; Cornell 1991: 77–8, 166–72; and Butler and Cornell 1998: 19–42. For a more recent reading of Irigaray's latter work that builds on Ziarek's insight, see Deutscher 2002.

3 Thomas Bestul notes Irigaray's eroticized and sexualized reading of Christ's side wound, without rendering explicit the latter's vulvic/vaginal quality. Karma Lochrie highlights the vulvic/vaginal quality of the wound without reference to Irigaray. I am deeply indebted to both studies in the work presented here. See Bestul 1996: 231 n. 71; and Lochrie 1997: pp. 180–200.

4 See especially Irigaray 1991: 164–90; Irigaray 1993a: 75–88; and Hollywood 2002: 203–6.

5 Already in 1949 Simone de Beauvoir makes a similar claim, although to very different ends. Foreshadowing arguments more recently (and it goes without saying, much more extensively) made by the historian of medieval spirituality, Caroline Walker Bynum, de Beauvoir suggests that Christ's suffering flesh is, as suffering, feminized. "In the humiliation of God she [the mystic] sees with wonder the dethronement of Man; inert, passive, covered with wounds, the Crucified is the reversed image of the white, blood-stained martyr exposed to wild beasts, to daggers, to males, with whom the little girl has so often identified herself; she is overwhelmed to see that Man, Man-God, has assumed her role. She it is who is hanging on the Tree, promised the splendor of the Resurrection" (de Beauvoir 1952: 751). For de Beauvoir, Christ's miming of suffering feminine flesh is not redemptive for women, but in its emphasis on suffering, abjection, and the body demonstrates the inadequacy of religion and mysticism as sites of women's agency (see Hollywood 2002: 120–45).

6 In making this assertion I make no definitive claim with regard to Irigaray's sources. As I will show, the language of devotion to Christ's blood and side wound and of entering into Christ's side runs throughout late medieval piety. Irigaray does explicitly cite Angela's *Book*, rendering it a possible source for the language of "*La mystérique*," but definitive attribution is both impossible and unnecessary. On Irigaray's "miming" technique and its philosophical implications, see Butler 1993: 36–49.

7 The transmission history of Angela's book is tremendously complex and has given rise to intense debates over the extent to which we can understand Angela as its author. According to the scribe who wrote the book, Angela dictated to him in her native dialect and he simultaneously translated into Latin and wrote down her words. At one point, when he reads a passage back to her, she claims to be unable to recognize it. Yet at the same time, she accepts his rendition and continues to work with him on the book (see Mooney 1994: 34–63; and Dalarun 1995: 59–97). For an argument about the collaborative nature of women's work with scribes, see Staley 1994: 36; and Summit 2003: 91–108. On the subject of women's use of scribes, see also Ferrante 1998: 12–35.

8 "Quartodecimo, dum starem ad orationem, Christus ostendit se mihi … Et tunc vocavit me et dixit mihi quod ego ponerem os meum in plagam lateris sui, et videbatur mihi quod ego viderem et biberem sanguinem eius fluentem recenter ex latere suo, et dabatur mihi intelligere quod in isto mundaret me" (Angela of Foligno 1985: 142–4).

9 "Et aliquando videtur animae quod tanta laetitia et delectatione intret intus in illud latus Christi" (Angela of Foligno 1985: 278). See also later in the text, where Angela is recorded exhorting others to enter into the wound in Christ's side (Angela of Foligno 1993: 246). For other examples of "possibly queer female desire for Christ's wounds" within the medieval period see Lochrie 1997: 199, n. 34.

10 I will focus here on a complex nexus of texts and images that emerge within the Latin tradition of Passion narratives. Meditation on Christ's side wound and devotion to the heart of Jesus also figures prominently in Latin hagiographies of holy women, particularly

among the Cistercians and early beguines, and in the many texts, in both Latin and the vernaculars, written by religious and semi-religious women in the later Middle Ages. Perhaps most important for the development of the devotion to Christ's side wound are Thomas of Cantimpre's *Life of Lutgard of Aywières* and the writings by and about Gertrude the Great (1256–1301). For these and a host of other relevant texts, see McGinn 1998: 60–1, 100–1, 118, 128, 141, 165, 172, 181, 189, 206, 230, 236, 274–81, 304–7, 312–16.

11 The most salient use of the apocryphal gospels with regard to the images discussed here is the *Gospel of Nicodemus's* identification of the Roman centurion who pierced Christ's side with a lance as Longinus. References to Longinus and his spear, then, are directly tied to devotion to Christ's side wound, for Longinus's action rendered that wound. Subsequent traditions will associate this action with Song of Songs 4:9: "vulnerasti cor meum soror mea sponsa vulnerasti cor meum in uno oculorum tuorum" ("You have wounded my heart, my sister, my spouse. You have wounded my heart with one of your eyes"). An image from a fourteenth-century florilegium discussed at length by Jeffrey Hamburger shows a woman (presumably the soul as bride of the Song) holding the lance with which Christ's side is wounded. Christ, on a stylized cross, displays his side wound as he looks lovingly on the lance-bearer (Hamburger 1990). For the image, see Rothschild Canticles, New Haven, Beinecke Rare Book and Manuscript Library, MS 404, fols 18v–19r.

12 "Quis est iste, qui venit de Edom, tinctis vestibus de Bosra? iste formosus in stola sua, gradiens in multitudine fortitudinis suae. Ego qui loquor justitiam, et propugnator sum ad salvandum. Quare ergo rubrum est indumentum tuum, et vestimenta tua sicut calcantium in torculari? Torcular calcavi solus, et de gentibus non est vir mecum; calcavi eos in furore meo, et conculcavi eos in ira mea; est aspersus est sanguis eorum super vestimenta mea, et omnia indumenta mea inquinavi. (Isaiah 63: 1–3). As cited and translated by Bestul 1996: 29.

13 The passage has further iconographical ramifications, as James Marrow shows. Images of Christ suffering under the beam of a winepress thus serve as pictorial allegories for the Passion (Marrow 1979: 76–94).

14 The image might also be related to Byzantine crucifixes, in which Christ wears a robe, and is also clearly tied to late medieval traditions in which hundreds of tiny wounds appear all over Christ's body (Areford 1998).

15 "Columba mea in foraminibus petrae in caverna maceriae ostende mihi faciem tuam sonet vox tua in auribus meis." For Biblical citations, I have used *Biblia Sacra Iuxta Vulgatam Versionem* 1969. Bestul rightly eschews any attempt to argue decisively for the influence of one text or group of texts on another or to pinpoint the absolute origin of any particular image or image cluster. Given the complexity of medieval manuscript cultures, Bestul argues, "it seems most useful to conceive of these Latin treatises on the Passion as the products of a productive and complex textual community built around mutual relationship and interdependence in which many works reveal the textual traces of many other works, and in which the texts themselves are not static, but, attributed to various authors, subject to revision, recension, and modification" (Bestul 1996: 51).

16 The Christological reading of the passage can also be found in Cassiodorus (d. c.580), Rabanus Maurus (d. 856), and Alan of Lille (d. 1202) (Gray 1963: 85, n. 19).

17 "Et revera ubi tuta firmaque infirmis requies, nisi in vulneribus Salvatoris? Tanto illic securior habito, quanto ille potentior est ad salvandum" (Bernard of Clairvaux 1957–77: Vol. 2, Sermon 61, 150).

18 "Licet mihi sugere mel de petra, oleumque de saxo durissimo, id est gustare et videre quoniam sauvis est Dominus" (Bernard of Clairvaux 1957–77: Vol. 2, Sermon 61, 150). Bernard here characteristically creates a collage of Biblical references. Deut. 32: 13: "constituit eum super excelsam terram ut comederet fructus agrorum ut sugeret mel de petra oleumque de saxo durissimo." Psalm 33:9: "gustate et videte quoniam bonus Dominus."

19 "Patet arcanum cordis per foramina corporis, patet magnum illud pietatis sacramen-
tum, patent VISCERA MISERICORDIA DEI NOSTRI, IN QUIBIS VISITAVIT NOS
ORIENS EX ALTO. Quidni viscera per vulnera pateant?" (Bernard of Clairvaux
1957–77: Vol. 2, Sermon 61, 150–1). See 1 Timothy 3:16 and Luke 1: 78.

20 "Tunc unus ex militibus lancea latus eius aperuit, et exiuit sanguis et aqua. Festina, ne
tardeueris, comede fauum cum melle tuo, bibe uinum tuum cum lacte tuo. Sanguis tibi
in uinum uertitur et inebrieris, in lac aqua mutatur ut nutriaris. Fact sunt tibi in petra
flumina, in membris eius uulnera, et in maceria corporis eius cauerna, in quibis instar
columbae latitans et deosculans singula ex sanguine eius fiant sicut uitta coccinea labia
tua, et eloquium tuum dulce" (Aelred of Rievaulx 1971b: 671).

21 For a eucharistic reading of this passage, see Dutton 1987: 1–31. For a reading of the
passage in light of medieval devotion to the Blood of Christ, see Bynum 2002: 685–8.

22 "Ut haurias aquas de fontibus Salvatoris" (Bonaventure 1882–1902: Vol. 8, 80; cited
by Bestul 1996: 45).

23 Bestul cites Bonaventure 1882–1902: Vol. 8, 188; and Bonaventure 1960: 203–4.
"Tandum accendendum est ad cor illud humillimum altissimi Iesu, per ianuam
videlicet lateris lanceati." Bestul also points the reader to Bonaventure's *On the
Perfection of Life to Sisters*: "non solum mitte manum tuam in latus eius, sed totaliter
per ostium lateris ingredere usque cor ipsius Iesu" ("not only put your hand into his
side, but enter with your whole being through the door of his side into Jesus' heart
itself") (Bonaventure 1882–1902: 120; and Bonaventure 1960: 239).

These passages demonstrate particularly clearly an additional source for the devotion to Christ's side wound: the gospel of John's account of Thomas's doubt that the
resurrected Jesus is indeed Jesus. "Deinde dicit Thomae infer digitum tuum huc et
vide manus meas et adfer manum tuam et mitte in latus meum et noli esse incredulus
sed fidelis." ("And then he said to Thomas, "Put your finger here and see my hands
and bring your hand and put it in my side do not be unbelieving but faithful.") John
20: 27.

24 For the text, see James of Milan 1905: 1–132. Wolfgang Riehle and Karma Lochrie go
so far as to argue that in James of Milan's text, mystical union is represented as the copulation of two wounds: that of Christ and the female soul. On the one hand, this works
to figure Christ's wound as vulvic/vaginal and the interpenetration of wounds as a site
of female same sex eroticism. At the same time, Christ's wound, Lochrie argues, is the
"gate of Paradise" evoked by Song of Songs 4:12: "My sister, my spouse, is a garden
enclosed, a garden enclosed, a fountain sealed up" ("hortus conclusus soror mea
sponsa hortus conclusis fons signatus"). Often taken as marking the soul or the female
religious' virginity, here the enclosed garden signifies Christ and the soul is invited to
penetrate into that protected and protecting space (Lochrie 1997: 189; and Riehle
1981: 46).

25 The Franciscan Ubertino da Casale's (1259–1329) *Arbor vitae crucifixae Jesu* (1305)
commands the reader to join Mary, the mother of Jesus, as she enters Christ's heart
through the wound made in his side by the lance. Ludolphus of Saxony's (d. 1377) *Vita
Christi*, as Bestul elegantly summarizes, compares "Christ's body pierced by wounds to
a dove house where Christians can take refuge in the holes, even building nests in those
openings" (Bestul 1996: 57–9). See Ubertino da Casale 1961: 322–35; and Ludolphus
of Saxony 1970: Vol. 2, p. 617. For more on the *Arbor vitae*, see Sticca 1988: 109–11.
For more examples of the theme, see Gray 1963; Lewis 1996; and Bestul 1996: 26–68.

26 On medieval attention to the dimensions of Christ's side wound, which was believed to
be known, see Areford 1998: 223–4. On the paradoxical interplay of narrativization (in
the texts dealing with Christ's Passion) and fragmentation (in the images often accompanying these and related texts), see Hollywood (forthcoming).

27 For more on Christ's side wound and its representation in devotional texts and images,
see Lewis 1996; Hamburger 1998: 111–48, 197–232; Morgan 1993–94: 507–18,
817–20; and the literature cited by Areford 1998: 213–14, nn. 6–8.

28 Areford goes on to describe the importance of the precise measurement of the side
wound for fourteenth- and fifteenth-century devotional practice.

29 "Medieval authors do not seem to have drawn as sharp a line as we do between sexual
responses and affective responses or between male and female. Throughout the Middle
Ages, authors found it far easier than we seem to find it to apply characteristics stereo-
typed as male or female to the opposite sex. Moreover, they were clearly not
embarrassed to speak of all kinds of ecstasy in language *we* find physical and sexual
and therefore inappropriate to God" (Bynum 1982: 162; cited by Lochrie 1997: 182).

30 Irigaray is not the only modern interpreter – or perhaps better mimer – of medieval
mystical traditions to see a correlation between God and women's sex. Georges
Bataille's evocations of female genitals as divine can be elucidated through attention to
the divinity of the wound in medieval Christian texts and images. So, in his novel
Madame Edwarda (closely aligned with his writings on mystical or inner experience
from the 1940s), a prostitute exposes her genitals to the unnamed narrator:

> You want to see my rags? she said.
> My two hands gripping the table, I turned toward her. Seated, she lifted her leg up
> high: to open her slit better, she pulled the skin apart with her two hands. Thus
> the "rags" of Edwarda looked at me, hairy and pink, full of life, like a repugnant
> spider. I stammered softly:
> Why are you doing that?
> You see, she said, I am GOD ...
> I am mad ...
> But no, you have to look: look!
> Her harsh voice softened, she became almost childlike, saying for me, with lassi-
> tude, with the infinite smile of abandon: "Oh, how I come [*joui*]."
> (Bataille 1970–88: Vol. 3, 20–1)

Angela of Foligno is a key figure for Bataille, a medieval purveyor of that inner, ecstatic experience he seeks to elicit through his own writing and meditative practices. Like
Angela, who presses her lips to Christ's side wound, *Madame Edwarda*'s unnamed narrator kisses Edwarda's genitals: "Finally, I knelt, I trembled, and put my lips on the
living wound" (Bataille 1970–88: Vol. 3, 20).

8 Early modern blazons and the rhetoric of wonder

Turning towards an ethics of sexual difference

Grant Williams

The blazon – a popular literary/rhetorical form which describes the beauty of the beloved's body parts by comparing them to desirable objects – has received over the last few decades sustained scholarly attention thanks to Nancy Vickers's groundbreaking and still influential work. Proffering fresh possibilities for the analysis of the gendered body in early modern culture, Vickers argued that Petrarch left "a legacy of fragmentation" to the Renaissance male poet, who effectively silences his beloved's voice through rhetorically fetishizing her body parts (Vickers 1981: 277). Vickers's thesis on the blazon has not only kindled feminist readings of Renaissance English literary texts that appropriate the female body on behalf of patriarchy (Baker 1991; Kahn 1991; Wall 1993), but has also been adapted by new historicism to examine Elizabethan and Jacobean ideological practices (Montrose 1986; Parker 1987; Sawday 1995; Betts 1998). As crucial as this work is in exposing the subtlety of patriarchal oppression, its exclusively political perspective neglects the ethical dimension to gender relations. The neglect arises, no doubt, from the difficulty of talking about gender without reproducing the essentializing proclivities of phallocentrism: early modern culture's dependence on Galenic homology necessitated the exaggeration of anatomical distinctions in order to rationalize the exclusion of women from dominant social practices and discourses. Luce Irigaray enables blazon criticism to push beyond this impasse, overcoming the limits of political approaches to the body without mitigating a critique of phallocentrism. Her ethics of sexual difference gives us the means of rethinking the blazon's engagement with female alterity. In particular, her theorization of the place of wonder in the encounter between the sexes helps us to fathom the strange rhetoric for which blazons are famous.

Vickers's analysis of the Petrarchan legacy to Renaissance poets detects in the blazon a conflictive relationship between the masculine and the feminine imaginary. She bases her argument on Petrarch's well-known textual strategy of fragmenting his beloved's body through praise, and elucidates the reasons behind this strategy with the myth of Actaeon-Diana, in which the goddess punishes a young hunter with dismemberment after he stumbles upon her bath and catches a glimpse of her naked body. In order to neutralize the castration threat symbolically suffered by his alter ego, the blazonneur preemptively fetishizes his beloved's body parts. The myth filtered through Petrarchan poetics conceives of the sexual relation as a Hegelian struggle between master and slave, the blazon-neur/Actaeon seeking the recognition of integration through disintegrating his rival, the beloved/Diana. Male identity is preserved only at the expense of annihilating a threatening female (m)otherness. But Vickers can pit the masculine against the feminine imaginary only because she has locked the blazon into a meta-narrative that already equates gender identity with power relations. Since blazons often appear in lyric form, readers may welcome Vickers's argument for filling in narrative gaps to explain the blazon's strangely ornate fabric.

However, when one sounds out the actual narrative settings in which numerous early modern blazons are embedded, feminine alterity does not always appear antagonistic to the masculine imaginary. At the beginning of Sidney's *Countess of Pembroke's Arcadia*, for instance, the sexual relation appears to be less a struggle with a castrating mother than an encounter with divine femininity. The romance opens with two shepherds Strephon and Claius coming upon the seashore where they first saw Urania, their beloved. Clauis celebrates her beauty by blazoning her face:

> Certainly as her eyelids are more pleasant to behold than two white kids climbing up a fair tree and browsing on his tenderest branches, and yet are nothing compared to the day-shining stars contained in them; and as her breath is more sweet than a gentle south-west wind which comes creeping over flowery fields and shadowed waters in the extreme heat of summer, and yet is nothing compared to the honey-flowing speech that breath doth carry, no more all that our eyes can see of her (though when they have seen her, what else they shall ever see is but dry stubble after clover's grass) is to be matched with the flock of unspeakable virtues laid up delightfully in that best-builded fold. But, indeed, as we can better consider the sun's beauty by marking how he gilds these waters and mountains than by looking upon his own face, too glorious for our weak eyes, so it may be our conceits, not able to bear her sun-staining excellency, will better weigh it by her works upon some meaner subject employed.
>
> (Sidney 1987: 5)

Clauis's blazon belongs to a narrative of remembering in which both shepherds recall a bethphany, a divine manifestation through a holy place (*OED*), in this case the seashore. Strephon recounts how the shore divided Urania's "heavenly beauty between the earth and the sea" at the moment she put one foot into the boat that took her away from the love-struck shepherds (Sidney 1987: 4). Strephon puns on the art of memory, for the memorable place is very much a mnemonic locus that not only haunts their thoughts but also reanimates fresh memories of Urania's alterity; he exclaims, "here we find that, as our remembrance came ever clothed unto us in the form of this place, so this place gives new heat to the fever of our languishing remembrance" (Sidney 1987: 3–4). For the shepherds, the shore is not simply a geographical location, but a phenomenological site of femininity that makes possible the sexual relation: the earth, the common ground so to speak, betokens proximity to otherness, while the sea suggests the self's separation and distance from otherness.

The place of divine femininity, upon which the narrative expands and Claius's blazon depends, speaks to the heart of an ethics of sexual difference. According to Irigaray, before there can be such an ethics, woman like man must occupy her own locus within the social imaginary. To develop a gender identity, a subject requires freedom, autonomy, and separateness from other gendered subjects. Because man has traditionally made the maternal-feminine his own place, woman, who ceaselessly serves his imaginary needs, has been denied the a priori condition of forming her own identity. Without her own place, there can be no authentic corporeal distinction between the sexes, an implication of Vickers's reading of blazons; in contrast, Sidney's blazon initiates an ethics of sexual difference. It posits a place of femininity at once preserving woman's autonomy within difference while opening an interval that gives male subjectivity the opportunity of relatedness (Irigaray 1993e: 13–14). Blazons locate and relocate – encounter and recall – feminine alterity on the seashore, the margin between earth and water, between phenomenological proximity and phenomenological distance.

The bethphanic place also makes possible a world of becoming for the masculine imaginary, not doomed to a Hegelian struggle of mastery or a Lacanian mirror stage of reflexive aggression. Clauis's blazon prefers over the Ovidian landscape of the hunt the pastoral setting of the Canticles, where the imagery of honey, sheep, and countryside tries to put into words a life-changing encounter with alterity. The fecundity of this pastoral setting may be elucidated with Theresa Krier's reading of the *Song of Songs*. Unsettling the popular view that the history of blazons records a fundamental alienation between the sexes, Krier deploys Winnicottian, as well as Irigarayan, psychoanalysis to throw into relief the creativity of potential space in the biblical poem. Such a space allows the lovers to "experiment with differing degrees of nearness to and distance from each other" to recreate themselves into generous beings (Krier 2001: 69). The place of Urania exhibits the same creativity. When recalling their bethphany, Strephon says, "hither we are now come to pay the rent for which we are so called unto by overbusy remembrance – remembrance, restless remembrance, which claims not only this duty of us but, for it, will have us forget ourselves" (Sidney 1987: 3). Urania has haunted their memories to the point that they have forgotten themselves, an early modern expression that reveals forgetting's close partnership with becoming: "To forget oneself" meant "to lose remembrance of one's station, position or character" (*OED*). At the place that now provides the architecture for their memories, the encounter with Urania begins their transformation from "silly ignorant shepherds" (Sidney 1987: 5) into lovers whose conversation learned clerks do not disdain. As suggested by the early modern language of interiority, namely, the art of memory, the blazon recalls the potential space of sexual difference, a mnemonic place that miraculously brings the male subject out of himself into new states of becoming.

Irigaray's work has much to offer the study of blazons. By recognizing the necessity of moving beyond the master/slave dialectic (Irigaray 1993e: 17),

Irigaray is able to ask questions of feminine alterity that are inconceivable to contemporary blazon scholarship, fixated as it is on equating gender relations with power relations. Her ethics of sexual difference describes how the sexes could relate to one another without forming "the mirror symmetry that annihilates the difference of identity" (Irigaray 1993e: 18). She avoids making femininity the mirror image of masculinity by implementing Emmanuel Levinas's phenomenology of alterity. For Levinas, ethics is first philosophy, because it precedes all philosophical enterprises, namely ontology and epistemology, which presuppose a self prior to otherness. The originary experience of the other, what he calls the face-to-face relation, constitutes the precondition of the self's identity. Irreducible and asymmetrical, otherness transcends being, throwing the "I" into question continually, since it embodies the idea of infinity, the limitless capacity to overflow the self's every effort at containing it within a totality. In her encounter with Levinas, Irigaray may be seen to create a "sexual or carnal ethics" (Irigaray 1993e: 17). Sensitive to the significance of corporeality, she aligns his asymmetry between self and other along a plane of sexual difference (Chanter 1995: 208).

And conversely Irigaray's ethics of sexual difference could not find a more amenable poetic genre than the blazon. Often written from the perspective of masculinity – sometimes femininity – the blazon describes the blazonneur's face-to-face encounter with his or her beloved. Blazons might be said to record an ethics as a "first poetics," insofar as they praise that which brings the male subject out of himself into a sexual relation. What makes the blazon so particularly receptive to questions of Irigarian ethics is that it incarnates, celebrates, and reveres the primary passion, upon which, Irigaray argues, a sexual relation is to be founded:

> To arrive at the constitution of an ethics of sexual difference, we must at least return to what is for Descartes the first passion: *wonder*. This passion has no opposite or contradiction and exists always as though for the first time.
>
> (Irigaray 1993e: 12)

Irigaray may very well be describing the formative passion felt by Claius, who can find no adequate experience or expression for capturing the incomparable beauty of Urania's face "too glorious for our weak eyes" (Sidney 1987: 5). The blazonneur exclaims the astonishment of encountering sexual difference unintelligible to his prior knowledge. Irigaray also attributes the wonder of sexual difference directly to the place of alterity. As with the shore/mnemonic locus in Sidney, the place of wonder is simultaneously intra-subjective and extra-subjective: the feeling of surprise and astonishment comes from meeting "the face of the unknowable" who resides in his or her separate locus "irreducible one to the other" (Irigaray 1993e: 13); and it marks a "new place of inscription" in the subject "not yet hardened by past impressions" (Irigaray 1993e: 77).

But Irigarian wonder has not been wholly accepted as an innocent, unmotivated passion. For Iris Young, the problem with adopting it for an ethics of sexual difference is that it may breed awe or curiosity, each of which "convert[s] the openness of wonder into a dominative desire to know and master the other person"

(Young 1997: 56). Young's reservations are more than warranted with conventional philosophical wonder, since Aristotle and Descartes make it an appetizer to knowing (Bishop 1996: 8, 26); however, her reservations underestimate the innovation of Irigarian wonder, which marks a rupture in the symbolic order – Lacan's term for the cultural/linguistic domain whose differences enable the subject to form identities, recognize objects, and generate knowledge. Ewa Ziarek and Krzysztof Ziarek have advanced Irigaray's radical conceptualization of the passions by carefully explicating how she revises Lacanian subjectivity along the gendered trajectory of becoming. For Ewa Ziarek, Irigarayan wonder exists in a disruptive temporality, much like Cornelius Castoriadis's notion of the radical imaginary (E. Ziarek 1998: 68), which, breaking from the past, asserts both the indeterminacy of history and the body in order to create new modes of life. For Krzysztof Ziarek, it exists beyond the subject of desire and the subject of knowledge, paralleling the later Lacan's "passion for ignorance," that third *jouissance* near the end of *Encore*, which reformulates the sexual relation "in terms of the futural vector of the possible" (K. Ziarek 1999: 10, 27). For both explicators, the subject's wondrous engagement with feminine corporeality does not absorb alterity into the symbolic or shape it according to the masculine imaginary but constitutes a transformative event that opens a passage, "between no longer and not yet" (E. Ziarek 1998: 69), toward new incarnations of sexual being.

To contend that the wonder of the blazon awakens a radical feminine imaginary may meet with some healthy skepticism from readers. Early feminist blazon criticism has been understandably wary of patriarchal rhetoric that worships female beauty. Young's suspicion of the passion is suggested by Vickers, who regards descriptive praise as narcissistically proclaiming the blazonneur's worth and simultaneously exciting possessiveness and envy among rivals (Vickers 1985b: 181). Refining this appraisal with a new historicist slant, Patricia Parker observes how the marvelous and the wondrous in the discursive practices of mercantile colonialism facilitate the commodification of female corporeality (Parker 1987: 148). But an Irigarayan approach to blazons may respectfully part company with, not negate, political critique if it avoids a key assumption found throughout feminist and new historicist work on the blazon: the assumption that Renaissance rhetoric operates according to a visual economy. The blazon's language is consistently characterized as an anatomical, voyeuristic, and telescopic tool used not just by poets but by courtiers, explorers, and scientists to master others, whether knowledge, subjects, or cultures (Vickers 1985b: 172; Baker 1991: 7; Montrose 1991: 13; Sawday 1995: 198; Gim 1998: 76). The rhetoric of display, notwithstanding its rapturous praise, can master the beloved because it supposedly leaves her body exposed at the intersection of two male gazes, the speaker's and the reader's (Parker 1987: 129; Miller 1989: 763).

While many critics have tacitly or openly adopted Laura Mulvey's theorization of cinematic spectatorship to discuss the politics of vision, this productive line of inquiry has operated at the expense of rhetoric. Blazons do not always feed scopophilia and, as counter intuitive as it may sound, do not always privilege the visual regime. Unlike a camera shot, the rhetoric of an individual blazon rarely adds up to a discrete visual image. The blazon's language regularly denies readers the option of identifying with the speaker's controlling gaze, since the typical speaker often admits to lacking the adequate words for describing his beloved: Clauis's "conceits" are "not able to bear her [Urania's] sun-staining excellency" (Sidney 1987: 5). The wonder of female corporeality is mediated less through a cinematic gaze than through figures of speech, such as the aforementioned paralipsis, and promotes more actively phonophilia and tropophilia rather than scopophilia. Consistent with Irigaray's emphasis on the first passion of ethics, the blazon's figures make one – and only one – concerted appeal to the reader, an appeal not to logos or ethos, but to pathos. They try to record the moment of intense wonder when the subject through an encounter with female alterity becomes transfigured into a lover.

Thomas Lodge's sonnet 22 from the sequence *Phillis* exemplifies the blazon's rhetorical appeal. I have not chosen his sonnet because of its originality; like numerous English sonnets, it is derived from a continental source (Paradise 1931: 224). I have chosen it expressly for its representative rhetoric. The sequence from which it hails was written by a non-canonical poet around the time Sidney and Daniel sparked the sonnet cycle craze in Elizabethan England. Thus, even a seemingly unremarkable blazon exhibits the deeply nuanced figurative language of wonder:

> Faire art thou Phillis, *I* so faire (sweet mayd)
> As nor the sunne, nor *I* have seene more faire,
> For in thy cheekes sweet roses are embayde,
> And golde more pure then gold doth guilde thy haire.
> Sweet bees have hiv'd their hony on thy tongue,
> And Hebe spic't hir Necter with thy breath:
> About thy necke do all the graces thronge,
> And lay such baites as might entangle death.
> In such a breast what heart would not be thrall?
> From such sweet armes who would not wish embraces?
> At thy faire handes who wonders not at all,
> Wounder it selfe through ignorance embases?
> Yet naithelesse tho wonderous giftes you call these,
> My faith is farre more wonderfull then all these.

> (Lodge 1593: F2r)

This sonnet clearly lends credence to Irigaray's insight that "Wonder must be the advent or the event of the other" (Irigaray 1993e: 75), for the blazon sets off in the final quatrain an astonishing chain-reaction of four interlinked wonders. The first wonder is experienced by those who embraced by Phillis realize that her miraculous touch has degraded the very idea of wonder – the second wonder. Referring to the blazon, the third wonder is the effect/quality of her gift-like body parts. And the fourth, apparently the most wonderful of all the wonders, is the speaker's religious-like experience.

As with hosts of blazons, sonnet 22 communicates the speaker's encounter with otherness less through mimetic representation than through figures of speech designed to appeal to pathos. Its hyper-ornate textuality signals the failure of the symbolic as though feminine alterity could not be securely positioned in conventional discourse. Generally speaking, linguistic ornament departs from everyday speech because words "used after some new or strange wise" define what figures are, as Thomas Wilson claims in his treatise *The Art of Rhetoric* (Wilson 1994: 195). But the blazon enacts a more pronounced linguistic astonishment insofar as it employs specific figures of speech that refuse to circumscribe alterity within the self-same. The blazonneur will forge similarities, equivalences, and parallels only to discard them as inadequate. In not supporting an equivalency between self and other, the figures underscore the irreducibility of sexual difference.

That said, blazons consistently rely upon implicit and explicit comparisons to make corporeal alterity known to the reader. The metaphor "Sweet Bees have hiv'd their hony on thy tongue" (Lodge 1593: F2r) is characteristic of the blazon's figurative language in that a corporeal member or attribute is compared to a sensual object for the purposes of praising beauty. Honey, the ambiguous metaphorical vehicle, betokens Phillis's sweet eloquence or her aromatic breath. Despite being clichéd, this metaphor discovers similarities between two different things not normally expected to have any kinship and thereby may afford linguistic surprise – as in the case of a metaphysical conceit. But the tropes of simile and metaphor, ethically speaking, forget sexual difference. The tongue's honey replicates a sweetness already familiar to the speaker. The language of comparison substitutes alterity with the self-same, forcing the unknown into a relationship of resemblance with the known.

One method of averting attacks on the blazon's language of comparison is to follow Irigaray's lead in recovering a metonymic, not a metaphoric, economy for the feminine imaginary. Theresa Krier's interpretation of the Canticles has done precisely that. Since metonymy, based on the contiguity and movement of the signifying chain, lends to the feminine imaginary a mechanics of fluids – in contrast to the solids typical of metaphorical substitutions – Krier reads the blazon's similes metonymically in order to ascertain the topographical dynamics of the poem. The poem's fluid spaces, especially the interval provided for maternal alterity, facilitate the exploration of sexual difference without collapsing distance into substitution (Krier 2001: 75–81). Although Krier points to a way of breaking the chokehold that political critique has on blazon criticism, there are shortcomings to reading blazons metonymically. As revolutionary as Irigaray's thinking has been in untangling a feminine from a masculine imaginary, conceiving the former in terms of metonymy buys into a tired binary inherited from a long line of structuralist thinkers. The opposition between metaphor and metonymy, popularized by Jakobson, Lévi-Strauss, and Lacan, subordinates the parameters of language to two master tropes or poles while eclipsing the figurative abundance inherent in textuality. To replace one master trope with another seems suspect when classical metonymy works by substitution too. Even in its capacity as the linguistic pole of the syntagmatic, metonymy may shorten distances by forging associations along a chain of otherwise separate signs. The self can exploit proximity to appropriate otherness into the space of the same.

Irigaray's suggestive yet inchoate comments on tropism in "Sex as Sign" are more compatible with the varied figuration of blazons. Irigaray tries to deconstruct metaphorism from within by reconceptualizing the as/like structure that substitutes one term for another; in representing sex, "Metaphor must remain a passageway, without resolution or resorption of the difference between the terms of its recurrence" (Irigaray 2002b: 147). Tropism, for which metaphor is the prototype, "exceeds or escapes from any predicate" and releases between two signifiers the play of between (Irigaray 2002b: 145). Judgments on the primacy of metaphor aside, her salutary thoughts on tropism are brought to fruition by the fertility of blazons, which regularly offset their extensive implementation of comparisons with a distinctly allotropic language. What I mean by "allotropic" is the propensity of certain figures to cut a passageway toward otherness without eliminating betweenness or distance. In sonnet 22, the fourth line, "And golde more pure then gold doth guilde thy haire" (Lodge 1593: F2r), appears to be a dissimile, a comparison of diverse qualities held by two dissimilar things: her hair and the precious metal have differing degrees of "purity" (also an oxymoron of sorts). But, in this figuratively complex line, the dissimile does not operate alone; it qualifies the line's initial metaphor, for Phillis's hair *is* compared to gold. How then do we reconcile the initial metaphor of gold with the dissimile of being more pure than gold? To state that either the metaphor or the dissimile dominates the line's configuration misreads the ethical dimension that the blazon communicates to the reader. Either assertion would insert Phillis within the totality of the self-same: her hair's golden sheen reproduces or does not reproduce a purity already perceived by the speaker. Yet the similitude/dissimilitude posits that the speaker views her hair as a gold that surpasses, not cancels out, the self-same vision of gold. This combination of figures, instead of actually negating comparison, envisions a place for feminine corporeality beyond comparison and thereby articulates a special relation to alterity embedded in Irigaray's thought and aptly expressed in Levinasian philosophical diction:

> Is not metaphysical alterity obtained by the superlative expression of perfections whose pale image fills the here below? But the negation of imperfections does not suffice for the conception of this alterity. Precisely perfection exceeds conception, overflows the concept; it designates distance: the idealization that makes it possible is a passage to the limit, that is, a transcendence, a passage to the other absolutely other. The idea of the perfect is an idea of infinity. The perfection designated by this passage to the limit does not remain on the common plane of the *yes* and the *no* at which negativity operates; on the contrary, the idea of infinity designates a height and a nobility, a transascendence.
>
> (Levinas 1998: 41)

The similitude/dissimilitude allotropically turns to feminine corporeality in such a way that alterity exceeds and overflows the known, that is, the totality encompassing the self-same and the self-same's negation. If the simile posits the other as the same and if dissimile posits the other as the non-same, then allotropic language seeks out a channel to the absolutely other through propagating a distance from the familiar world of comparison. Without destroying the sexual relation, it discloses the infinite height that the other's separate, perfect, and incomparable place holds over the self.

Put simply, allotropic language generates the wonder of otherness in and through language. If Irigarayan "Wonder is the passion that can express this [sexual] relation because it does not involve judgment and comparison" (La Caze 2002: 6), then the blazon accordingly inscribes wonder in a rhetoric that refuses to measure alterity by a predetermined legal (moral) or similative standard. Just as the two sexes cannot be substituted for one another (Irigaray 1993e: 13), the rhetoric of wonder does not as*simil*ate female corporeality into the language of the self, that is, a system structured by substitution and centered on the self-same. Alterity requires its own point of reference, its own measurement, its own divine, transascendent place.

Take, for example, hyperbole, another figure frequently occurring throughout blazonic literature. According to George Puttenham, an early modern rhetorician who calls this figure "the Over reacher," a poet deploys it when speaking "in the superlative and beyond the limites of credit" (Puttenham 1869: 202). Although Puttenham distrusts its potential to distort the truth, the blazonneur regularly adopts it to praise his beloved's beauty. Lodge's blazon begins with hyperbole: "Faire art thou, *Phillis*, *I* so faire (sweet mayd)/As nor the sunne, nor *I* have seene more faire" (Lodge 1593: F2r). In much the same manner as the similitude/dissimilitude, this instance of hyperbole elevates the advent of feminine corporeality above the range of everyday comparison and substitution. There is no one as fair as the fairest Phillis, whose incomparable corporeality is set apart from all others in the world under the sun. What often is dismissed as calculated flattery, even lies, of how the beloved's looks measure up in a social context is really the ascendant plane of the other in the ethical relation. For an ethics of sexual difference, the feminine other appears irreplaceable and superlative to the masculine self.

In implementing the allotropic, ethical blazons cannot be said to operate according to the scopic economy that Vickers along with Parker has famously advocated. What the gaze masters can be measured, exchanged, and made known – inserted into a system of equivalences and substitutions. Allotropic language, actually preventing the male subject from freeze-framing feminine corporeality, underscores her transascendence to the visible, the comparable, and the known. It bears out Irigaray's argument that "sexual difference is not reducible to the quantitative" (Irigaray 1993e: 76), but also bears out, on the level of rhetoric, her general ethical critique of vision and the visible in her chapter "The Invisible of the Flesh" (Irigaray 1993e). The space of wonder is always too bright, catching the subject off guard with the surprise of the first time and dazzling the senses with shocking intensities. It touches the eye, as flesh, not image. In other words, blazons release the Irigarian wonder carefully formulated by Ewa Ziarek: allotropic language posits a radical female imaginary. Femininity escapes predication in the symbolic order and capture in the masculine imaginary, both of which belong to the scopic economy (E. Ziarek 1998: 61). The blazon's advent of sexual difference, instead, effects a discontinuous temporality that catapults subjectivity into a present, contingent becoming, vectored neither toward past determinations nor toward future certainties, neither nostalgic nor apocalyptic (Irigaray 1993e: 75; E. Ziarek 1998: 68).

Sonnet 22's last noteworthy example of allotropic language evinces the radical imaginary that sets subjectivity on the track of becoming. In the final quatrain, the paroxysm of wonders, a response to the blazoned body, not coincidentally communicates an ethics of sexual difference through paradox: Puttenham anglicizes paradox as "the wondrer" because it reports a marvelous or incredible phenomenon contrary to received opinion (Puttenham 1869: 233). The second rhetorical question declares that those whom Phillis embraces experience a wonder of which Wonder itself has no knowledge: "At thy faire handes who wonders not at all/Wounder it selfe through ignorance embases?" (Lodge 1593: F2r). Lacking this experience of Phillis, Wonder thus diminishes in value, indicated not only by the action of abasement but by the curious spelling of wonder with a "u." If wonder's etymology is indeed related to "wound" as T. G. Bishop argues (Bishop 1996: 183), the sonnet registers both the wounding potential of wonder and the wounded nature of Wonder as an abstraction. But really, how could the abstraction of wonder, the genus that logically makes possible all of the individual species of wonder, not include within its ken Phillis's wondrous touch? Again, allotropic language gestures toward the superlative place of alterity. The advent of feminine corporeality has exposed the poverty of the phallocentric discourses of Aristotelianism, Platonism, and Christianity, whose logic of wonder subordinates the specific, terrestrial, and carnal body to the abstract, the metaphysical, and the spiritual. The everyday logic of wonders fails to put into words the passion aroused by the experience of Phillis's touch. Because Wonder is now itself depreciated, the reader is given to believe, moreover, that the advent of feminine alterity has revealed a new incarnation of wonder, which no doubt prompts the ignorant Wonder, now wounded, to wonder. Wonder always exceeds previous formulations, since it is a passion that, as Irigaray observes, involves surprise at the extraordinary as though seen for the first time.

However, after wonder has reached what seems to be its apotheosis, the sonnet continues the paradox with a surprising twist: "Yet naithelesse tho wonderous giftes you call these,/My faith is farre more wonderfull then all these" (Lodge 1593: F2r). As transcendent as Phillis's wonder appears, the speaker's wonderful faith surpasses even that. This compound paradox dramatizes two points about the ethical dimension of blazons.

First, the paradox recreates on the plane of language the surprising experience of wonder. The paradox goes beyond itself as though the wondrous response to feminine corporeality always exceeds the limits of the self's knowledge. That which is impossible to surpass has been surprisingly surpassed by something that, in turn, has been surprisingly surpassed by something else. At the level of the material signifier, the quatrain's implementation of polyptoton, a repetition of words which share the same root but possess different endings, presents the idea of wonder continually differing from itself. In terms of figures, then, wonder is language continually transcending itself, turning outwardly toward otherness.

Second, the compound paradox enunciates the repercussions of wonder for the blazonneur. Denoting the coming or incarnation of sexual difference, Irigaray's "advent" of feminine presence (parousia) is by no means an indifferent experience for male subjectivity (Irigaray 1993e: 147–50) but impacts him with a religious force, described throughout her work. "The first passion [wonder] is indispensable not only to life but also or still to the creation of an ethics" (Irigaray 1993e: 74), because it opens up recalcitrant male subjectivity to feminine alterity. As such, it initiates "the mourning for the self as an autarchic entity" (Irigaray 1993e: 75) and designates "the place of man's second birth" (Irigaray 1993e: 82). Mediated by eros, this birth amounts to what Irigaray describes elsewhere as a "state of becoming with no objective other than becoming" (Irigaray 1993e: 33). By the final line of this sonnet, the speaker has clearly entered into a new era of being: the advent of the other has left him with the life-changing gift of faith. Contrary to orthodox Christian faith, whose energies direct subjectivity toward an otherworldly telos (1 Peter 1:9), the speaker's faith elicits a plenitude of wonder at the present moment of enunciation. Here it is reminiscent of the story of the centurion whose faith actually made Christ marvel (Luke 7) insofar as it betokens the startling presence of divine-like alterity within the human. Unqualified by any eschatological fulfillment, the speaker's faith is wondrous to him because it bears witness to the incursion of the other into the self. The advent of feminine alterity has exposed the poverty and hopelessness of solipsistic self-sufficiency and opened up for the subject the fecund possibilities of a new sexual relation.

As much as the blazon points to a utopia of gender relations, there are limits to its engagement with female alterity. The many passages of poetry and prose where blazons occur attest to the failure of the blazonneur to realize the fecundity of a sexual relation, which for Irigaray reveals itself on the intimate level of the caress and on the social level of a recreated world – where "man and woman may once again or at last live together, meet, and sometimes inhabit the same place" (Irigaray 1993e: 17). Lodge's sonnet sequence ends with an ode that terminates the sexual relation, exposing Phillis to be a siren, whose deception, treason, and cruelty authorize the speaker to take pleasure in the eventual decay of her beauty; the place posited for female alterity has been violently effaced. But the aborted assignations, failed expectations, and defensive postures punctuating the climaxes of early modern erotic poetry should not detract from what the blazon does indeed accomplish. The blazon speaks of wonder with the first, irreplaceable words of an ethics of sexual difference.

Challenging us to rethink early modern gender relations, Irigarian ethics dislodges the blazon from the discourse of political critique popularized by feminist and new historicist scholarship. Only because this scholarship assumes rhetoric to advance a scopic economy can it lock the blazonneur and the beloved into a Hegelian dialectic of master and slave – a Lacanian mirror stage in which the male gaze seeks integration through fragmenting his castrating female imago. But allotropic rhetoric opens up the possibility that ethical blazons do not blindly reflect the Petrarchan language of fetishism. Through its appeal to the pathos of wonder, the blazon's figures of speech posit an incomparable place of alterity for the feminine and thereby move the masculine self to relinquish narcissism for a world of becoming. The allotropic – that rhetorical turn toward otherness – gives a compelling account of the strangely superlative language that blazons, such as the *Song of Songs*, consistently deploy to praise the beloved.

The allotropic also suggests another genealogy for the blazon, one more attuned to its rhetorical rather than its generic modalities and one less concerned with poetic origins whether it be Petrarchanism or the *Song of Songs*. The popularity of the English blazon coincides with the emergence of elocutionary wonder, as evinced by the proliferation of early modern handbooks devoted to figures of speech. Richard Sherry's *Treatise of Schemes and Tropes*, George Puttenham's *Arte of English Poesie*, and Henry Peacham's *Garden of Eloquence* elicit rhetorical fecundity by gathering up a profusion of figures and as such continue in the vernacular Eramus's program of teaching writing through providing an abundant variety of textual devices, what he calls after Quintilian "copia." These handbooks conceive rhetoric as a miraculous cornucopia, the mythological horn of plenty renown for its endless capacity to pour forth sustenance of infinite variety. Operating under the auspices of copia, the blazon's figures impart the infinite sensual appeal of feminine alterity and its concomitant possibilities for generating a sexual relation. Its figures propose endless ways of relating to the female body: Phillis's corporeal presence unfolds through similitudes, dissimilitudes, hyperboles, paradoxes, rhetorical questions, polyptotons, etc.

But copia cannot fully trace the genealogy of figuration out of which the blazon emerges. Longinus's *On Sublimity*, though not a direct participant in Renaissance debates over rhetoric, articulates most effectively what the blazon is aiming to achieve through its appeal of pathos. The allotropic does not merely persuade or delight the reader; it tries to transport him or her with the force of amazement and wonder (Longinus 1989: 143). Extensively explicating this rhetorical appeal, the treatise's attempts to imagine figures of speech that go beyond themselves in attaining a height, a grandeur, and a sublimity properly describe the efforts of the blazon to inscribe the transascendance of femininity (Longinus 1989: 164). It is only the wonder of rhetoric as it flashes out at various points in the history of figuration that could ever make possible the blazon's rhetoric of wonder – language allotropic enough to ethically engage with the wondrous wonders of feminine alterity.

9 Gynephobia and culture change

An Irigarayan just-so story

Harry Berger, Jr.

There used to be a tendency in criticism by feminist scholars and others to use the term "misogyny" to denote the whole antifeminist position rather than merely the hostility, contempt, and dismissal expressed in conventional denigrations of woman. Yet it isn't hard to show that antifeminist discourse has a divided structure of which misogyny is but one side, and, in my opinion, the less important side for interpretive purposes. Misogyny may be no more than the reaction to or surface manifestation of a deeper anxiety, *gynephobia*. There is a gynephobia of gender and a gynephobia of sex: the former is fear of effeminization, fear of the woman within the man, and the latter is fear of impotence, emasculation, or infantilization, fear of the woman outside the man; the former is fear of a threat to man's possession of the power signified by the phallus, the latter is fear of a threat to man's possession of the power signified by the penis; the former is a fear of having one's status reduced *to* that of woman but not necessarily *by women*; the latter is specifically a fear of having one's status reduced or usurped *by women*. To be unmanned by "the system"; to be politically or socially unmanned by other males or by women in positions of power or authority; to be sexually unmanned by women's insatiability, infidelity, and promiscuity: these "sources" of gynephobia may interact or signify each other, but they are both analytically and empirically distinct, and their conjunction in any particular case must be demonstrated.

The distinctions between misogyny and gynephobia, and between the two kinds of gynephobia, lead directly to the founding political premise of my study: gynephobia is basic to the structure of society as we know it; it is an originary motive of male fantasy, patriarchal discourse, and the political, economic, and cultural organization of all the social formations about which history or our own experience gives evidence. The very conditions of male fantasy, discourse, and society thus make it impossible for any particular sample of discourse to avoid gynephobia. Gynephobia is a universal of human society. In order to demonstrate why and how this is so, I want to engage in an exercise that has a long and distinguished pedigree and goes back at least as far as one of the all-time favorite targets of postmodern and feminist discourse, Plato. This is the exercise of aetiological fantasy, the construction of a myth of origins that "explains" a state of structural equilibrium (or equilibration) by means of a fiction of diachronic and dialectical process. The particular myth I have chosen is in fact one that has already been invented, and which I propose to adopt as the basis for a somewhat revised version. Its inventor is Luce Irigaray.

Irigaray argues in *This Sex Which Is Not One* that since "all systems of exchange that organize patriarchal societies and all the modalities of productive work that are recognized, valued, and rewarded in these societies are men's business," and since the "production of women, signs, and commodities is always referred back to men," it follows that the very:

> possibility of our social life, of our culture, depends upon a hom(m)o-sexual monopoly. ... What the anthropologist calls the passage from nature to culture thus amounts to the institution of the reign of hom(m)o-sexuality. Not in an "immediate" practice, but in its '"social" mediation.

> Women, signs, commodities, and currency always pass from one man to another; if it were otherwise, we are told, the social order would fall back upon incestuous and exclusively endogamous ties that would paralyze all commerce. ... This means that the *very possibility of a sociocultural order requires homosexuality* as its organizing principle. Heterosexuality is nothing but the assignment of economic roles. ... Why is masculine homosexuality considered exceptional, then, when in fact the economy as a whole is based upon it? Why are homosexuals ostracized, when society postulates homosexuality? Unless it is because the *"incest" involved in homosexuality has to remain in the realm of pretense.*[1]

> (Irigaray 1985a: 171, 192)

Eve Sedgwick and Judith Butler have criticized this conception because it is not "historically responsive" but totalizing – its "failure to acknowledge the specific cultural operations of gender oppression [is] itself a kind of epistemological imperialism ... that uncritically mimics the strategy of the oppressor" – and because Irigaray accords "actual sex between men ... the same invariable, tabooed status for her larger, 'real' 'homosexuality' that incest has in principle for Lévi-Straussian kinship in general."[2] As Sedgwick reminds us, examples of instituted pederasty and sanctioned homosexuality in ancient Greek and other societies demonstrate "that while heterosexuality is necessary for the maintenance of any patriarchy, homophobia, against males at any rate, is not" (Sedgwick 1985: 4). Sedgwick therefore prefers to Irigaray's model a variable structure of male "homosocial continuums" in which the degree of continuity or discontinuity between homosocial and homosexual desire is "culturally contingent" (Sedgwick 1985: 5). With this proviso, she grants "that in any male-dominated society, there is a special relation between male homosocial (*including* homosexual) desire and the structures for maintaining and transmitting patriarchal power" (Sedgwick 1985: 25).

I think this critique misses an important point: Irigaray's vision of the hom(m)o-sexual economy is offered not as a totalizing transhistorical truth but as a critique and myth of origins that negotiates with and polemically re-engenders a dominant model of precapitalist social formation: the tradition of analysis that includes Malinowski, Mauss, Lévi-Strauss, and Bourdieu, and derives from a more general paradigm various versions of which have been developed by (for example) Marx, Weber, Polanyi, and Parsons. This is a paradigm of institutional and cultural change from precapitalist to capitalist structure. In its simplest version it postulates that economic and political practices and discourses are first embedded in, then differentiated from, social and religious practices and discourses. Thus the initial state of this diachronic system is depicted as one in which commodity trade is embedded in – and misrecognized as – social interaction and coded as gift exchange; one in which abstract signifiers of value and equivalence receive the concrete form not of currency or writing but of embodied and often personified exchange objects, and in which the items exchanged are treated not as commodities but as presents.

Lévi-Strauss extended Mauss's version of this system to the traffic in women, and Irigaray, like Gayle Rubin, begins her critique there. In her own analysis of the traffic as policed by homosocial interests Rubin argues that since "reciprocal exchange confers its quasi-mystical power of social linkage" on the male partners in exchange, not on the women who are the presents, this difference produces gender asymmetry. It "entails the constraint of female subjectivity" and also establishes, as a precondition of the incest taboo, "a prior, less articulate taboo on homosexuality" (Rubin 1975: 174, 183, 180). This taboo should not be confused with homophobia because its function is to discourage obstacles not to heterosexuality per se but to *exogamy*, which is another term for the traffic that subordinates heterosexuality and women to the interest of widening and solidifying homosocial ties and control. Where homosexuality is sanctioned it serves exactly the same purpose, defending the homosocial interests of male corporate groups against the disruptive effects of women's sexual, reproductive, and nurturant power. Whether sanctioned or prohibited, therefore, homosexuality is a factor, a "player," in a homosocial game, one objective of which is to control what men do with their penises. Even if "hom(m)o-sexuality" is interpreted as merely figurative homosexuality, the figure is more metonymic than metaphoric since actual sex between men is part of the fantasmatic spectrum of possibilities policed by homosocial ideology.

This point can be made another way. The notion that sex between men and women is a displaced and degraded simulacrum of sex between men may be sheer hyperbole but it conveys a truth about the ideological fantasy of hom(m)o-sexuality. This truth has less to do with the forms of sexuality per se than with the relation of sexuality to the traffic in women, which can be expressed as a relation of the penis to the phallus. The power of the penis is a power *of* penetration for pleasure, for dominance, and for insemination, which may be a contingent and unwanted byproduct of the desire for pleasure and dominance. The power of the phallus is a power *over* penetration exerted in the homosocial strategies of gift exchange that shape the traffic in women. In this context insemination is not a *byproduct* of penetration but its *objective*, the end to which penetration is the means. The power of the phallus turns out to be the power of donation in Mauss's classic formulation of the "rule" of gift exchange: "To give is to show one's superiority, to show that one is something more and higher, that one is *magister*. To accept without returning or repaying more is to face subordination, to become ... *minister*" (Mauss 1967: 72). If we substitute "to penetrate" for "to give" in the first sentence we may comprehend both the difference and the resonance between penis power and phallic power. Reversing the relation of penetration to insemination, the phallic power of donation extends the power of the penis from individual agents to corporate groups. But it also regulates that power by means of prohibitions, practices, and discourses that police the unruly desire of the penis. The traffic in women produces a perpetual need in men to keep from being disempowered, made *minister*, defeated, therefore effeminized, by the men they compete with. But it is *through* women – and, by an easy displacement, *from* women – that men face this peril of castration embedded in the system of exchange.

As a myth of origins Irigaray's argument gestures toward an ironic and subversive recapitulation of the logic elaborated by Freud in *Civilization and its Discontents*. The phallic power of donation secures the network of gift exchange by repressing, inhibiting, or channeling the power and desire of the penis. The truth of hom(m)o-sexuality is that men would identify the power of the phallus with the pleasure of the penis if they could. Irigaray claims that homosexuality is forbidden not only because it threatens to expose the law of hom(m)o-sexuality but also because it "might lower the sublime value of" the *étalon*, which means both "standard" and "stallion": "Once the penis itself becomes merely a means to pleasure, pleasure among men, *the phallus loses its power*" (Irigaray 1985a: 193). The prophylactic reaction to this autoseductive threat – in the Irigarayan logic I am teasing out – is to move through the moment of sublimation (from homosexual to homosocial bonding) toward the gynephobic displacement of the source of danger: "Sexual pleasure, *we are told*, is best left to those creatures who are ill-suited for the seriousness of symbolic rules, namely women" (Irigaray 1985a: 193, my italics). As a fantasmatic ideal, then, sublimation secures the power of the phallus from both forms of sexuality since both are centered in the desire of the penis. Yet sublimation doesn't simply separate phallic power from the penis. It is "not desexualization," Jane Gallop writes, "but a more mediated, represented, mastered form of sexuality" (Gallop 1982: 28). It involves a conflict between the two aspects of a single process of displacement, *extension* and *abstraction* or *alienation*. We may say, continuing this development of Irigaray's myth of origins, that the homosocial economy comes into being when the power of the penis is symbolically extended from individual sexual actors to the corporate group. But the condition of this extension of power is that it be abstracted, differentiated, alienated from those actors, taken "out of their hands" and conferred on the system of gift exchange, where sexual control *of* women is instrumental to the more difficult control of the traffic *in* women.

The difficulty in controlling this alienated power is increased by the unruly force of sexuality, which can disrupt homosocial negotiations by setting the penis against the phallus. Organized homosociality protects against the danger by first defining and then prohibiting what counts as unruliness. Its targets of definition and prohibition are the behavior and desire of those who participate, as nominal agent and patient, in the act of penetration. This includes both men and women, both heterosexual and homosexual activity:

> A prohibition against *some* heterosexual unions assumes a taboo against non-heterosexual unions. … The suppression of the homosexual component of human sexuality, and by corollary, the oppression of homosexuals, is therefore a product of the same system whose rules and relations oppress women.
>
> (Rubin 1975: 180)

Homosocial ideology thus defends its male subjects against the fear of losing control of the power of donation by conferring value on both male homophobia and gynephobia. Why is the latter more widespread and important than the former? "The ethnographic record is littered with practices whose effect is to keep women 'in their place' – men's cults, secret initiations, arcane male knowledge, etc.," whereas there are many documented instances and forms of "institutionalized homosexuality" (Rubin 1975: 163, 181). Why should women, already oppressed, need to be policed? In the regime of hom(m)o-sexuality and its homosocial economy, where do they get enough power to make men anxious?

It's here that Irigaray's myth of origins reveals its generative power. For as soon as we take a close look at it, we can discern under the assertive simplicity of its rhetoric a fundamental contradiction between the two aspects of what seems to be a single structure: a homosocial system of exchange and a heterosexual "assignment of economic roles" (Irigaray 1985a: 192). In its homosocial dimension the originary fantasy constructs woman only as an object suitable for exchange on the alliance market. Conspicuously reductive, mischievously parodic, Irigaray's language accentuates the degraded, disempowered status of female subjectivity and desire. Woman's sexual power is de-emphasized, male desire is oriented toward the art of exchanging women as commodities: "heterosexuality has been up to now just an alibi for the smooth working of man's relations with himself, of relations among men" (Irigaray 1985a: 172). This is the paradise of the homosocial imaginary, the fantasmatic idyll of domination in which woman is objectified as pure gift, a mirror of the value of the giver, possessed of little more subjectivity or autonomy than a statue.

From this paradisal dream of origin every deviation that animates the statue is marked with the sense of its loss.[3] The dream thus persists. It is only swept under the rug in the shift from the homosocial to the heterosexual dimension. This shift of fantasy reempowers woman by making her not only the object of male desire but also its cause, and not only the object of exchange, but also a custodian of the orderly transmission of phallic power. As custodian she gains just enough volitional autonomy to become a responsible – and therefore culpable – agent in the processes of exchange and transmission. She is made less than a partner, perhaps, but more than an object. She is allowed to be a subject so that she may be capable of resisting integration into the system, capable of resisting identification with the normative role functions or subject positions that articulate the female "life cycle," capable, indeed, of representing herself to herself and others, and therefore of representing herself falsely. She is invested with the natural unruliness that makes her, like the penis, a threat to both economies. This functional analogy gives her added value: it makes her available as a scapegoat for the unruliness of the penis. Thus re-empowered and fetishized, the heterosexual construction of woman is marked with the loss of the homosocial statue's innocence. Correspondingly, the desire to recuperate this loss by restoring woman to her first statuesque objectivity marks a regressive response to the traumatic threat to the phallus that is itself the logical consequence of the fantasy of loss.

In my expanded Irigarayan model the ideological fantasy inscribed in male discourse is layered and dialectically interactive: it shuttles back and forth between the illusion that hom(m)o-sexuality is (we are told) the way things really are and the illusion that heterosexuality is (we are told) the way things really are. The tension, negotiations, and adjustments between the claims of the hom(m)o-sexual ideal of undisputed male phallocracy and those of the heterosexual injunction to alienate more phallic power to female subject positions (virgin, wife, mother, whore, virago, goddess, woman warrior, witch) maintain the model in this oscillatory structure as its permanent state. The obvious effect of the shuttle would seem to be the two forms of gynephobia – the gynephobia of gender produced by the threat to the phallus and the gynephobia of sex produced by the threat to the penis.

However, a moment's thought will disclose that to conceive of gynephobia as an effect of the system is part of the ideological illusion. We can see this by putting into play the paralogism of inverse causality, which is the classic structure underlying all metaleptic or genealogical construction: the effect is the cause of its cause, or the cause is the effect of its effect, for if A is the cause of B then B is the cause of A's being a cause. One shouldn't be deceived by the purely logical status of this circular inversion. If it is only a trick in logic it is a truth in psycho-logic, which is to say that it is the basic truth of the metapsychological construction of the sex–gender shuttle. Gynephobia is the cause of the shuttle and the cause that the shuttle causes it. The ideological fantasy of hom(m)o-sexuality is an illusion because, although we are told it is the way things really are, the way things really really are is that the telling is motivated by fear of the power of woman, the fear inscribed in the homosocial objectification that reduces her to a statue. This fear then justifies itself as merely the effect of the fall from the homosocial paradise to the heterosexual subjectification and reempowerment of woman. Finally, the whole shuttle – and this is the way things really really really are – reveals by its structure that what men fear is their inability to maintain control of their desire, their sexuality, the power of the penis, and the power of the phallus. It isn't women men are afraid of; it is themselves. Thus the origin of the sex–gender shuttle is not in gynephobia but in autophobia; gynephobia is its displacement and scapegoat.

From the Irigarayan standpoint in which this genealogy of male fantasy is grounded, the shuttle is a representation that conceals its "inner" workings. Autophobia and gynephobia are the unconscious of the system, its principles of structuration. The aim of the feminist critique is to bring these hidden motives to the surface and to show how all the componential aspects of the system –

hom(m)o-sexual monopoly, homosocial objectification, and heterosexual subjectification – betray their real functions as strategic effects of gynephobia,
institutional and ideological mechanisms of defense against the imaginary loss of
power, the trauma or wound of castration of which the signifier is woman. In
Irigaray's deployment of the critique these mechanisms are deconstructed by a
method calculated to breach the hom(m)o-sexual representation and revive the
anxiety that structures it. She does this in part by exploring the possibility of "a
female sexuality 'other' than the one prescribed in, and by, phallocratism," an
"other woman," a "female imaginary," repressed or unrepresented by male discourse (Irigaray: 1985a: 119, 30), in part by refusing to represent the other woman
in the available language of the hom(m)o-sexual symbolic order, hinting at but
withholding its secret, insisting on its unrepresentability by that language.

   The anxiety this refusal evokes is an anxiety central to all representation,
including self-representation. To suggest how it arises requires the addition of two
further touches to the model. The first is Judith Butler's observation that whatever
is "understood as 'within' the body" – subjectivity, identity, soul, self, mind, etc. –
"is signified through its inscription *on* the body, even though its primary mode of
signification is through its very absence, its potent invisibility," and that this
inscription is "a social fabrication that perpetually renounces itself as such."
Butler applies this Foucauldian insight to sexuality and gender which, she argues,
are performed by repetitive:

> acts, gestures, and desire [that] produce the effect of an internal core or sub-
> stance ... *on the surface* of the body. ... That the gendered body is
> performative suggests that it has no ontological status apart from the various
> acts which constitute its reality. This also suggests that if that reality is fabri-
> cated as an interior essence, that very interiority is an effect and function of a
> decidedly public and social discourse, and public regulation of fantasy
> through the surface politics of the body. ... The displacement of a political and
> discursive origin of gender identity onto a psychological "core" precludes an
> analysis of the political constitution of the gendered subject and its fabricated
> notions about the ineffable interiority of its sex or of its true identity.
>
> (Butler 1990: 136–6)

The second touch I want to add to the model is a Lacanian caution about the
extent to which the "potent invisibility" of this "'core'" may be said to be domes-
ticated, colonized, interpellated by such fabrications. For doesn't the public
discourse that produces this absence and invisible interiority represent it *as* absent
and invisible? If the hom(m)o-sexual and heterosexual regimes constitute the
female subject as an ego-ideal – which is to say, from the male standpoint of those
regimes, as an alter-ideal – do their representations fully saturate the invisible
space of subjectivity "fabricated as an interior essence" or do they fall short, leave
an unrepresented excess, a remainder that they nevertheless adumbrate *as* unrepresented? If the ideological police construct an other, an alter-ideal, and map this
interior on the body from the point of view of the other of that other, don't they

constitute at the same time the permanent possibility of a suspicion that some prior alterity "within" that body has been repressed or scotomized? What I am looking for in the discourses of hom(m)o-sexuality are traces of representation anxiety, traces of bad conscience, accents of failed or incomplete interpellation, sluices in the fabric that reveal glimpses of some uncolonized space behind the double inscription of subjectivity and gender, signals that mark the fictiveness of inscription as well as its shallow depth.

One might seem to find such a recognition in the Lacanian thesis that "in the phallic order of patriarchal culture and its theory, woman is unrepresentable except as representation." But as Teresa de Lauretis, whose paraphrase this is, goes on to suggest, a discourse that represents woman as unrepresentable in or by its own terms constitutes her unrepresentability as an effect of representation, therefore constitutes an excess *beyond* representation as part *of* representation. Proposing a dialectical method of moving between the represented and unrepresented female subject of male discourse, de Lauretis counsels against the tendency toward ontological closure: "*not* ... a movement ... from the space of a representation ... to the space outside the representation, the space outside discourse, which would then be thought of as 'real' ... or again, from the symbolic space constructed by the sex-gender system to a 'reality' external to it," but rather "a movement back and forth between the representation of gender (in its male-centered frame of reference) and what the representation leaves out or, more pointedly, makes unrepresentable" (de Lauretis 1987: 20, 25–6).

In male discourse that encourages this shuttling the unrepresented *She* materializes as the hidden agent to stir up renewed desire and anxiety, renewed efforts to penetrate the veil and capture the excess in representation; the excess is continuously reconstituted "outside discourse as a potential trauma which can rupture or destabilize ... any representation" (de Lauretis 1987: 3) and which thereby motivates the renewal of the efforts to domesticate it:

> Of course, we might – we were supposed to? – exhibit one "truth" while sensing, withholding, muffling another. Truth's other side – its complement? its remainder? – stayed hidden. Secret. Inside and outside, we were not supposed to be the same. That doesn't suit their desires. Veiling and unveiling: isn't that what interests them? What keeps them busy? Always repeating the same operation, every time. On every woman.
>
> (Irigaray 1985a: 210)

Notes

1 Luce Irigaray, *This Sex Which Is Not One*, trans. Trans. Catherine Porter, with Caroline Burke (Ithaca: Cornell University Press, 1985), 171, 192.
2 Sedgwick 1985: 26; Butler 1990: 13. Other criticisms of Irigaray, especially of her "essentialism," are conveniently collected and analyzed (and often refuted) by Fuss 1989: 55–72.
3 See, for example, Lévi-Strauss 1969: 496–7.

10 The commodities dance

Exchange and escape in Irigaray's "Quand nos lèvres se parlent" and Catherine Des Roches's "Dialogue d'Iris et Pasithée"

Ann Rosalind Jones

> As soon as a table emerges as a commodity, it changes into a thing which transcends sensuousness. It not only stands with its feet on the ground, but, in relation to all other commodities, it stands on its head, and evolves out of its wooden brain grotesque ideas, far more wonderful than if it were to begin dancing of its own accord.
>
> (Karl Marx 1867: from "The Fetishism of the Commodity and Its Secret" in *Capital*, Ch. 1, trans. Fowkes 1976: 63–4)

I hope to show in this essay how a late sixteenth-century text, Catherine Des Roches's "Dialogue d'Iris et Pasithée," dramatizing an encounter between a learned, independent woman and a daughter crazed by the search for a husband, can be illuminated by Luce Irigaray's gendered re-theorization of the exchange of women in the late 1970s. In two essays toward the end of *Ce Sexe qui n'est pas un* (1977), Irigaray took up Lévi-Strauss and Marx on the topic of women as objects of exchange, that is, as commodities circulated for profit among men. In several ways, her essays resemble the brilliant inter-reading of anthropology, Marxist economic theory and psychoanalysis written a few years earlier by the American social critic Gayle Rubin, "The Traffic in Women: Notes on the 'Political Economy' of Sex" (Rubin 1975). But Irigaray adds the realm of the Symbolic – language and imagery, both unconscious and social – to the structures under analysis. Then, in the final essay of the collection, "Quand nos lèvres se parlent," she constructs a lyrical alternative, a poetic/polemical invitation to another woman to escape the objectifying system of family, economic, and symbolic bonds analyzed in the preceding essays.

In "Le Marché des femmes," Irigaray draws out the parallels between Lévi-Strauss' analysis of endogamous marriage in *The Elementary Structures of Kinship*, in which brides are exchanged by and for men, and the system of commodity exchange analyzed by Marx in the first chapter of *Capital*, in which the value of goods is measured in relation to an external standard invented by their dealers. She argues that these two circuits, constructed and dominated by men, produce a double sexual and symbolic alienation for women: their bodies have exchange and use value for men (as marriageable daughters, as mothers of sons) but not for women themselves as sexual or social subjects. Moreover, men make this market more competitive by accumulating as many women as possible, because possessing them in quantity (all at once, or sequentially, as for the Don Juan) translates into a sign of their owner's power in the structure. A man's ownership of women proves his wealth and gives him the symbolic prestige of the phallus. Women, as a result of their triple objectification as wives, commodities and measures of male potency, are not "interested," in any sense, in one another. Hence Irigaray's attempt in "Quand nos lèvres se parlent" to imagine and verbalize a space outside male exchange, in which women exist in and for each other.

"Le Marché des femmes" and "Des Marchandises entre elles" are remarkably different in tone from "Quand nos lèvres se parlent." Irigaray's exploration of women as commodities in the first two essays, inflected by the destabilizing questions and sarcasm typical of her earlier confrontations with male authorities such as Plato and Freud (as in *Speculum de l'autre femme*), belongs to a cooler, more critical register than does the warmly seductive rhetoric of "Quand nos lèvres se parlent." Here, in lyrical prose, she evokes two mouths, two pairs of feminine lips, those of a speaker and a listener, in order to invite a feminine counterpart into a utopian collaboration that would allow them, together, to escape the masculine Symbolic that turns them both into abstract, speechless tokens identified only by their value to men.

Irigaray links the two extremes of this trio by focusing on the systemic isolation of women from one another in a passage mid-way through "Le Marché des femmes." As commodities made exchangeable by reference a common, external standard – men's definition of femininity – women lose their particularity, are generalized into goods oriented toward a measure of value outside themselves. They have no identity in themselves and no meaning for one another:

> L'équivalent général des marchandises ne fonctionne plus lui-même comme marchandise. Miroir éminent, transcendant à leur monde, il assure la possibilité d'échange universel entre elles. Chacune peut devenir équivalente à chacune au regard de cet étalon sublime. ... mais ce suspens de l'estimation de leur valeur à quelque transcendentale les rend, pour l'immédiat, inéchangeable entre elles. Elles s'échangent dans l'équivalent général. ... Cette référence ek-statique les sépare radicalement l'une de l'autre. Une valeur abstraite et universelle les soustrait à l'usage et l'échange entre elles.
> (Irigaray 1977b: 177; 1985e: 181)

A "merchandise" (this noun, feminine in French, allows Irigaray to underline the gendered power asymmetry of the market in a way that the neutral English word "commodity" makes impossible [Irigaray 1985a: 219–20]), in order to be traded for something else, must be assigned a value derived from an external standard – bride price, a certain sum of cash, or "femininity," in the sense of a unit of evidence for the power of the man who owns her. As a result of being assessed in this quantified, abstract way, she loses any intrinsic value that would allow her to recognize and speak to such intrinsic value in another "merchandise."

In "Les Marchandises entre elles," Irigaray points out how unimaginable this psychic economy makes links between women. Reading Freud's account of the lesbian painter who desired women, in which he can account for feminine homosexuality only by defining her as masculine in both libido and physiology, she concludes:

> L'homosexualité feminine a donc échappé au psychanalyste. ... L'économie socio-culturelle dominante ne laisse aux homosexuelles ... *que le mime de modèles masculins.* La mise en jeu des désirs entre corps, sexes, paroles des femmes y est inconcevable. ... Les marchandises ne peuvent entrer en relations que sous le regard de leurs "gardiens." Pas question qu'elles aillent seules au "marché," qu'elles jouent de leur valeur entre elles, qu'elles se parlent, se désirent, sans le contrôle de sujets vendeurs-acheteurs-consommateurs.
>
> (Irigaray 1977c: 192–3; 1985b: 196)

Then she poses one of her provocative questions: "Et si les 'marchandises' refusaient d'aller au 'marché'? Entretenant entre elles un 'autre' commerce?" In answer, she sketches out a Marxist/feminist utopia in which economic terms have simultaneous psychic and erotic overtones, in a series of puns that provides a conceptual map and stylistic fore-sample of "Quand nos lèvres se parlent":

> Échanges sans termes identifiables, sans comptes, sans fin. ... Sans un(e) plus un(e), sans série, sans nombre. Sans étalon. ... Où l'usage et l'échange se confondraient. Où le plus de valeur serait, aussi bien, le moins de réserve. Où la nature se dépenserait, sans épuisement; s'échangerait, sans travail; se donnerait – à l'abri des transactions masculines – pour rien: plaisirs gratuits, bien-être sans peines, jouissances sans possessions.
>
> (Irigaray 1977c: 193; 1985b: 197)

She concludes in a neat prolepsis by accepting a likely challenge – "Utopie? Peut-être – " and then adds an intriguing remark about history: "A moins que ce mode d'échange mine depuis toujours l'ordre du commerce" (Unless this mode of exchange has undermined the order of commerce from the beginning). Assuming she means here that both the exchange of women and women's resistance to it are practices of *longue durée*, I offer her riddling proposal as a useful path backward into early modern literary history.

THE *BLASON*: POEMS AS/ON THE BEAUTY FETISH

Irigaray's critique, particularly in its focus on the Symbolic order that names, categorizes and abstracts women in relation to their male owners, makes it possible to recognize a poetic version of men's trade in women in the Renaissance *blason* tradition. Her analysis provides an uncannily apposite description of male poets doing business in the competitive exchange of poems typified in the contest

organized by Clément Marot at the court of Renée de France in Ferrara in 1536
(Saunders 1981: 121; Charpentier 1983: 118–34; Vickers 1985b: 172, 1996:
171–5). Each participant in the contest composed a poem on a single part of a
woman's body: hair, breast, foot. Maurice Scève won, with a poem on the mathe-
matical perfection of his lady's eyebrow.

What's striking about this contest, and the printed anthology of its poems that
followed in 1536, is, first, the bonds that the part-poems established among its
poets socially as well as in print. Their rivalry brought them cultural prestige, as
shown by the five expanded editions of the collection, in which the eleven poems
of the first printing grew to over thirty by the third edition of 1536 (Saunders
1981: 138–9). Everyone wanted to get into the act (the male kinship display?) of
the original courtly *blasonneurs*. Indeed, the name of their shared genre has
affinities with modern advertising: *blasonner*, in its first sense, meant to blow a
trumpet and call out the name of a knight as he proceeded into a tournament, to
win him attention in the public arena (Vickers 1985b: 175–6). In the Ferrara contest, what was trumpeted was not the poet's historical beloved but an isolated part
of an anonymous female body – illustrated, in every printed edition, by a woodcut
– and, more emphatically, the skill and daring with which the man publicizing that
body part had made it into his poetic product.

Such poems, as has frequently been pointed out, involved the anatomization of
women, their fragmentation into discursively and psychologically manageable
corporeal tidbits (Charpentier 1983: 117; Vickers 1985b: 26; Parker 1987;
Fumerton 1991; Jones 2000). An Irigarayan perspective reveals that, like the commodity in Marx, such texts are elaborated through a process of abstraction. The
woman's body is departicularized: the poems describe not *Laura's* knee, for
example (no woman's name is mentioned in any of them), but a version of it. An
Irigarayan perspective reveals further that – exactly like a commodity – this
abstract typicality makes it desirable to all men. A representation of one body part
as a public, generally sought after commodity is worked out in the first lines of
Victor Brodeau's "La Bouche":

> Bouche belle, Bouche bénigne,
> Courtoise, claire, coralline,
> Douce, de mine désirable,
> Bouche à tous humains admirable,
> Bouche, quand premier je te vis,
> Je fus sans mentir tout ravi
> Sur le doux plaisir et grand aise
> Que reçoit l'autre qui te baise. …
>
> (Charpentier: 142: 1–8)

[Lovely Mouth, kindly Mouth,/Courteous, shining, coral-hued,/Sweet, desirable in its outward show,/Mouth admired by all human [men],/Mouth, when I
first saw you,/I was – I lie not – totally ravished/By the sweet pleasure and
great delight/That another, kissing you, receives. (my translation)]

Senſuiuent

LES BLASONS A-
natomiques du corps feme
nin, enſemble les contreblaſons de
nouueau compoſez, & additionez, auec
les figures, le tout mis par ordre:compo
ſez par pluſieurs poetes contempo-
rains.Auec la table deſdictz Bla-
ſons & contreblaſons,Im-
primez en ceſte
Année.

Pour Charles Lan-
gelier.

1 5 4 3.

Figure 10.1   Title page, *Les Blasons anatomiques du corps femenin* (Paris: Charles
Langelier, 1543). Albert and Shirley Small Special Collections Library.
Reproduced by permission of the University of Virginia Library.

Twice in this invocation Brodeau refers to other viewers/consumers of the mouth: all the humans (masculine, by a linguistic convention that Irigaray would offer as proof of men's domination of the Symbolic) who admire the mouth visually, and the "other" – which we can safely assume is a man's mouth – that enjoys it tactilely. The feminine mouth has value not as the feature of a single woman (Brodeau withholds any concrete details about the size or shape of this mouth) but as a public good: a commodity consumable in one way by onlookers and in another by the unspecified man who kisses it. The lack of exclusivity in these poems sharply distinguishes the *blason* as genre from the record of personal obsession and jealous scrutiny in lyric sequences such as Scève's and Shakespeare's. Brodeau's "Mouth" gains value in the market place because everybody wants it. The poet's labor produces it (and his poem) not as his own private treasure but as a good increased in value by its visibility throughout a wide system of exchange. No particular source, no particular purchaser: this "Mouth" transforms nature into a cultural artifact via miniaturization and advertises it as desirable because it is already desired.

In the next section of Brodeau's poem, he adds value by celestializing the mouth:

> Mais après que t'oius parler,
> Je pensais entendre par l'air
> Les dits de Junon la seconde,
> Et de Minerve la faconde:

(9–12)

[But after I heard you speak,/I thought I heard in the air/The words of the second Juno,/And the eloquence of Minerva.]

It might appear here that the poet is reanimating the woman, giving her active speech as a subject in this discourse. On the contrary, it is not her speech he invokes, but the divine language of two goddesses, whose absolute power over mankind he goes on to attribute to the mouth he describes:

> Bouche à qui tu veux ennemie,
> Bouche qui fait vivre ou mourir
> Tous ceux qu'elle peut secourir ...

[Mouth, enemy to whom you please,/Mouth that gives life or death/To all the men whom she might succor ...]

This nervous compliment to an omnipotent "enemy" repays consideration from Irigaray's point of view, particularly her take on Marx's metaphor of the commodity as a fetish.

His point, briefly, is that in capitalism, the material, sensuous work that genuinely gives value to a commodity (the weaver's and tailor's skills that go into a coat) becomes confused with the market value of the object, that is, with the purely relational price the coat commands in the market. What men make themselves,

Blafon de la Bouche.

BRODEAV.

B Ouche belle, Bouche benigne,
Courtoife, clere, coralline,
Doulce, de myne defirable.
Bouchɇ à to᷈ humains admirable
Bouche quand premier ie te veis
Ie fuz fans mentir tout rauis
Sur le doulx plaifir & grand ayfe
Que reçoit l'autre qui te baife:
Mais aprés que t'ouys parler,
Ie penfoys entendre par l'air
Les dictz de Iuno la fecondɇ,
Et de Minerue la faconde,
Parquy ie dis, o bouchɇ amye,
Bouchɇ à qui tu veulx ennemye,
Bouche que faict viurɇ ou mourir
Tous ceulx quelle peult fecourir.
Bouchɇ amyable, bouchɇ entiere,
Non variable, non legiere.

                          B iiii

Figure 10.2   Victor Brodeau, "Blason de la bouche," from *Les Blasons anatomiques du corps femenin* (Paris: Charles Langelier, 1543). Albert and Shirley Small Special Collections Library. Reproduced by permission of the University of Virginia Library.

other men misread as goods inhabited by an extra-human value. This is why Marx remarks that the absolute value attributed by liberal economists to goods in the market parallels the divinity that early believers believe dwells physically inside their fetishes – amulets or free-standing figures they have made themselves, but that they see as animated by the gods. He adds a mock passage in which commodities speak through deluded economists who confuse their market and their intrinsic value (1867/1977: 176–7). Irigaray genders the human delusion engendered under capitalism: men are so conditioned by the "meta-physical" system of exchange that they resemble the compulsive saver who, as Marx says, "sacrifices to this fetish [of gold, or cash, or the limited feminine role he has elaborated for women] all the penchants of his flesh" (quoted in Irigaray 1977b: 184–5). The male fantasy of a phallic self endowed with women subordinates the variety of erotic pleasures available to the male body to fixed rituals of ownership (breaking the bride's hymen) and reproduction (limiting sexual practice only to procreative coupling). But because ownership of the fantasized phallus assures men of their position in the socio-sexual economy, they are willing to sacrifice a wide range of erotic pleasures to the solid masculine identity the system assures them. Irigaray suggests, moreover, that men's unconscious anxiety about the symbolic rather than innately corporeal status of masculinity/the phallus means that "women unwittingly come to represent the danger of a misappropriation of masculine power" (Irigaray 1977b: 188). Hence the "mirage" that women have the phallus.

Fetishization and mirage-making both structure Brodeau's *blason*. He animates the mouth not with human words but with those of two goddesses – in fact, the cultural invention of the Greeks and Romans. Interestingly, he does not choose Venus to animate his mouth. Juno and Minerva are more frightening figures: Minerva's resentment of the Trojans governs the *Iliad*, Juno's curse propels the *Aeneid*. By invoking these menacing deities to classicize and thus to add cultural capital to his invention, he elevates the mouth far above everyday bodily realities. Turning his own invention – a standard of female beauty – into an absolute, he then falls to his knees before it. At the same time he signals his participation in the humanist courtly culture inhabited by the male élite of his time, trademarking his product as coming from a distinguished company.

Then, as though he believed his own deification of the mouth, he mollifies its power to bless or reject suitors through the wishful, propitiatory tone of his next lines. He ends, however, with a less than awestruck request:

> Bouche amiable, bouche entière,
> Bouche variable, non légère …
> Bouche riante, plaisante bouche,
> Qui baille devant qu'on la touche.
> Bouche, voudrais-tu emboucher
> Celui qui voudrait te boucher?
> Bouche où gît mon repos,
> Bouche pleine de bons propos, . .

(17–26)

[Lovable mouth, mouth complete unto itself,/Variable, but not flighty mouth
.../Laughing mouth, joking mouth,/That opens wide before someone touches
it./Mouth, are you willing to take in/He who'd like to close you up?/Mouth in
which lies my rest,/Mouth, filled up with worthy words.]

This section of the poem suggests that building an idol and then worshipping it
produces an anxiety that the male speaker must dispel. The goddess-inspired
mouth is attributed a discourse of its own ("variable," "entière") but then transformed into an aperture accessible to one man who would plug or shut it/her up,
as one corks a bottle. Brodeau here is playing on the Renaissance conflation of
mouth and vagina, "the two interchangeable thresholds of female appetite and
vulnerability," as Gail Kern Paster puts it (Paster 1993: 55). Given this fantasy of
possession, which reestablishes the blasoned mouth as a single man's private territory, it is hard not to read the mouth's fullness as a metaphor for pregnancy and
its "good words" as the echo or reproduction of the words of its author/maker. The
mouth may be fetishized and worshipped, but it is then violently re-inserted into
the male-dominated system via the fantasy through which its closure, as alluring
to every man as female virginity, leads to penetration by one man and a labeling
and identification with his Nom – his name, language and prohibition of access to
other men.

This kind of reflex, through which the male speaker recovers from adulation
of the abstract beauty he has invented, can be seen in other poems in the Ferrara
collection in which the literary imperative to produce *blasons* as exchangeable
commodities runs up against the sex–gender system centered on male property.
The poet plucks the body part out of the abstract circulation from which all
writers/readers benefit and recovers it for ownership by one man. Marot's well
known *blason*, "Le Tétin," typically abstracts the lauded breast by isolating it
from its mate, then assigns it market value by naming the "envie dedans les
mains ... de maints" (the desire in the hands of many men) to touch it. But this
advertising of the breast to all hearers is cut short as the poet imagines a more
restricted scene: the breast is suddenly given voice, but a voice to which only
one man can respond: "Mariez-moi tôt, mariez!" (line 28: "Marry me quickly,
marry me!"). The focus then shifts to the single husband, "heureux" because
"de lait [il] t'emplira,/Faisant d'un Tétin de pucelle,/Tétin de femme entière et
belle" (148: with milk he will fill you up,/Making from a maiden's breast/A
woman's breast, full and fair). The anonymous *blasonneur* of "Le Ventre" (the
belly) accomplishes a similar privatization of the goods ("private," be it remem-
bered, is related to "deprivation," loss of a possession). After praising the belly's
appeal as a cool, ivory-hued exterior alluring to "chacun" (every man") and,
more specifically, to old and new lovers, he shifts focus inward to imagine a
reproductive future that implies single ownership of what he has previously represented as a pleasure to many:

O ventre habile a recevoir
Cela de quoi peux concevoir. ...

Ventre qui es si digne chose
Que dedans toi l'enfant repose. . .

(23–24, 26–27)

[Oh belly, skillful in receiving/What you can conceive with. .../Belly, who's such a deserving thing/That within you, a child rests.]

It could be argued that such turns from abstract, intricate composition to the facts of procreation re-nature the woman's body, replace it in a less fabricated and commercial world. But, as Irigaray points out, in a social and symbolic system that defines feminine embodiment only as the site of sexual and maternal services men expect from women, the reproductive synecdoche (woman as womb) is no more liberating than poetic synecdoche and metaphor (womb as ivory treasure-chest). However inventively and self-enhancingly the poets in the *blason* circuit embellish and proffer their goods, they cannot risk the possibility that women might circulate as freely as poems. In this market, endless competition is intolerable. Exchange finally must give way to possession.

Irigaray condemns the sex–gender system that makes women into erotic and reproductive commodities because this economy prevents women from exploring or even imagining their bodies as a field for their own exploration: "Neither as virgin nor wife nor prostitute has woman any right to her own pleasure." To oppose "what is required of a 'normal' feminine sexuality ... oddly evocative of the characteristics of the status of a commodity" (Irigaray 1977b: 187), she argues that a complete transformation of social and symbolic forms is necessary. Toward that end, she composes "Quand nos lèvres se parlent" as a counter-fantasy, putting new language, images and symbolic exchange experimentally into practice.

PEDAGOGY, PROSOPOPEIA, POETRY

"Quand nos lèvres se parlent" sets up a tête-à-tête, a private exchange between a female "je" and a "tu," as a contrast to the public trade in standardized women. In the form of a prose monologue, the text dramatizes and thematizes resistance to the commodification of women. And the intimately persuasive voice of this text resonates in many ways with the voice of Pasithée in the maneuvers of Catherine Des Roches's "Dialogue d'Iris et Pasithée." This dialogue appeared in her second collection of prose and poems, published, along with poems by her mother, in Poitiers in 1583: *Les Secondes Oeuvres de Madeleine et Catherine Des Roches*. In the cross-reading that follows, I want to interweave some common threads that link both texts as invitations to their female addressee to escape the economic and symbolic network that reduces women to commodities.

Catherine Des Roches lived her life in a way that allowed her to escape the reproductive imperative summed up by Irigaray as the "use value" assigned to women. Madeleine married twice, Catherine never: her central loyalty appears to have been to her mother. In her "Epistre à sa mere" in *Les Secondes Oeuvres*, she kidnaps the language of neoplatonic love poetry, in which the beloved woman, as body, raises the man from physical lust to spiritual illumination (an ideational system that corresponds to Irigaray's analysis of women's bodies as the ground for men's social/symbolic power). Des Roches reverses these terms in a complex way. Inserting the body/spirit hierarchy into a same-sex circuit, she constructs a metaphor of herself as the disembodied shadow to her mother's body. Defined by her mother's physical silhouette, she is also illuminated by Madeleine's light, which leads them indivisibly along a new path: "je vous suys partout comme l'ombre le corps … [et] la vive clarté de vostre entendement nous fait voir par un sentier gueres fréquenté." (Larsen 1998: 118). This is indeed a path rarely taken in sixteenth-century French poetry, even in lyrics written by women. Pernette Du Guillet, for example, compares her male beloved to the Sun and herself to the day, the short-lived, human measure of time created by the Sun in its heavenly course (*Rithmes*, Chanson 9); Louise Labé, in a typically scandalous rejection of the chastity assigned to women, willingly adopts the role of body to her beloved as spirit (*Euvres*, Sonnet 7). In Des Roches's letter, body and spirit are not opposed but re-symbolized as a union of two women moving to a new place.

The single state allowed Catherine to produce literary work by herself and in collaboration with another woman. But she did, at one moment, experience a violent commodification by men in a poetic contest that recalls the *blason* contest at the Ferrarese court: the flurry of poems collected under the title *La Puce*, initiated by the Paris lawyer Etienne Pasquier when, in the Des Roches's Poitiers salon, he claimed to have seen a flea on Catherine's breast. His poem on the subject generated a number of others, increased in number, as was the case with the Ferrarese *blasons*, when they reached print in Paris in 1582 and again in 1583. To the extent that the flea targeted Catherine synecdochally (its imagined travels around her body supplied blasonnable sites and also provided an aggressive alter-ego for the authors of the sixty-plus poems in the collection), her body and name were circulated throughout the composite male-authored text and its readers. The first two times the set of poems was published, it appeared as a commodity detached from any individual maker, though Abel l'Angelier was named as its editor. Its title, *La Puce de Madame Des-Roches*, was ambiguous: it could be taken to mean either that the flea belonged to Catherine or that she was the author of the collection. But L'Angelier's explanatory subtitle reestablished the gender norm, identifying its authors as "plusieurs doctes Personnages aux Grans Jours tenus à Poitiers." Catherine's half-dozen poems are rendered invisible by this title, which advertises only the competitive and complimentary interplay of men – local Poitevins and visitors to the city.

Her defense was to publish her responses alone, withdrawn from the raillery and quasi-obscenity of the men's poems, in *Les Secondes Oeuvres*. Eliminating the men's poems, she pulled her own out of the textual network that elaborated Pasquier's fantasy and her name in more and more elaborate, witty performances. But the battle over ownership of the book as commodity did not end there; finally, the masculine circuit of exchange won out (Jones 1995: 126–7). In 1610, when Pasquier published the whole collection in an anthology of his early writing, *La*

Jeunesse d'Etienne Pasquier, published by Jean Petipas in Paris, he reappropriated Catherine's name, body, and flea as the men's topic and her writing as his work.

Competition over the ownership and use of literary texts, not surprisingly, plays an important role in Catherine Des Roches's dialogue. Speaking in the voice of a humanistically educated bourgeoise, the character Pasithée welcomes Iris, the daughter of a neighbor, to a private conversation in which she encourages Iris to escape the economic and erotic system organized by and profited from by men. Catherine's text opens up a magical privacy closely akin to the intimacy voiced by the speaker of "Nos Lèvres." Both writers frame their chamber of women by acknowledging the power of men to isolate women one from another in the epistemological and linguistic circuits that make them into counters circulated among actual men and in the male Imaginary. In Des Roches's dialogue, the sex–gender system is personified by Iris's father and mother, and her suitors, several of whom are poets. Irigaray and Des Roches counter this power structure in similar ways: through a sly, devastating form of citation or mimicry that discredits the enunciators of the male-ordered Symbolic, and through invitations to resistance based on a tenderly imagined alternative way of being – and communicating – between women.

Irigaray and Des Roches both begin by refusing the last names through which men identify and claim daughters and wives. Irigaray warns her listener that unless they escape the language of men, they will remain "env(i)olées dans des noms propres. Pas le tien, ni le mien. Nous n'en avons pas … Sors de leur langage. Essaie de retraverser les noms qu'ils t'ont donné" (1977d: 205, 1985d: 205). Significantly, Des Roches omits last names from her text: in the dialogue preceding "Iris et Pasithée" she gives symbolic first names but no last names to the humanist father, Placide, and the misogynist father of Iris, Sévère. Neither of the two daughters has a last name to identify her as belonging to her father: they call each other by their first names, effacing paternal authority in their form of address.

Both writers also reject the patterns of exchange in which men give and take women for profit. Irigaray denounces gendered interactions as the same old stories. Only in the restorative retreat of a scene between women can any of them find relief from a sex–gender system all the more rigid to the extent that it is patently inimical to human happiness:

> Tu ne le sens pas? Autour de nous, les hommes et les femmes, on dirait que c'est pareil. Mêmes discussions, mêmes disputes, mêmes drames. Mêmes attraits, et ruptures. Mêmes difficultés, impossibilités de se joindre … Tu restes ici, et tu ne t'abstrais pas en scenes déjà jouées, en phrases déjà entendues et redites, en gestes déjà connues.
>
> (Irigaray 1977d: 205, 1985d: 205)

Des Roches gives Irigaray's all-too familiar disputes and recycled sentences a local habitation in the story told by Iris, who gradually reveals to Pasithée that her family and love lives are equally catastrophic. Her parents squabble about everything except their shared fury at seeing her leave the house. Her mother has refused one of her suitors as too poor; her father opposed her second choice because he asked for too big a dowry; the man she loves, Eole, writes her a poem confessing his fear of her paternal owner, "vostre imploiable père" (your unbending father, 233). Nirée, another suitor, plies her with second-rate poems, rehashing conventional metaphors and *carpe diem* formulas. Surrounded on all sides by noisy, insistent representatives of the male-driven social economy, Iris is stalled amidst a traffic in women going nowhere.

Both writers focus in detail on the danger of being trapped in masculine discourse, which attributes unintelligible mutability to women. For the masculine ego, rigid in its distinctions between I/not I and committed to other oppositions that shore it up (light/dark, solid/fluid, closed/open), women's greater flexibility looks like confusion. Irigaray refuses the opposition between symbolic colors traditionally associated with women – the white of virginity, the red of hymeneal and menstrual blood – in a rapturous list of multiple, coexistent female hues:

> Le sang nous est familier. Le sang: proche. Tu est toute rouge. Et tellement blanche. L'une et l'autre. Tu ne deviens pas rouge en perdant ta candeur. Tu es blanche de ne pas t'être éloignée de ton sang. De nous, blanches tout en restant rouges, naissent toutes les couleurs: roses, brunes, blondes, vertes, bleues ...
>
> (Irigaray 1977d: 206, 1985d: 207)

Like Irigaray, Des Roches's Pasithée warns her listener to beware of men's logic and discourse. Masculine incomprehension of the woman not fixed in subjection to men or in poetic traditions formulated by men similarly deprecates feminine inconstancy. Des Roches's Pasithée, like Irigaray, reverses the values attributed to this term: she celebrates mutability. She opens by defending Sévère's change of mind: from forbidding Iris to visit Pasithée, he has ordered her to do so. Inconstancy, Pasithée says, is the natural principle of the universe: the sun's course, the phases of the moon, the shifting colors of the rainbow, and the Heraclitan transformation of fire into air, air into water, water into earth and so on, all prove that humans, too, should embrace inconstancy; indeed, without variety, the beauty of human faces and of gardens would be reduced to monotonous sameness (224–5; Larsen 1998: 225 n7). Similarly, in her critique of Nirée's contemptuous comparison of Iris to the rainbow, she rejects his negative take on the simile: the rainbow predicts rain, i.e. tears, it is bent, in the sense of crooked, contrary to the sun as Iris is contrary to Reason, and as "changeante" as she is "variable." She transforms it into a compliment: God gave the rainbow to men as a presage of peace, Iris's arc-shaped spirit allows her to contemplate her own soul from every angle, the rainbow looks toward the sun as Iris looks toward reason, and the rainbow reflects the changing colors of the world; it is not changeable in itself, but reflects the marvelous variety of colors actually present in light (229–30). Deconstructing the speech Nirée gave Iris and that Iris repeated to her, Des Roches sets up an exchange of men's texts between women that reverses the exchange of texts among male *blasonneurs*. She judges Nirée's claim that Iris's beauty is as false as the rainbow's by firmly asserting that any "oeil juste" (discerning eye) would take pleasure in looking at Iris. With equal confidence, she dismisses his angry poem of farewell to Iris – "Je voi au fil des ans,/Et voz beautez, et mes amours passées" (I see with the passage of the years/Both your beauty and my love passed away) – as simply inaccurate: "Mais pourquoy dit-il cela, Iris? Vous ne fûtes jamais plus belle que vous êtes" (240: But why does he say that, Iris? You were never more beautiful than you are now).

The citations of men's language in Irigaray's and Des Roches's texts are never reverent; they are the first step toward deflating male authority. Both writers ironize men's statements about women by juxtaposing them with a celebration of female fluidity. Irigaray sounds strikingly like Des Roches, though more telegraphic, when she writes: "ce corps sans bords arrêtés. Cette mobilité, sans cesse. Cette vie. Ce qu'on appelera peut-être nos agitations, nos folies, nos feintes ou nos mensonges." She concludes, "Ne pas nous laisser, encore, en(vi)oler dans leur langage" (Irigaray 1977d: 214, 1985d: 215).

Beyond rejecting men's scorn for behavior alien to their rigid logic, both writers offer positive alternatives to their interlocutrices: the warming recovery of feminine bodily pleasure, delight in proximity, a quick understanding prior to words, followed by experiments in a new feminine language. Irigaray writes: "Je t'aime, toi qui n'es mère ... ni soeur ... Je t'aime: ton corps ici maintenant. Je/tu me touches, c'est bien assez pour que nous nous sentions vivantes" (Irigaray 1977d: 208, 1985d: 209). Later, she associates this shared bodily delight with freedom from men's discourse and with a tentative beginning of speech between women: "Attends. Mon sang revient. De leur sens. Il fait à nouveau chaud en nous. Entre nous. Leurs mots se vident ... Tu veux dire? ... Oui. Sois patiente. Tu diras tout" (Irigaray 1977d: 212, 1985d: 212).

Calls to intimacy as erotic as Irigaray's would be startling in Des Roches's 1583 text, but the Renaissance writer finds other ways to draw her listener into the pleasures of feminine intimacy. Pasithée reads Iris a poem that she saw in the hands of man, Philide (clearly Des Roches's own composition), in which comparisons between the various flowers in a garden and the multiple hues and shapes of a woman's face and body celebrate life, variety and change: the growing white lily, the yellow flame inside the iris, the long-lived laurel all share the vivacity of the young beauty to whom they are addressed (226–8). When Iris responds coolly to a poem Pasithée recites to her as proof that a woman can write well, Pasithée sympathetically guesses her objection before she can articulate it and gives her instead a more rhythmic song that she can dance to:

P: Et bien, Iris, qu'en dites-vous? Est-elle aisée à danser?
I: Nenny pas beaucoup, Pasithée, il m'est advis qu'elle est trop, là, je ne sçay comment, elle n'est pas assez ...
P: Voulez-vous dire qu'elle n'est pas assez gaie?
I: Oui, oui, c'est cela mesme!
P: En diray-je une plus gaillarde.

(255–6)

P: Well, Iris, what do you think of it? Is it easy to dance to?

I: Well, no, not very, Pasithée, my view is that it's too – oh, I
    don't know, exactly – it's ... it's not ...

P: Do you mean it's not gay enough?

I: Yes, yes, that's exactly it!

P: Then I'll recite a livelier one.

Responding to Iris's request, Pasithée also plays the *vielle* to accompany her: this ex-commodity is genuinely dancing. And she enjoys it so much that she promises to come back the next day. A range of discourses, music, light-hearted collaboration, physical pleasure, a sense of the future: like Irigaray, Des Roches's heroine uses her erudition to create delight sharable with another woman. And she, too, points toward the pleasures of freedom. Encouraging Iris to read, write and play the lyre, she assures her, tactically, that such accomplishments will attract better men. More important, she assures her, "faisant ce que je vous conseille amiablement, sans être aimée d'un Serviteur, vous pourrez vivre *commodément*" (249, emphasis mine: by doing what I advise you to, as a friend, without being loved by any suitor, you can live comfortably, as it suits you to do). This last word turns the English word *commodity* on its head. Outside the reign of fathers and husbands, Iris can live at her ease, at her own convenience. Des Roches's adverb and the English version of Marx's and Irigaray's crucial noun have antithetical meanings. The French adverb sums up the pleasures for women that the mercantile term, in English, denies them. But both women's texts make such *commodité* imaginable.

CONCLUSION: TALKING TO HERSELF?

In their different ways, through feminist interpretation of powerful social theory and an educated heroine's understanding of a marriageable girl's dead-ended life, Irigaray and Des Roches convincingly illustrate the reduction of women to exchangeable units. And in the choice of woman-to-woman dialogue as a form, they both intend to demonstrate an escape from male/male discourse. But does either one of them construct a two-sided conversation?

In fact, Pasithée lectures Iris from a superior position, as we'd expect in a pedagogic dialogue of the sixteenth century; Des Roches cannot imagine that Pasithée could learn anything from Iris. (I have not cited the instances of Iris's comic ignorance in which the text abounds.) Even more, Irigaray interrogates and commands her listener/reader without imagining any identity for her outside the text created by her own monologue. Neither writer gives her interlocutrice a voice firm enough to participate in a genuine dialogue.

But if this is a failing, it is a symptomatic one. In 1570, as in 1970, the entrapment of most women in the phallogocentric circuit foreclosed a mutuality differentiated enough to make real argument among the escapees and the commodities possible. Both texts, in fact, aim their arguments as much or more toward men as toward women. Even so, they both mark a new refusal of sexual norms, and they both register a crucial political fact: women must draw other women into shared resistance before such norms can be dislodged. In spite of the differences in time between these pedagogical dramas, Irigaray's question toward the end of "Quand nos lèvres se parlent" captures their deep connection: "Comment attendre que tu reviennes si, distante, tu ne peux aussi être proche?" How can you be expected to return, if, though distant, you cannot be close at the same time?

11 Afterword

Rosi Braidotti

For Irigaray, feminism is the process of bringing into representation the female feminine subject, that is to say that which is coded as unrepresentable within the dominant discourse of subjectivity. Bringing the unrepresentable into representation in a non-dialectical manner which would not result merely in a reversal of the poles of the gendered opposition Masculine/Feminine, is a work of the imagination. It requires both conceptual and affective creativity. Irigaray translates this problem into the issue of "women's language," i.e. of how to find adequate expression for the margin of difference that female feminist subjects can draw from revisiting the site of the feminine. As the contributors to this volume show in different ways, this process of speaking the silence of women within the language which is one and the same for everyone implies both retrieval (memory) and creation (imagination). The difficulty consists in thinking through and expressing the in-between spaces, the transit-areas, the transitions and the shifts which make up the nomadic itinerary. It's these moments of nomadic transit that are both crucial to the process of theoretical creation and also quite resistant to representation: how does one configure that which goes in-between A and B and does not coincide with either? What counts in the project of sexual difference is the in-between spaces, the itinerary, rather than the final destination. The 'feminine' in question is the trace of this journey, not its arrival-point.

SEXUALITY IN FEMINIST DISCOURSE: TRANS-ATLANTIC DIS-CONNECTIONS

The embodied structure of the subject is a key-term in feminist struggle, and it is not accidental that many of these essays consider embodiment. It is to be understood as neither a biologically nor sociologically fixed category, but rather as a point of overlapping between the physical, the symbolic and the material social conditions. The body is an inter-face, a threshold (an idea that animates Jane Bellamy's essay), a field of intersecting material and symbolic forces, it is a surface where multiple codes (race, sex, class, age, etc.) are inscribed; it is a cultural construction that capitalizes on energies of a heterogeneous, discontinuous, and affective or unconscious nature. This vision of the body contains sexuality as a process and as a constitutive element.

Being embodied means being in and of sexualized matter. This sexual fibre is intrinsically and multiply connected to social and political relations; thus, it is anything but an individualistic entity. Sexuality is simultaneously the most intimate and the most external, socially-driven, power-drenched practice of the self. Sexuality as a social and symbolic, material and semiotic institution is singled out as the primary location of power, in a complex manner which encompasses both macro- and micro-relations. Sex/gender is the social and morphological mode of dualistic assignation of identity and suitable form of erotic agency to subjects that are socialized/sexualized in the polarized dualistic model of Masculine/Feminine implemented in our culture. Sexual difference, the sexualized bi-polarity, is another word for power in both the negative or repressive (*potestas*) and the positive or empowering (*potentia*) meaning of the term. Accordingly, for Irigaray (1985a) the body, and especially sexuality, is perceived as the site of power struggles and contradictions and, consequently, it is viewed critically. But it is also re-visited creatively as a site of re-constitution of the subject.

The feminist theory of sexual difference gives sexuality a central place as the matrix for power-relations in the broad but also most intimate sense of the term. This is a major point of divergence with American feminism. In the USA through the 1990s, the sex/gender dichotomy swung towards the pole of gender with a vengeance, embracing it either as the preface to liberal individual "rights" or in terms of social constructivist "change." In both cases gender occupies the center of the political spectrum to the detriment of issues of sexuality and of sexual difference. It was left to the gay and lesbian and queer campaigners to try and re-write sexuality into the feminist agenda. In this framework, homosexuality is almost always synonymous with transgression or subversion. The tendency is also to critique heterosexuality as the dominant matrix of power and to target specifically the maternal roots of female sexuality for critique. Judith Butler (1990, 1993), following on from the work of Gayle Rubin (1975) and Monique Wittig (1992), makes an important intervention, pointing out that the distinction sex/gender is not only untenable, but also complicitous with structural patterns of exclusion. If anything, argues Butler, it is the always-already sexualized matter that constructs the possibility of this dichotomy in the first place. Butler then proceeds to propose her own theory of performativity as a form of affirmative deconstruction of all identities, even those they taught us to despise.

The 1990s in European feminism, by contrast, are marked by a number of very explicit and politically motivated experimentations around the theme of alternative forms of sexuality, including heterosexuality. Under the impact of psychoanalysis, post-structuralism and other radical critical theories many European feminist movements make sexuality into a public issue, both in terms of political debates concerning regulations of new family forms, gay and lesbian marriages, and in terms of reproductive rights (Griffin and Braidotti 2002). Whereas, as a sequel to the "sex wars," in American public discourse heterosexuality is either silenced or made into the site of litigious court cases focused on male abuse and violence. In Irigaray's work but also in European feminism as a whole this issue is not abandoned to its own static fate, but is rather challenged from a variety of critical corners. One of these is Irigaray's radical feminist call for a different heterosexuality. Because of her psychoanalytic frame of reference, Irigaray states that women's self-love, or primary narcissism, has to be reconstructed as the necessary premise to a redefinition of the terms of heterosexual encounter in our society. The project of regrounding female sexuality in an empowered sense of self-esteem requires love for and recognition by another woman. This homosexual moment is constitutive of a woman's sense of empowerment in so far as it enables the exploration and the redefinition of sexuality in its wide range of choices and applications (Grosz 1994).

Irigaray is a thinker who places full emphasis on radical heterosexuality and the need to reconstruct a heterosexual social-symbolic contract that does not rest on femino-phobia and hence not on a patriarchal social unconscious, an idea that Harry Berger's contribution considers in detail. Irigaray denounces the delusional nature of identities postulated on the phallogocentric signifier and digs deeper than the sociological expressions of everyday sexism and culturally-enforced misogyny. Her critique touches upon the in-depth roots of a subject whose foundations rest on the rejection of the feminine as the site of an irreparable loss and an unrepresentable grief. This is a structure of "unrepresentability" – which expresses the patriarchal unconscious' unease with all the attributes, qualities, and entitlements which are cast/projected on the feminine: embodiment, natality and hence mortality (this complex connection between mortality and natality is the subject of Theresa Krier's essay), generative powers, and sexual vitality. How to recast these elements in a new socio-symbolic contract is the question which lies at the core of Irigaray's feminist politics by calling for a radically new form of sexuality. In other words, for Irigaray, both heterosexual and homosexual identities are equally problematic in a phallocentric system which reduces everything to the criteria of evaluation and selection of sexual Sameness, or the power of One. Irigaray's emphasis on heterosexuality stresses the radical difference and the role it plays in the constitution of sexuality: we need an "other" sexuality which breaks from the male homosocial bonding induced by the reduction of all human sexualities to a phallic model. The dissymmetry between heterosexuality and homosexuality is made more complex by Irigaray, who introduces instead the notion of differentiation within different forms of homosexuality – first and foremost the difference between homosexuality in women and homosexuality in men.

This radical position also grants a significant role to men in reconstructing their own attachment to phallic parameters of sexual identity. Far as this may sound from the claims of deconstruction and sexual in-between-ness which are advanced by queer theorists, Irigaray's political project is however neither incompatible with nor opposed to homosexual, gay, and lesbian discourses (Braidotti 2002). Her position refuses to place all the burden of the transformation onto gay and queer people and calls into question instead the great majority of self-perpetuating sexually "normal" individuals. Irigaray shows both the intrinsic dysfunctionality and the enduring violence of heterosexual love under the power of the phallic signifier and calls for a drastic realignment of all parties concerned. In so doing she emphasizes the extent to which "feminophobia" still functions in our world and of how some feminist theories are complicitous with it.

In Irigaray's scheme of things, the other-woman (including the mother–daughter dyad) is like a data-bank of missing information which the feminist subject can draw from. Indeed, Ann Rosalind Jones makes this crucial mother–daughter relationship central to her analysis of an early modern dialogue. This exchange repairs ontological losses and accelerates the state of change, transforming the collective space between politicized women into a laboratory of becoming. This is not to say that this subject draws only from other women; on the contrary, Irigaray's heterosexual scheme gives a very ample margin and a high priority to the wealth of exchanges that are possible between the sexes. The ethics of sexual difference has to do with more than differences within each woman and among women: it is marked by sets of irreducible differences which construct the singularity of the subject. In other words: identification with the Feminine and the Masculine is necessary for the constitution of female and male subjects respectively, but it is not sufficient. More is needed – such as concrete and imaginary relations to ethnicity, religion, and other variables – the "other" remains for Irigaray a moving, ungraspable horizon. The yearning for the other – or desire – is also described by Irigaray as the passion of wonder.

The theoretical core of the feminism of sexual difference is the assertion of not-One-ness at the origin of the subject, and hence also within each subject (Braidotti 2002). This non-unitary or complex vision of subjectivity also affects the diversity or multiple differences among women. Both on political and on logical grounds (Frye 1996) the assumption that emphasizing sexual difference is a totalizing move that denies all other differences among women is mistaken. Sexual difference is a marker of multiple differences, first and foremost within each one (radical anti-essentialism) and then also among different "others" (radical politics of difference). I concur with both Whitford (2003) and Deutscher (2003) that Irigaray's conceptual schemes offer important points of cross-reference and applicability to the analysis of other differences, notably ethnic and religious ones.

What is at stake in this feminist project is the redefinition of the entire framework of the subject, not only of its gendered or sexed identity. It is a symbolic transformation of far broader appeal. From self-love to and through the recognition of an-other who is like me, to the engagement in a political project of social and ethical transformation all the way to a new universal that will no longer be colonized by the Same. A vital bond of recognition of woman by woman is the crucial starting point for this process. It is an elemental, basic process of becoming. It's a way of re-processing what Deleuze and Guattari (1980) call the "stolen body" of the little girl under patriarchy. Primary narcissism repairs this ontological theft, in such a way as to re-assert the asymmetry between the sexes.

BODILY MATERIALISM(S)

As the essays in this collection richly demonstrate, this body is a multi-layered text where different meanings and attributes related to the "feminine" have historically sedimented. Psychoanalysis shows that the female body is the screen where male fantasies and castration fears have been projected and performed. As such, it has been metonymically displaced and replaced over and over again. The radical edge of Lacanian politics consists in exploring this reduction of the feminine (imaginary) to women (empirical) and the masculine to men, stressing instead the instability of any subject and the impossibility of being anchored to the imaginary and binary institutions of masculinity and femininity. Exposing this imposture is Lacan's political gesture. What to do about changing any of it, however, is an off-limits question for psychoanalysis. Not so for feminism, of course (Irigaray 1974, 1977a, 1984), where the female body becomes the site for feminist reinscriptions and symbolic reappropriations of woman's subjectivity.

At the core of the debate over sexual difference lies the notion of embodied matter (a question that Jonathan Crewe's essay engages), or bodily materialism in our age, which could be described as one of advanced post-humanism. Even the most convinced social constructivists today argue that the performances of bodies cannot be ascribed exclusively to the social codes or to symbolic and imaginary orders – nor can they be read back into the Holy Scriptures of the DNA Scrolls. Both "nature" and "the body" are slippery categories – that tend to slide towards essentialism; get caught into positivist reductions – or in their opposite: new-age naïve celebrations. In the age of the politics of bio-diversity, the inter-dependence of the natural and the social needs to be explored outside classical, dualistic habits of thought. I prefer a deeply embedded vision of the embodied subject. In the light of contemporary genetics and molecular biology, it is more than feasible to speak of the body as a complex system of self-sustaining forces. The DNA and the cells communicate effectively with each other, transferring vital information. In terms of bio-diversity, we humans are actively and destructively involved in manipulating our environment. Neuro-sciences have increased our understanding of memory and the extent to which the storage and retrieval of information is essential to the progress of the self. This is evidence which can no longer be ignored by critical, Left-leaning intellectuals. Nor need it be left to the delusions of grandeur of professional scientists and their industrial, financial backers. Irigaray's approach to bodily materiality can be of inspiration to develop new levels and forms of understanding about being embodied humans in the age of intelligent machines.

The effect of the contemporary technological revolution – which is marked by the convergence of bio-technologies and information technologies is such, in fact, as to institutionalize the decline of dualistic oppositions between bodily matter and materialized intelligence – mind/body; brain/muscle – which our culture has adopted since the eighteenth century as the dominant model of representation. Contemporary science and technology in fact have reached right into the most intimate layers of the living organism and the structures of the self, dissolving boundaries that had been established by centuries of humanistic thinking. This means that we can now think of the body as an entity that inhabits different material spheres and time-zones simultaneously, and is animated by different speeds and a variety of internal and external clocks which do not necessarily coincide.

As the site of our conscious self-representation and the motor of unconscious self-styling, the "body" remains a central factor for both processes of identification and forms of libidinal and social investment. The body is intelligent matter endowed with the capacity to be affected and to affect and thus to inter-relate. Temporally speaking, on the other hand, a body is an enfleshed memory, that is an organism that endures, lasts – albeit temporarily – by undergoing constant internal modifications following the encounter with other bodies and forces. The key terms are affectivity and inter-relation. A body is an entity which yearns for, and thus actively desires, encounters and inter-relations with others. Irigaray, not unlike Deleuze on this score, supports the vision of desire as the positive longing for inter-connections. In so doing, she goes beyond the psychoanalytic idea of desire as lack structured within a phallocentric economy of self-representation. Affectivity is the heart of the subject, an idea whose early modern roots Harvey elaborates, and this desire to be moved by others is motivated by wonder – the passion of admiration – and by the love of "others": it is therefore hetero-directed, though not normatively hetero-sexual. Love, or positive affectivity, happens in encounters with different bodies and forces which propel the subject forward towards a dynamic horizon of shifting and multiple encounters.

The feminist subject of knowledge is an intensive, multiple subject, functioning in a net of inter-connections. It is non-unitary, non-linear, web-like, embodied and therefore perfectly artificial. As an artifact it is machinic, complex, endowed with multiple capacities for inter-connectedness in the impersonal mode. It is sexed, but it's all over the place. It is abstract and perfectly, operationally real, and one of the main fields of operation is sexual difference. The "feminine" at stake in sexual difference is neither one essentialized entity, nor an immediately accessible one: it is rather a virtual reality, in the sense that it is the effect of a project, a political and conceptual project of transcending the traditional subject position of Woman as the Other of the Same, so as to express her as the multiple other of the Other. This transcendence, however, occurs through the flesh, into embodied locations and not in a flight away from them.

Feminist theory is about multiple and potentially contradictory locations and differences, among women but also within each woman. To account for them, locations are approached as geo-political, but also as time-zones, related to personal, historical, and cultural memory. Feminism is not about restoring another dominant memory, but rather about installing a counter-memory, or an embedded and embodied genealogy. Feminist thinking takes place between the no longer and the not yet, in the in-between zone between wilful, conscious political practice and the not-necessarily conscious yearning for transformation and change. I see feminist theory as the activity aimed at articulating the questions of individual gendered identity with issues related to political subjectivity, the production of knowledge, diversity, and epistemological legitimation.

FEMINIST ETHICS

Irigaray has argued passionately for an ethics of empirically based sexualized subjects involved in processes of transformation. As Alison Martin (2003) points out, the political culture of sexual difference is not only leftist and radical in that it aims at social justice, civil rights, the empowerment of women in public life, but also ethical – in that it wants to keep in mind the larger picture. Thus issues of sustainable development, adequate technologies and respect for nature enter the agenda, but so also does the need to have an ethical system of indexation for the changes and transformations which are induced by the shifting relations within a new socio-symbolic contract – aka "radical heterosexuality." A philosopher of change first and foremost, Irigaray stresses the importance of marking the limits of changes, which are often linked to how much the embodied subject can sustain, process and be empowered and not wounded by. The idea of transcendence through the flesh or the sensible empirical is crucial to the project of transformation which finds both its site and its limit in the body itself.

Of special concern to me and the writers of these essays is the affirmative dimension of this ethical project, namely how to move beyond the aporia of deconstruction, or a post-Lacanian hystrionic exacerbation of the guilt and aggression that fuel the phallic symbolic (Žižek 1992). How can we grab the historic chance to create the new and thus avoid repetitions of the Same? Affirming sexual difference is a positive passion that implies loyalty, not so much to what one is, or could be, as to what one will have been. This is a new form of activism, which takes seriously the active force of affects understood as affirmative ethical inputs. I call them positive processes of becoming which are neither abstract nor disengaged from concrete material and historical situations. They are processes of actualization or materialization of qualitative shifts that occur across a number of interrelations, or in-between spaces: between different species; human/non-human actors; different categories; masculine/feminine, or European/native; and between different forces: negative/positive or reactive/active. This transformative project is utopian only in the sense that it traces a path of becoming or transformation. It implies the transcendence of the present, not in a flight away from the body but rather as a radical exploration of the immanence of the flesh. Indeed, Irigaray's interest in the vitalism and materialism of early periods contributes possibilities to this hope for the future. This utopian impulse in turn implies a different approach to the spatio-temporal co-ordinates that we have learnt to recognize as "the body," and of its immense vitality – which redefines the boundaries between life, death and the many degrees of in-between.

This is where the question of time becomes crucial, as Barbara Estrin's essay, for example, implies. One of the many positive sides of feminist ethics is that one gets used to time loops, or a permanent state of jetlag. A feminist critical position assumes the dislocation of the linearity of time and hence the necessity to inhabit different and even potentially contradictory time zones at the same time: a sort of trip through chrono-topia. On the theoretical level, feminists have developed crucial critiques of ideologies, revisions of the symbolic and a vast array of counter-models and paradigms to configure the shifts of subjectivity actually in progress in our globalized world. Those who were still hoping to use such immense creativity to correct the mistakes of the patriarchal order soon realized they would run out of time before they could reach their aim. One of the possible figurations of oppression is being systematically behind: living in one time zone behind the times – like reading yesterday's paper. It is not so much being second-best as being minus-one.

Irigaray's feminism affirms political and ethical passions. It designs tools and road maps by which to establish values, not in the normative mode, but in the sense of evaluation of the interaction with a large variety of others, including external objects and projects. This 'intensive' reading of feminist theory expresses a non-unitary – in my terms 'nomadic' subject – that is opposed to classical humanism, or liberal notions of the individual, but also to facile postmodern celebrations of fragmentation for its own sake. In opposition to the urge to complete the loss of specification or marking of the subject, this position expresses also my desire to defend the relevance of that historically obsolete institution known as the "feminine." As I suggested earlier, it is neither as an essentialized entity, nor as an immediately accessible one, femininity is rather a virtual reality, in the sense that it is the effect of a political and conceptual project aimed at transcending the traditional subject position of Woman as other. This transcendence, however, occurs through the flesh, into enfleshed locations and not in a flight away from the body, in an embodied and embedded manner.

Feminism, like all critical theories, can express affirmative forces and thus liberate in those who partake of it a yearning for freedom, dignity, justice, lightness, and joyfulness. These values can also be translated both into dogmatic gloom and into more constructive rational beliefs and policies. They form in any case a substratum of affect that activates the movement in the first place. In feminism, as elsewhere in critical theory and practice, the wager is to move beyond the negative stasis and the slave morality of an oppositional culture. One must avoid the deadly serious priestly revolutionary zeal of *dogma* and *doxa* joining forces within the gravitational pull of a new normative order. If politics begins with our passions, then what I yearn for is the gay knowledge of an affirmative critical spirit.

SEXUAL DIFFERENCE AS THE PRINCIPLE OF NOT-ONE

Sexual difference, understood as the principle of not-one, in Lévi-Strauss's sense of "zero institution," fulfills the essential function of making a fundamental break at and as the site of origin of the subject. What needs to be broken is the fantasy of unity, totality, and one-ness. This is what the psychoanalytic idea of the original loss stands for: it is the pound of flesh one needs to hand over in order to enter the socio-symbolic contract. What is knocked out from the subject's psychic landscape is the delusion of One-ness, the phantasy of omnipotence, which leans upon the empirical referent that is the closest for the newly-born, namely the mother. This "leaning-upon," however, and the symbolic marking it operates, must not be confused with the symbolic function it enacts. The difference between poststructuralist, Lacanian psychoanalysis and other psychoanalytic schools, as for instance object-relation theory, rests precisely on this point: in Lacanian terms, the empirical does not equate or comprehensively include the symbolic, but it merely props it up. The mother is the logical operator of a number of symbolic functions which are structural. A mere focus on this empirical level, therefore, is likely to miss the point altogether and thus leave the symbolic system untouched. To recognize this basic, ego-deflating principle is a gesture that marks a syntactical necessity, a zero-level out of which an interactive vision of the subject can begin to emerge. That recognition of alterity in the sense of incommensurable loss and an unpayable outstanding debt to others entails the awareness that one is the effect of irrepressible flows of encounters, interactions, affectivity, and desire, which one is not in charge of.

This humbling experience of not-Oneness, far from opening the doors to relativism, anchors the subject in an ethical bond to alterity, to the multiple and external others that are constitutive of that entity which, out of laziness and habit, we call the "self." The split, or not-one nature of the subject, entails the recognition of a pre-discursive structure of the "self," of a necessary loss of that which is always already there – an affective, interactive entity endowed with intelligent flesh and an embodied mind. The totality and the always-already-thereness of the corporeal self is that which must become foreclosed, and thus remain inaccessible to the reduced, but more functional unit that will become the socialized subject. As such, the totality and priority of the enfleshed corporeal subject – rooted in desire – is that which remains un-thought at the heart of the thinking subject, because it is what drives him/her in the first place.

As I argued previously (Braidotti 2002) the pathetic-despotic face of femininity in the historical era of advanced technologies bears a privileged link to whiteness as a term that signifies Sameness and thus indexes access to power and to the structural advantages that being white entails. This mutation takes place in the spectral economy of globalization, propelled by the convergence between the new media and information technologies and bio-technologies. In such a context, I want to plead most definitely for a new brand of vitalistic materialism that would address these contradictions and instaurate a materialist culture of affirmation, not of euphoria. I see radical immanence and sustainable ethics as a strategy to dis-intoxicate ourselves from the fumes of prosthetic promises of perfectibility and face instead the specific complexities of our embodied subjectivity in the age of *zoe-power*.

In this framework, I want to defend sexual difference as a political project for the following reasons. First, as a cartography of contemporary geo-political relations, which see the return of essentialized forms of sexual dichotomy and hence a resurgence of discrimination against women on a global scale. Second, as a political platform to articulate and empower the female feminist subjects towards alternative social and symbolic spaces. I see sexual difference as a political project and hence as a site of transformation of the subject. I call this the project of the "virtual feminine" and of "'virtual/masculinities." This alternative subject position is multi-layered and implicated with complex sites of articulation of its complexities. It is inter-relational and intersectional, but also split within itself, in a myriad of internal self-differentiations and discrepancies. It is a resolutely non-unitary subject.

This enchanted, anti-essentialist, high-tech vitalism echoes the ideas of Irigaray about the subject as a bodily human entity, sensitive flesh framed by the skin (a notion that has affinities with Hollywood's discussion of the erotics of surface). I find it significant that Irigaray turns to non-Christian religions, notably Judaism in the philosophy of Levinas and Buddhist practices like yoga in her more recent work. In the reading of Levinas, which Grant Williams uses in his examination of the blazon, Luce Irigaray writes an apology of the caress as a mode of approaching the other – the erotic, respectful touching of the other's skin is distinctly posed as the basis for an ethics of sexual difference. This respectful contemplation of the contained boundaries of an other's life – his skin-cloud, enfleshed existence – is also a response to the philosophy of excess in Bataille. This cruel and violent attempt to break beyond the enclosed space of the embodied self leads him to theorize both the inevitability of violence, and also the desirability of a transcendence which requires – ontologically – the consumption of an other's body. As in Bataille's un-reconstructed phallogocentrism, an other's body is preferentially the body of the other, of woman as "other-of-the-same" – the specular, necessary and necessarily devalorized other – Bataille's theory of transcendence is also an apology of female sacrifice.

Irigaray's emphasis on the "enchanted materialism" of feminine morphology constitutes a parallel but dissonant project in relation to the nomadic anti-foundationalism of Deleuze. The ethics of sexual difference and the ethics of sustainable nomadic subjectivity are two faces of the same coin: that of an enfleshed, immanent subject-in-becoming, for whom life is embodied, embedded, and eroticized. To present them as mutually incompatible is not doing justice to either. I think instead that a parallel reading of Irigaray's ethics of sexual difference (and the notion of the sensible transcendental) and Deleuze's sustainable nomadic ethics (transcendental empiricism) can be mutually illuminating. Both predicate the reversal of the tide of dialectical negativity and support an ethics of affirmation and positive desire. Deleuze's empirical transcendental and Irigaray's sensible transcendental are bodily locations for the elaboration of embodied, situated ethics of sustainability. The model of alternative ethics proposed by radically immanent philosophies of difference such as Irigaray's, Deleuze's, or my own feminist brand of philosophical nomadism implies a non-hierarchical idea of transcendence and a non-binary model of inter-relation or inter-subjectivity. That Irigaray chooses to focus her priority on the reconstruction of the female imaginary in order to work towards the empowerment of women, whereas Deleuze postulates the feminine as the threshold to a more generalized becoming-minoritarian, does not alter the commonalities between their two projects.

Therefore, what is at stake in sustainable ethics is not the feminine as codified in the phallogocentric code of the patriarchal imaginary, but rather the feminine as project, as movement of destabilization of identity and hence of becoming. I call this the "virtual feminine," and I connect it to the social and symbolic project of redefinition of female subjectivity which is undertaken by feminism. Irigaray's discussion of a virtual feminine "symbolic" expresses both theoretically and ethically the desire to find a transmissible form for this feminine voice. Crucial to this project is the empowerment of the embodied female subject, in flesh as well as in word. While holding on to the empirical foundations of a feminist subject that is in a process of becoming other – than the eternal feminine of Man – the feminist practice of sexual difference nomadizes the subject. The feminine gets redefined as a moving horizon, a fluctuating path, a recipe for transformation, motion, becoming. This non-teleological understanding of the feminist process of redefining the feminine is combined in Irigaray's work with close attention to the body and to bodily morphology, to the flesh and blood of female embodiment and the specific sensorial experiences related to it, including the importance of touch and feeling over seeing and the scopic. This passionate, intelligent, and memory-driven flesh is at the heart of Irigaray's carnal materialism. Moreover, the "virtual feminine" project opens up to issues of universality and transcendence. Irigaray locates this corporeal universal in the specifically situated efforts by female feminist subjects to re-conceptualize the spatio-temporal territory of the feminine as a transit-zone between themselves.

The reference to the "universal" is a qualitative leap from individual experience to collective practice that aims to generate representations of general relevance. In other words, the universal is located in the specific singularity of an immanent subject. More importantly, the political project of feminism consists in framing the space between different women, conscious of their differences, who both recognize each other's efforts and empower one another to go further. In other words, for Irigaray, "virtual feminine" is a collective project that rests upon the presence of at least another subject, first of all another woman as the threshold through which to activate paths of becoming-subject in alternative ways. As both an ethical and political quest, it is a project fit for the third millennium.

Bibliography

Adelman, Janet (1992) *Suffocating Mothers: Fantasies of Maternal Origin in Shakespeare's Plays*, Hamlet *to* The Tempest, London and New York: Routledge.

Adelman, Janet (1997) "Iago's Alter Ego: Race as Projection in *Othello,*" *Shakespeare Quarterly* 48 (2): 125–44.

Aelred of Rievaulx (1971a) *Treatises and Pastoral Prayer*, trans. T. Berkeley, M. P. Macpherson, and R. P. Lawson, Kalamazoo, MI: Cistercian Publications.

Aelred of Rievaulx (1971b) *Opera Omnia I: Opera Ascetica*, A. Hoste and C. H. Talbot (eds) in *Corpus Christianorum Continuatio Mediaevalis*, Turnhout: Brepols.

Agamben, Giorgio (1998) *Homo Sacer: Sovereign Power and the Bare Life*, trans. Daniel Heller-Roazen, Stanford: Stanford University Press.

Alpers, Paul J. (1967) *The Poetry of* The Faerie Queene, Princeton: Princeton University Press.

Angela of Foligno (1985) *Il Libro della Beata Angela da Foligno*, L. Their and A. Calufetti (ed.), Grottaferrata: Editiones Collegii S. Bonventurae ad Claras Aquas.

Angela of Foligno (1993) *The Complete Works*, trans. P. Lachance, New York: Paulist Press.

Anzieu, Didier (1989) *The Skin Ego: A Psychoanalytic Approach to the Self*, trans. C. Turner, New Haven: Yale University Press.

Areford, David S. (1998) "The Passion Measured: A Late-medieval Diagram of the Body of Christ" in A. A. MacDonald, H. N. B. Ridderbos and R. M. Schlusemann (eds) *The Body Broken: Passion Devotion in Late-medieval Culture*, Groningen: Egbert Forsten.

Arendt, Hannah (1958) *The Human Condition*, Chicago: University of Chicago Press.

Arendt, Hannah (1987) "Labor, Work, Action" in J. W. Bernauer (ed.) *Amor Mundi: Explorations in the Faith and Thought of Hannah Arendt*, Dordrecht and Boston: Martinus Nijhoff Publishers.

Aristotle (1957) *On Sense and Sensible Objects*, trans. W. S. Hett, Cambridge, MA: Harvard University Press.

Ascoli, Albert (1987) *Ariosto's Bitter Harmony: Crisis and Evasion in the Italian Renaissance*, Princeton: Princeton University Press.

Bailey, Cyril (1928) *The Greek Atomists and Epicurus*, Oxford: Clarendon Press.

Baker, Moira P. (1991) "'The Uncanny Stranger on Display:' The Female Body in Sixteenth- and Seventeenth-Century Love Poetry," *South Atlantic Review* 56 (2): 7–25.

Bartels, Emily C. (1990) "Making More of the Moor: Aaron, Othello and Renaissance Refashionings of Race," *Shakespeare Quarterly* 41 (4): 433–54.

Bataille, Georges (1970–88) *Oeuvres Complètes*, 12 vols, Paris: Gallimard.

Bateson, F. W. (1951) "Contributions to a Dictionary of Critical Terms," reprinted in John R. Roberts (ed.) *Essential Articles for the Study of John Donne's Poetry*, Hassocks, Sussex UK: Harvester, 1975.

Batstone, William (1997) "Virgilian Didaxis: Value and Meaning in the *Georgics*" in C. Martindale (ed.) *The Cambridge Companion to Virgil*, Cambridge: Cambridge University Press.

Benhabib, Seyla (1992) *The Situated Self*, Cambridge: Polity Press.

Berger, Harry, Jr. (1989) "The Fight for the Future Perfect," in his *Imaginary Audition: Shakespeare on Stage and Page*, Berkeley: University of California Press, 104–37.

Berger, Harry, Jr. (1996) "Impertinent Trifling: Desdemona's handkerchief," *Shakespeare Quarterly* 47 (3): 235–50.

Bernard of Clairvaux (1957–77) *Sancti Bernardi Opera*, J. Leclercq, C. H. Talbot, and H. M. Rochais (eds) 8 vols, Rome: Editiones Cistercienses.

Bernard of Clairvaux (1979) *On the Song of Songs III*, trans. K. Walsh and I. M. Edmonds, Kalamazoo: Cistercian Publications.

Berry, Philippa (1994) "The Burning Glass" in C. Burke, N. Schor, and M. Whitford (eds.) *Engaging with Irigaray*, New York: Columbia University Press: 229–46.

Bestul, Thomas (1996) *Texts of the Passion: Latin Devotional Literature and Medieval Society*, Philadelphia: University of Pennsylvania Press.

Betts, Hannah (1998) "'The Image of This Queene so Quaynt': The Pornographic Blazon 1588–1603" in Julia M. Walker (ed.) *Dissing Elizabeth: Negative Representations of Gloriana*, Durham, North Carolina: Duke University Press.

Biblia Sacra Iuxta Vulgatam Versionem (1969) Stuttgart: Deutsche Bibelgesellschaft.

Biow, Douglas (1996) *Mirabile Dictu: Representations of the Marvelous in Medieval and Renaissance Epic*, Ann Arbor: University of Michigan Press.

Bishop, T. G. (1996) *Shakespeare and the Theatre of Wonder*, Cambridge, New York: Cambridge University Press.

Bollas, Christopher (1987) *The Shadow of the Object: Psychoanalysis of the Unthought Known*, New York: Columbia University Press.

Bollas, Christopher (1995) *Cracking Up: The Work of Unconscious Experience*, New York: Hill and Wang.

Bollas, Christopher (1992) "Aspects of Self-Experiencing" in *Being a Character: Psychoanalysis and Self-Experience*, New York: Hill and Wang.

Bonaventure (1882–1902) *Bonaventurae Opera Omnia*, PP. Collegii S. Bonaventurae (ed.), 11 vols., Quaracchi: Collegium S. Bonaventurae.

Bonaventure (1960) *The Works of Bonaventure ... I Mystical Opuscula I*, trans. J. de Vinck, Paterson, N J: St Anthony Guild Press.

Bordo, Susan R. (1987) *The Flight to Objectivity: Essays on Cartesianism and Culture*, Albany, NY: State University of New York Press.

Bourdieu, Pierre (1990) *The Logic of Practice*, trans. Richard Nice (*Le sens Pratique*, Les Éditions de Minuit, 1980), Stanford, CA: Stanford University Press.

Braidotti, Rosi (1998) "Sexual Difference Theory" in Alison M. Jaggar and Iris Marion Young (eds.) *A Companion to Feminist Philosophy*, Oxford: Blackwell.

Braidotti, Rosi (2002) *Metamorphoses: Towards a Materialist Theory of Becoming*, Cambridge: Polity Press.

Braidotti, Rosi (2003) "Becoming-Woman: Or Sexual Difference Revisited," *Theory, Culture & Society* 20 (3): 43–64.

Brennan, Teresa (2000) *Exhausting Modernity: Grounds for a New Economy*, London and New York: Routledge.

Brown, Peter (1988) *The Body and Society: Men, Women and Sexual Renunciation in Early Christianity*, New York: Columbia University Press.

Burke, Carolyn (1989) "Romancing the Philosophers: Luce Irigaray" in Dianne Hunter (ed.) *Seduction and Theory*, Chicago: University of Illinois Press.

Burke, Carolyn (1994a) "Translation Modified: Irigaray in English," in C. Burke, N. Schor and M. Whitford (eds) *Engaging with Irigaray: Feminist Philosophy and Modern European Thought*, New York: Columbia University Press: 249–61.

Burke, Carolyn (1994b) "Irigaray Through the Looking Glass" in C. Burke, N. Schor, and M. Whitford, eds, *Engaging with Irigaray: Feminist Philosophy and Modern European Thought*, New York: Columbia University Press: 37–56.

Butler, Judith (1990) *Gender Trouble: Feminism and the Subversion of Identity*, New York: Routledge.

Butler, Judith (1993) Bodies That Matter: On the Discursive Limits of 'Sex', London and New York: Routledge.

Butler, Judith (1994) "Bodies that Matter" in C. Burke, N. Schor and M. Whitford (eds) *Engaging with Irigaray: Feminist philosophy and Modern European Thought*, New York: Columbia University Press: 141–73.

Butler, Judith and Cornell, D. with Cheah, P. and Grosz, Elizabeth (1998) "The Future of Sexual Difference: An Interview with Butler and Cornell," *Diacritics*, 28: 19–42.

Bynum, Catherine Walker (1982) *Jesus as Mother: Studies in the Spirituality of the High Middle Ages*, Berkeley: University of California Press.

Bynum, Catherine Walker (1987) *Holy Feast and Holy Fast: The Religious Significance of Food to Medieval Women*, Berkeley: University of California Press.

Bynum, Catherine Walker (1991) *Fragmentation and Redemption: Essays on Gender and the Human Body in Medieval Religion*, New York: Zone Books.

Bynum, Catherine Walker (1995) "Why All the Fuss About the Body?: A Medievalist's Perspective," *Critical Inquiry* 22: 1–33.

Bynum, Catherine Walker (2002) "The Blood of Christ in the Later Middle Ages," *Church History* 71: 685–714.

Caciola, N. (2000) "Mystics, Demoniacs, and the Physiology of Spirit Possession in Medieval Europe," *Comparative Studies in Society and History* 42: 268–306.

Callaghan, Dympna (2000) *Shakespeare Without Women: Representing Gender and Race on the Renaissance Stage*, London: Routledge.

Caretti, Lanfranco (ed.) (1954) *Ludovico Ariosto: Orlando Furioso*, Milan: Riccardo Ricciardi.

Carruthers, Mary (1998) *The Craft of Thought: Meditation, Rhetoric, and the Making of Images*, 400–1200, Cambridge: Cambridge University Press.

Castoriadis, Cornelius (1987) *The Imaginary Institution of Society*, trans. Kathleen Blamey (Institution Imaginaire de la Société, Editions de Seuil, 1975) Cambridge: Polity Press.

Castoriadis, Cornelius (1997) *World in Fragments: Writings on Politics, Society, Psychoanalysis, and the Imagination*, ed. and trans. David Ames Curtis, Stanford, CA: Stanford University Press.

Cavarero, Adriana (1995a) *In Spite of Plato: A Feminist Rewriting of Ancient Philosophy*, trans. Serena Anderlini-D'Onofrio and Áine O' Healy, New York: Routledge.

Cavarero, Adriana (1995b) "Thinking Difference," *Symposium* 49 (2): 120–30.

Cavell, Stanley (1995) *Contesting Tears: The Hollywood Melodrama of the Unknown Woman*, Chicago: University of Chicago Press.

Cavell, Stanley (1981) *Pursuits of Happiness: The Hollywood Comedy of Remarriage*, Cambridge: Harvard University Press.

Chambers, Ross (1991) *Room for Maneuver: Reading Oppositional Narrative*, Chicago: University of Chicago Press.

Chanter, Tina (1995) *Ethics of Eros: Irigaray's Rewriting of the Philosophers*, New York: Routledge.

Charpentier, Françoise (ed.) (1983) "Les Blasons Anatomiques (1536–43)" in Louise Labé, *Oeuvres Poétiques* & Pernette du Guillet, *Rymes*, Paris: Gallimard.

Clay, Diskin (1983) *Lucretius and Epicurus*, Ithaca: Cornell University Press.

Clément, Catherine (1983) *The Lives and Legend of Jacques Lacan*, trans. Arthur Goldhammer, New York: Columbia University Press. (First French publ. 1981, *Vies et Legendes de Jacques Lacan*, Editions Bernard Grasset).

Clements, A. L. (ed.) (1966) *John Donne's Poetry*, New York: Norton.

Coffin, Charles Monroe (1958) *John Donne and the New Philosophy*, New York: The Humanities Press.

Cornell, Drucilla (1991) *Beyond Accommodation: Ethical Feminism, Deconstruction, and the Law*, New York: Routledge.

Corthell, Ronald (1997) *Ideology and Desire in Renaissance Poetry: The Subject of Donne*, Detroit: Wayne State University Press.

Dalarun, Jacques (1995) "Angèle de Foligno a-t-elle Existé?" in *Alla Signoria: Mélanges Offerts à Noëlle de la Blanchardière*, Rome: École Française de Rome.

de Beauvoir, Simone (1952) *The Second Sex*, trans. H. M. Parshley, New York: Vintage.

De Grazia, Margreta (2001) "Spenser's Antic Disposition," keynote speech at the Spenser Conference, Cambridge, July 2001; summarized in *The Spenser Review* 32 (3): 20–1.

de la Primaudaye, Pierre (1594) *The French Academie*, trans. T. B., London: Eliot's Court Press.

de Lauretis, Teresa (1987) *Technologies of Gender: Essays on Theory, Film, and Fiction*, Bloomington: Indiana University Press.

Debus, Allen G. (1965) *The English Paracelsians*, London: Oldbourne Book Co., Ltd.

Deleuze, Gilles and Felix Guattari (1972) *L'anti-Oedipe: Capitalisme et Schizophrénie I*, Paris: Minuit; trans. R. Hurley, M. Seem and H. R. Lane (1977) *Anti-Oedipus: Capitalism and Schizophrenia*, New York: Viking Press/Richard Seaver.

Deleuze, Gilles and Felix Guattari (1980) *Mille Plateaux: Capitalisme et Schizophrénie II*, Paris: Minuit; trans. Brian Massumi (1987) *A Thousand Plateaus: Capitalism and Schizophrenia*, Minneapolis: University of Minnesota Press.

Des Roches, Catherine and Madeleine (1583) *Les Secondes Oeuvres de Mes-Dames Des Roches de Poictiers, Mere et Fille*, Poitiers: Nicolas Courtois; reprinted in Anne R. Larsen (ed.) (1998) *Les Secondes Oeuvres*, Geneva: Droz.

Despres, Denise (1989) *Ghostly Sights: Visual Meditation in Late Medieval Literature*, Norman: Pilgrim Books.

Detienne, Marcel and Vernant, Jean-Pierre (1974) *Les Ruses de l'intelligence: La Mètis des Grecs*, Paris: Flammarion.

Deutscher, Penelope (2002) *A Politics of the Impossible Difference: The Later Work of Luce Irigaray*, New York: Routledge.

Deutscher, Penelope (2003) "'Between East and West' and the Politics of 'Cultural Ingenuity': Irigaray on Cultural Differences'" in *Theory, Culture & Society* 20 (3): 65–76.

Donne, John (1959) *Devotions Upon Emergent Occasions*, Ann Arbor: University of Michigan Press.

Donne, John (1969) *Ignatius His Conclave*, T. S. Healy, S. J. (ed.) Oxford: Clarendon Press.

Donne, John (1985) *The Complete Poems*, C. A. Patrides (ed.) London: J. M. Dent & Sons, Ltd.

Donne, John (2001) *The Complete Poetry and Selected Prose of John Donne*, Charles Coffin (ed.) New York: Modern Library.

Dubrow, Heather (1995) *Echoes of Desire: English Petrarchism and its Counterdiscourses*, Ithaca and London: Cornell University Press.

Dutton, M. (1987) "Eat, Drink and Be Merry: The Eucharistic Spirituality of the Cistercian Fathers" in John R. Sommerfeldt (ed.) *Erudition at God's Service*, Kalamazoo: Cistercian Publications.

Elliott, D. (1997) "The Physiology of Rapture and Female Spirituality" in Peter Biller and A. J. Minnis (eds) *Medieval Theology and the Natural Body*, Woodbridge: York Medieval Press.

Empedocles (2001) *The Poem of Empedocles*, ed. and trans. Brad Inwood (rev. ed.), Toronto: Univerity of Toronto Press.

Empson, William (1993) "Donne the Space Man" in John Haffenden (ed.) *Essays on Renaissance Literature, vol. I: Donne and the New Philosophy*, Cambridge: Cambridge University Press, 1993.

Erasmus, Desiderius (1512) *De Copia*, trans. B. I. Knot in C. R. Thompson (ed.) (1978) *Literary and Education Writings 2*, vol. 24 of *The Collected Works of Erasmus*, Toronto: University of Toronto Press.

Erickson, Peter (2002) "Images of White Identity in *Othello*" in Philip C. Kolin (ed.) Othello: *New Critical Essays*, New York: Routledge.

Farrell, Joseph (1991) *Vergil's* Georgics *and the Traditions of Ancient Epic: The Art of Allusion in Literary History*, Oxford: Oxford University Press.

Ferrante, Joan (1998) "'Scribe quae vides et audis': Hildegard, Her Language and Her Secretaries" in D. Townsend and A. Taylor (eds) *The Tongue of the Fathers: Gender and Ideology in Twelfth-century Latin*, Philadelphia: University of Pennsylvania Press.

Findlen, Paula (2002) "Ideas of Mind: Gender and Knowledge in the Seventeenth Century," *Hypatia: A Journal of Feminist Philosophy* 17 (1): 183–96.

Fineman, Joel (1994) "The Sound of O in *Othello*: The Real of the Tragedy of Desire" in Gerard Barthelemy (ed.) *Critical Essays on Shakespeare's* Othello, New York: G. K. Hall.

Finucci, Valeria and Schwartz, Regina (eds) (1994) *Desire in the Renaissance: Psychoanalysis and Literature*, Princeton: Princeton University Press.

Fleming, J. V. (1977) *An Introduction to Franciscan Literature of the Middle Ages*, Chicago: Franciscan Herald Press.

Fletcher, Angus (1991) *Colors of the Mind: Conjectures on Thinking in Literature*, Cambridge: Harvard University Press.

Fletcher, Angus (2003) "Living Magnets and the Legacy of Paracelsianism in Donne's 'An Anatomie of the World'," paper presented at the annual meeting of the Modern Language Association of America, San Diego, December 2003.

Foucault, Michel (1985; repr. 1990) *The Use of Pleasure,* New York: Vintage Books.

Foucault, Michel (1986; repr. 1988) *The Care of the Self,* New York: Random House.

Fowler, Alastair (1975) *Conceitful Thought: The Interpretation of English Renaissance Poems,* Edinburgh: Edinburgh University.

Freud, Sigmund (1900) *The Interpretation of Dreams*, trans. James Strachey in James Strachey (ed.) (1953) *The Standard Edition of the Complete Works of Sigmund Freud*, vols. IV-V, London: Hogarth Press.

Freud, Sigmund (1920) *Beyond the Pleasure Principle*, trans. James Strachey in James Strachey (ed.) (1942) *The Standard Edition of the Complete Works of Sigmund Freud*, vol. XVIII, London: Hogarth Press.

Frye, Marilyn (1996) "The Necessity of Differences: Constructing a Positive Category of Women," *Signs* 21 (4): 991–1010.

Frye, Susan (2000) "Staging Women's Relations to Textiles in Shakespeare's *Othello* and *Cymbeline*," in Peter Erickson and Clark Hulse (eds) *Early Modern Visual Culture: Representation, Race and Empire in Renaissance England*, Philadelphia: University of Pennsylvania Press.

Fulton, R. (2002) *From Judgment to Passion: Devotion to Christ and the Virgin Mary, 800–1200*, New York: Columbia University Press.

Fumerton, Patricia (1991) "'Secret Arts': Elizabethan Miniatures and Sonnets" in *Cultural Aesthetics: Renaissance Literature and the Practice of Social Ornament*, Chicago: University of Chicago Press.

Fuss, Diana (1989) *Essentially Speaking: Feminism, Nature, and Difference*, New York: Routledge.

Gage, John (1993) *Color and Culture: Practice and Meaning from Antiquity to Abstraction*, Boston, Toronto, London: Brown, Little, and Co.

Gallop, Jane (1982) *The Daughter's Seduction: Feminism and Psychoanalysis*, Ithaca: Cornell University Press.

Gallop, Jane (1988) *Thinking Through the Body,* New York: Columbia University Press.

Gatens, Moira and Lloyd, Genevieve (1999) *Collective Imaginings: Spinoza Past and Present*, London and New York: Routledge.

Gerson, Lloyd P. (1994) *Plotinus*, New York: Routledge.

Gerson, Lloyd P. (ed.) (1996) *The Cambridge Companion to Plotinus*, Cambridge: Cambridge University Press.

Gim, Lisa (1998) "Blasoning 'the Princesse Paragon': The workings of George Puttenham's 'False Semblant' in his *Partheniades* to Queen Elizabeth," *Modern Language Studies* 28 (3): 75–89.

Goldberg, Jonathan (1985) "Shakespearean Inscriptions: The Voicing of Power" in Patricia Parker and Geoffrey Hartman (eds) *Shakespeare and the Question of Theory*, London: Methuen.

Goldhill, Simon (1995) *Foucault's Virginity: Ancient Erotic Fiction and the History of Sexuality*, New York: Cambridge University Press.

Graham, Jorie (2000) *Swarm*, New York: Ecco Press.

Grant, W. L. (1965) *Neo-Latin Literature and the Pastoral*, Chapel Hill: University of North Carolina Press.

Gray, D. (1963) "The Five Wounds of Our Lord," *Notes and Queries*, n. s. 10.

Griffin, Gabriele and Braidotti, Rosi (eds) (2002) *Thinking Differently: A Reader in European Women's Studies*, London: Zed Books.

Grosz, Elizabeth (1989) *Sexual Subversions: Three French Feminists*, Sydney: Allen & Unwin.

Grosz, Elizabeth (1994) "The Hetero and the Homo: The Sexual Ethics of Luce Irigaray" in C. Burke, N. Schor and M. Whitford (eds) *Engaging with Irigaray: Feminist Philosophy and Modern European Thought*, New York: Columbia University Press.

Guibbory, Achsah (ed.) (1990a), "Interpreting 'Aire and Angels'," special issue of the *John Donne Journal* 9 (1).

Guibbory, Achsah (ed.) (1990b) "Donne, The Idea of Woman, and the Experience of Love" in Achsah Guibbory (ed.) (1990a), "Interpreting 'Aire and Angels'," special issue of the *John Donne Journal* 9 (1): 105–12.

Guss, Donald L. (1966) *John Donne, Petrarchist: Italianate Conceits and Love Theory in the* Songs and Sonnets, Detroit: Wayne State University Press.

Hall, H. M. (1914) *Idylls of Fishermen: A History of the Literary Species*, New York: Columbia University Press.

Halperin, David M., Winkler, John J. and Zeitlin, Froma I. (eds) (1990) *Before Sexuality: The Construction of Erotic Experience in the Ancient Greek World*, Princeton: Princeton University Press.

Hamburger, J. (1990) *The Rothschild Canticles: Art and Mysticism in Flanders and the Rhineland Circa 1300*, New Haven: Yale University Press.

Hamburger, J. (1997) *Nuns as Artists: The Visual Culture of a Medieval Convent*, Berkeley: University of California Press.

Hamburger, J. (1998) *The Visual and the Visionary*, New York: Zone Books.

Hamilton, A. C. (ed.) (1977) *Edmund Spenser: The Faerie Queene*, London and New York: Longman.

Haraway, Donna (1991) *Simians, Cyborgs and Women: The Reinvention of Nature*, London: Free Association Books.

Harris, Jonathan Gil (1998) *Foreign Bodies and the Body Politic: Discourses of Social Pathology in Early Modern England*, Cambridge: Cambridge University Press.

Harris, Victor (1949) *All Coherence Gone*, Chicago: University of Chicago Press.

Harvey, Elizabeth D. (1992/1995) *Ventriloquized Voices: Feminist Theory and English Renaissance Texts*, New York: Routledge.

Harvey, Elizabeth D. (ed.) (2003) *Sensible Flesh: On Touch in Early Modern Culture*, Philadelphia: University of Pennsylvania Press.

Hayles, Katherine (1999) *How We Became Posthuman: Virtual Bodies In Cybernetics, Literature and Informatics,* Chicago: University of Chicago Press.

Heidegger, Martin (1968), *What Is Called Thinking?* trans. J. Glenn Gray, New York: Harper & Row. (Original German publ. 1954.)

Heidegger, Martin (1959) *Discourse on Thinking*, trans. John M. Anderson and E. Hans Freund (1966), New York: Harper & Row.

Heidegger, Martin (1977) "Modern Science, Metaphysics, and Mathematics" in David Krell (ed.) *Basic Writings*, New York: Harper & Row.

Herbert, George (1974) *The English Poems of George Herbert*, ed. C.A. Patrides, London: Dent.

Hirsch, David A. Hedrich (1991) "Donne's Atomies and Anatomies: Deconstructed Bodies and the Resurrection of Atomic Theory," *SEL 1500–1900* 31 (1): 69–94.

Hodge, Joanna (1994) "Irigaray Reading Heidegger" in C. Burke, N. Schor and M. Whitford (eds) *Engaging with Irigaray: Feminist Philosophy and Modern European Thought*, New York: Columbia University Press.

Hollywood, Amy (2002) *Sensible Ecstasy: Mysticism, Sexual Difference, and the Demands of History*, Chicago: University of Chicago Press.

Hollywood, Amy (forthcoming) "Mysticism and Mourning: Margaret Ebner's Revelations."

Holmberg, I. E. (1997) "The Sign of Mètis," *Arethusa* 30 (1): 1–33.

Homer (1951) *The Iliad*, trans. Richmond Lattimore, Chicago: University of Chicago Press.

Homer (1967) *The Odyssey*, trans. Richmond Lattimore. New York: Harper & Row.

Hunter, Dianne (ed.) (1989) *Seduction and Theory: Readings of Gender, Representation, and Rhetoric,* Chicago: University of Illinois Press.

Huntington, P. (1998) *Ecstatic Subjects, Utopia, and Recognition: Kristeva, Heidegger, Irigaray*, Albany: State University of New York Press.

Jabès, Edmond (1963) *Le Livre des Questions*, Paris: Gallimard.

James of Milan (1905) *Stimulus Amoris Jacobi Mediolanensis*, PP. Collegii S. Bonaventurae (ed.), Quaracchi: Collegium S. Bonaventurae.

James, Susan (1997) *Passion and Action: The Emotions in Seventeenth-century Philosophy*, Oxford: Clarendon Press.

Jameson, Fredric (1981) *The Political Unconscious: Narrative as a Socially Symbolic Act*, Ithaca: Cornell University Press.

Jay, Martin (1993) *Downcast Eyes: The Denigration of Vision in Twentieth-century French Thought,* Berkeley: University of California Press.

Jonas, Hans (1977) "Acting, Knowing, Thinking: Gleanings from Hannah Arendt's Philosophical Work," Social Research 44: 25–43.

Jonas, R. (2000) *France and the Cult of the Sacred Heart: An Epic Tale for Modern Times*, Berkeley: University of California Press.

Jones, Ann Rosalind (1993) "The Muse of Indirection: Feminist Ventriloquism in the Dialogues of Catherine Des Roches" in Colette Winn (ed.) *The Dialogue in Early Modern France, 1547–1630: Art and Argument*, Washington, DC: Catholic University of America Press.

Jones, Ann Rosalind (1995) "Contentious Readings: Urban Humanism and Gender Difference in *La Puce de Madame Des-Roches* (1582)," *Renaissance Quarterly* 48 (1): 109–28.

Jones, Ann Rosalind (2000) "'*Blond Chef, Grande Conqueste*': Feminist theories of the gaze, the *blason anatomique*, and Louise Labé's Sonnet 6" in John O'Brien and Malcolm Quainton (eds) *Distant Voices Still Heard: Contemporary Readings of French Renaissance Literature*, Liverpool: Liverpool University Press.

Jowett, Benjamin (trans.) (1931; 4th edn 1953) *The Dialogues of Plato*, 5 vols., Oxford: Oxford University Press.

Kahn, Coppèlia (1991) "Lucrece: The Sexual Politics of Szubjectivity" in *Rape and Representation*, New York: Columbia University Press.

Kalkavage, Peter (trans.) (2001) *Plato's Timaeus*, Newburyport: Focus Books.

Kennedy, W. J. (1983) *Jacopo Sannazaro and the Uses of Pastoral*, Hanover and London: University Press of New England.

Kermode, Frank (1957) "Dissociation of Sensibility," reprinted in John R. Roberts (ed.) (1975) *Essential Articles for the Study of John Donne's Poetry*, Hassocks: Harvester.

Keynes, Geoffrey (1958) *A Bibliography of Dr John Donne*, Cambridge: Cambridge University Press.

Kitts, Margo (2000) "The Wide Bosom of the Sea as a Place of Death: Maternal and Sacrificial Imagery in *Iliad* 21," *Literature and Theology*, 14 (2): 103–24.

Krier, Theresa (2001) *Birth Passages: Maternity and Nostalgia, Antiquity to Shakespeare*, Ithaca: Cornell University Press.

Krier, Theresa (2003) "Daemonic Allegory: The Elements in Late Spenser, Late Shakespeare, and Irigaray," Theresa Krier, John Watson, and Patrick Cheney (eds) *Spenser Studies XVIII*: 315–42.

Kristeva, Julia (1980) "Place Names" in *Desire in Language: A Semiotic Approach to Literature and Art*, trans. T. Gora, A. Jardine, and L. Roudiez, New York: Columbia University Press.

Kristeva, Julia (1988) *Etrangers à Nous-memes*, Paris: Fayard.

La Caze, M. (2002) "The Encounter Between Wonder and Generosity," *Hypatia* 17 (3): 1–19.

Labriola, Albert C. (1990) "'This Dialogue of One': Rational Argument and Affective Discourse in Donne's 'Aire and Angels'" in Achsah Guibbory (ed.) (1990a), "Interpreting 'Aire and Angels'," special issue of the *John Donne Journal*, 9 (1): 77–83.

Lacan, J. (1998) *On Feminine Sexuality, the Limits of Love and Knowledge, 1972–73* in trans. Bruce Fink, *Encore: The Seminar of Jacques Lacan, Book XX*, New York: W. W. Norton.

Lacan, J. (1977a) "The Mirror Stage as Formative of the Function of the I as Revealed in Psychoanalytic Experience" in *Écrits: A Selection*, trans. Alan Sheridan, New York: Norton: 1–7.

Lacan, J. (1977b) "The Function and Field of Speech and Language in Psychoanalysis" in *Écrits: A Selection*, trans. Alan Sheridan, New York: Norton, 30–113.

Lamberton, Robert (1986) *Homer the Theologian: Neoplatonist Allegorical Reading and the Growth of the Epic Tradition*, Berkeley: University of California Press.

Larsen, Anne R. (1998) "Introduction" in Anne R. Larsen (ed.) *Les Secondes Oeuvres de Madeleine and Catherine Des Roches*, Geneva: Droz.

Lawrence, Henry (1646) *Of our Communion and Warre with Angels*, London: G. Calvert.

Lemay, H. R. (ed. and trans.) (1992) *Women's Secrets: A Translation of Pseudo-Albertus Magnus' De Secretis Mulierum with Commentaries*, Albany: State University of New York Press.

Lemnius, Levinus (1576; 2nd edn 1633) *The Touchstone of Complexions*, trans. Thomas Newton, London: Thomas Marsh.

Levinas, Emmanuel (1998) *Totality and Infinity: An Essay on Exteriority*, trans. Alphonso Lingis, Pittsburgh: Duquesne University Press.

Lévi-Strauss, Claude (1969) *The Elementary Structures of Kinship*, trans. James Harle Bell; John Richard von Sturmer, and Rodney Needham (eds), Boston: Beacon Press.

Lewis, F. (1996) "The Wound in Christ's Side and the Instruments of the Passion: Gendered Experience and Response" in L. Smith and J. H. M. Taylor (eds) *Women and the Book: Assessing the Visual Evidence*, London and Toronto: The British Library and University of Toronto Press.

L'Hermite-Leclercq, P. (1999) "Le Lait et le Sang de la Vierge" in M. Faure (ed.) *Le Sang au Moyen Âge: Actes du Quatrième International de Montpellier Université Paul-Valéry (27–29 novembre 1997)*, Montpellier: Université Paul Valéry.

Little, Arthur L., Jr. (2000) *Shakespeare Jungle Fever*, Stanford: Stanford University Press.

Lochrie, Karma (1997) "Mystical Acts, Queer Tendencies" in K. Lochrie, P. McCracken and J. A. Schultz (eds) *Constructing Medieval Sexuality*, Minneapolis: University of Minnesota Press.

Lodge, Thomas (1593) *Phillis: Honoured with Pastorall Sonnets, Elegies and Amorous Delights*, London: Printed for John Busbie.

Longinus (1989) "On Sublimity," trans. D. A. Russell in D. A. Russell and M. Winterbottom (eds), *Classical Literary Criticism, World's Classics*, Oxford; New York: Oxford University Press, 143–87.

Ludolphus of Saxony (1870) *Vita Christi*, L.-M. Rigollot (ed.) 4 vols, Paris: Palme.

Lyotard, Jean-Francois (1988) *L'Inhumain: Causeries sur le Temps*, Paris: Galilee; trans. Geoffrey Bennington and Rachel Bowlby (1992) *The Inhuman: Reflections on Time*, Stanford: Stanford University Press.

McGinn, B. (1998) *The Flowering of Mysticism: Men and Women in the New Mysticism – 1200–1350*, New York: Crossroad.

Maclean, Ian (1980) *The Renaissance Notion of Woman: A Study in the Fortunes of Scholasticism and Medical Science in European Intellectual Life*, New York: Cambridge University Press.

Marrow, J. H. (1979) *Passion Iconography in Northern European Art of the Late Middle Ages and Early Renaissance: A Study of the Transformation of Sacred Metaphor into Descriptive Narrative*, Kortrijk: Van Ghemmert.

Martin, Alison (2003) "Introduction: Luce Irigaray and the Culture of Difference," *Theory, Culture & Society* 20 (3): 1–12.

Martin, Ellen (1982) "The Romance of Anxiety in Chaucer's Franklin's Tale" in *Voices in Translation: The Authority of 'Olde Bookes' in Medieval Literature. Essays in Honor of Helaine Newstead*, ed. Deborah M. Sinnreich-Levi *et al.*, New York: AMS Press, 117–36.

Marx, Karl (1867) "On Commodities," trans. Ben Fowkes (1997) *Capital: Volume One*, New York: Vintage.

Maus, Katharine Eisaman (1995) *Inwardness and the Theater in the English Renaissance*, Chicago: University of Chicago Press.

Mauss, Marcel (1967) *The Gift: Forms and Functions of Exchange in Archaic Societies*, trans. Ian Cunnison, New York: Norton.

Mazzio, Carla and Hillman, David (eds) (1997) *The Body in Parts: Fantasies of Corporeality in Early Modern Europe*, New York and London: Routledge.

Mazzio, Carla and Trevor, Douglas (eds) (2000) *Historicism, Psychoanalysis, and Early Modern Culture*, New York and London: Routledge.

Mazzoni, Cristina (2002) *Maternal Impressions: Pregnancy and Childbirth in Literature and Theory*, Ithaca: Cornell University Press.

Meakin, H. L. (1998) *John Donne's Articulations of the Feminine*, Oxford: Clarendon Press.

Miles, Margaret R. (1999) *Plotinus on Body and Beauty: Society, Philosophy and Religion in Third-century Rome*, Oxford: Blackwell.

Miller, David Lee (1989) "The Death of the Modern: Gender and Desire in Marlowe's 'Hero and Leander'," *South Atlantic Quarterly* 88 (4): 757–87.

Miller, David Lee (2003) *Dreams of the Burning Child: Sacrificial Sons and the Father's Witness*, Ithaca: Cornell University Press.

Moi, Toril (1985) *Sexual/Textual Politics*, London: Methuen.

Montrose, Louis (1986) "The Elizabethan Subject and the Spenserian Text," in Patricia Parker and David Quint (eds) *Literary Theory/Renaissance Texts*, Baltimore: Johns Hopkins University Press.

Montrose, Louis (1991) "The Work of Gender in the Discourse of Discovery," *Representations*, 33: 1–41.

Mooney, C. (1994) "The Authorial Role of Brother A. in the Composition of Angela of Foligno's Revelations" in E. A. Matter and J. Coakley (eds) *Creative Women in Medieval and Early Modern Italy: A Religious and Artistic Renaissance*, Philadelphia: University of Pennsylvania Press.

Morgan, N. (1993–94) "Longinus and the Wounded Heart," *Wiener Jahrbuch für Kunstgeschichte*, 46–7: 507–18, 817–20.

Mueller, Janel (1989) "Women Among the Metaphysicals: A Case, Mostly, of Being Donne for," *MP*, 87: 142–58.

Mueller, Janel (1993) "Troping Utopia: Donne's Brief for Lesbianism," in James Grantham Turner (ed.) *Sexuality and Gender in Early Modern Europe: Institutions, Texts, Images*, Cambridge: Cambridge University Press.

Murnaghan, Sheila (1992) "Maternity and Mortality in Homeric Poetry," *Classical Antiquity* 11 (2): 242–64.

Murrin, Michael (1980) *The Allegorical Epic: Essays in its Rise and Decline*, Chicago: University of Chicago Press.

Nagy, Gregory (1979) *The Best of the Achaeans: Concepts of the Hero in Archaic Greek Poetry*, Baltimore: Johns Hopkins University Press.

Neely, Carol Thomas (1994) "Women and Men in *Othello*," Gerard Barthelemy (ed.) in *Critical Essays on Shakespeare's* Othello, New York: G. K. Hall.

Newman, Karen (1987) "'And Wash the Ethiop White': Femininity and the Monstrous in *Othello*," in Jean Howard and Marion F. O'Connor (eds) *Shakespeare Reproduced: The Text in History and Ideology*, London: Routledge.

Nicols, Thomas (1659) *Gemmarius Fidelius, or The Faithful Lapidary*, London.

Nohrnberg, James (1976) *The Analogy of* The Faerie Queene, Princeton: Princeton University Press.

Norbrook, D. (1993) "Introduction" in H. R. Woudhuysen (ed.) *The Penguin Book of Renaissance Verse 1509–1659*, Harmondsworth: Penguin.

O'Brien, Dennis (1996) "Plotinus on Matter and Evil" in Lloyd P. Gerson (ed.) *The Cambridge Companion to Plotinus*, Cambridge: Cambridge University Press.

Paradise, N. B. (1931) *Thomas Lodge: The History of an Elizabethan*, New Haven: Yale University Press.

Parfitt, George A. E. (1971) "Renaissance Wombs, Renaissance Tombs," *Renaissance and Modern Studies* 15: 23–33.

Parker, Patricia (1987) *Literary Fat Ladies: Rhetoric, Gender, Property*, London and New York: Methuen.

Parker, Patricia (1993) "Preposterous Reversals: *Love's Labor's Lost*," *Modern Language Quarterly*, 54 (4): 435–82.

Parker, Patricia (1994) "Fantasies of 'Race' and 'Gender': Africa, *Othello* and Bringing to Light" in Margo Hendricks and Patricia Parker (eds) *Women, "Race," and Writing in the Early Modern Period*, New York: Routledge.

Paster, Gail Kern (1993) *The Body Embarrassed: Drama and the Disciplines of Shame in Early Modern England*, Ithaca: Cornell University Press.

Paster, Gail Kern (2001) "The Body and Its Passions," *Shakespeare Studies* 29: 44–50.

Pender, Stephen (2003) "Essaying the Body: Donne, Affliction, and Medicine," in David Colclough (ed.) *John Donne's Professional Lives*, Woodbridge: D. S. Brewer.

Plato (1931) *Timaeus*, trans. Benjamin Jowett, *Dialogues of Plato*, 3, Oxford: Oxford University Press.

Plotinus (1956) *Enneads*, trans. Stephen McKenna and rev. B.S. Page, London: Faber & Faber.

Plumwood, Val (2002) *Environmental Culture: The Ecological Crisis of Reason*, London and New York: Routledge.

Puttenham, G. (1869) *The Arte of English Poesie*, E. Arber (ed.), London: Alexander Murray and Son.

Quint, David (1983) *Origin and Originality in Renaissance Literature: Versions of the Source*, New Haven: Yale University Press.

Rambuss, R. (1998) *Closet Devotions*, Durham: Duke University Press.

Reynolds, B. (trans.) (1977) *The Orlando Furioso*, Harmondsworth UK: Penguin.

Riehle, W. (1981) *The Middle English Mystics*, trans. Bernard Standring, London: Routledge and Kegan Paul.

Rist, John (1996) "Plotinus and Christian Philosophy" in Lloyd P. Gerson (ed.) *The Cambridge Companion to Plotinus*, Cambridge: Cambridge University Press.

Roberts, John R. (1990) "'Just Such Disparitee': The Critical Debate About 'Aire and Angels'" in Achsah Guibbory (ed.) (1990a), "Interpreting 'Aire and Angels'," special issue of the *John Donne Journal* 9 (1): 43–64.

Robinson, F. N. (ed.) (1957) *The Works of Geoffrey Chaucer*, Boston: Houghton Mifflin.

Roche, T. P. (1964) *The Kindly Flame: A Study of the Third and Fourth Books of Spenser's* Faerie Queene, Princeton: Princeton University Press.

Rorty, Richard (1979) *Philosophy and the Mirror of Nature*, Princeton: Princeton University Press.

Ross, David O., Jr. (1987) *Virgil's Elements: Physics and Poetry in the* Georgics, Princeton: Princeton University Press.

Rubin, Gayle (1975) "The Traffic in Women: Notes Toward a Political Economy of Sex" in *Toward an Anthropology of Women*, ed. Raina Reiter, New York: Monthly Review Press.

Sallis, John (1999) *Chorology: On Beginning in Plato's* Timaeus, Bloomington: Indiana University Press.

Saunders, Alison (1981) *The Sixteenth-Century Blason Poétique*, Durham/Bern: University of Durham and Peter Lang.

Sawday, Jonathan (1995) *The Body Emblazoned: Dissection and the Human Body in Renaissance Culture*, London: Routledge.

Scarry, Elaine (1985) *The Body in Pain: The Making and Unmaking of the World*, Oxford: Oxford University Press.

Scarry, Elaine (1988) "Donne: 'But Yet the Body is his Booke'" in Elaine Scarry (ed.) *Literature and the Body: Essays on Populations and Persons*, Baltimore: Johns Hopkins University Press.

Schoenfeldt, Michael C. (1999) *Bodies and Selves in Early Modern England: Physiology and Inwardness in Spenser, Shakespeare, Herbert, and Milton*, Cambridge: Cambridge University Press.

Schor, Naomi (1994a) "This Essentialism That Is Not One: Coming to Grips with Irigaray" in C. Burke, N. Schor and M. Whitford (eds) *Engaging with Irigaray: Feminist Philosophy and Modern European Thought*, New York: Columbia University Press: 57–78.

Schor, Naomi (1994b) "Previous Engagements: The Receptions of Irigaray" in C. Burke, N. Schor and M. Whitford (eds) *Engaging with Irigaray: Feminist Philosophy and Modern European Thought*, New York: Columbia University Press: 3–14.

Sedgwick, Eve Kosofsky (1985) *Between Men: English Literature and Male Homosexual Desire*, New York: Columbia University Press.

Sedley, David (1998) *Lucretius and the Transformations of Greek Wisdom*, Cambridge: Cambridge University Press.

Selleck, Nancy (2001) "Donne's Body," *SEL 1500–1900* 41 (1): 149–74.

Shakespeare, William (1992a) *As You Like It*, Agnes Latham (ed.) London: Routledge.

Shakespeare, William (1992b) *King Lear*, Kenneth Muir (ed.) London: Routledge.

Shakespeare, William (1993) *Romeo and Juliet*, Brian Gibbens (ed.) London: Routledge.

Shakespeare, William (2001) *Othello*, E.A. Honigman (ed.) London: Routledge.

Sidney, Philip (1987) *The Countess of Pembroke's Arcadia*, V. Skretkowicz (ed.) Oxford: Clarendon Press.

Silverman, Kaja (1988) *The Acoustic Mirror: The Female Voice in Psychoanalysis and Cinema*, Bloomington: Indiana University Press.

Slatkin, Laura (1991) *The Power of Thetis: Allusion and Interpretation in the* Iliad, Berkeley: University of California Press.

Smith, Ian (1998) "Barbarian Errors: Performing Race in Early Modern England," *Shakespeare Quarterly* 49 (2): 168–86.

Spenser, Edmund (1947) *Amoretti* in E. Greenlaw (ed.) *Minor Poems: Part Two* in C. G. Osgood and H. G. Lotspeich (eds) *The Works of Edmund Spenser: A variorum edition*, vol. 8, Baltimore: Johns Hopkins Press.

Staley, L. (1994) *Margery Kempe's Dissenting Fictions*, University Park: Pennsylvania State University Press.

Sticca, S. (1988) *The Planctus Mariae in the Dramatic Tradition of the Middle Ages*, trans. J. R. Berrigan, Athens: University of Georgia Press.

Summit, J. (2003) "Women and Authorship" in C. Dinshaw and D. Wallace (eds) *The Cambridge Companion to Medieval Women's Writing*, Cambridge: Cambridge University Press.

Tatum, James (ed.) (1994) *The Search for the Ancient Novel*, Baltimore: Johns Hopkins University Press.

Teskey, Gordon (2003) "'And Therefore as a Stranger Give it Welcome': Courtesy and Thinking," *Spenser Studies XVIII*: 343–59.

Thomas, Richard F. (1999) *Reading Virgil and His Texts: Studies in Intertextuality*, Ann Arbor: University of Michigan Press.

Trumbull, Grace H. (ed.) (1934) *The Essence of Plotinus: Extracts from the Six* Enneads *and Porphyry's "Life of Plotinus,"* trans. Stephen Mackenna, New York: Oxford University Press.

Tuana, N. (ed.) (1994) *Feminist Interpretations of Plato*, University Park, PA: Pennsylvania State University Press.

Tuve, Rosemond (1947) *Elizabethan and Metaphysical Imagery*, Chicago: University of Chicago Press.

Urbertino da Casale (1961) *Arbor Vitae Crucifixae Jesu*, with an introduction and bibliography by Charles T. Davis, Turin: Bottega d'Erasmo.

Vickers, Nancy J. (1982) "Diana Described: Scattered Woman and Scattered Rhyme" in *Writing and Sexual Difference*, ed. Elizabeth Abel. Chicago: University of Chicago Press: 95–109.

Vickers, Nancy J. (1981) "Diana Described: Scattered Woman and Scattered Rhyme." *Critical Inquiry* 8.2: 265–79.

Vickers, Nancy J. (1985a) "'The Blazon of Sweet Beauty's Best': Shakespeare's Lucrece" in Patricia Parker and Geoffrey Hartman (eds) *Shakespeare and the Question of Theory*, New York: Methuen: 95–115.

Vickers, Nancy J. (1985b) "'This Heraldry in Lucrece's Face'," *Poetics Today* 6 (1): 171–84.

Vickers, Nancy J. (1996) "The Unauthored 1539 Volume in which is Printed the *Hecatomphile, The Flowers of French Poetry*, and *Other Soothing Things*" in Margaret De Grazia, Maureen Quilligan and Peter Stallybrass (eds) *Subject and Object in Renaissance Culture*, Cambridge, Cambridge University Press.

Vickers, Nancy J. (1997) "Members Only: Marot's Anatomical Blazons," in David Hillman and Carla Mazzio (eds) *The Body in Parts: Fantasies of Corporeality in Early Modern Europe*, New York: Routledge.

Virgil (1990) *Georgics*, R. A. B. Mynors (ed.), Oxford: Clarendon Press.

Virgil (1982) *The Georgics*, trans. L. P. Wilkinson, Harmondsworth: Penguin.

Vitkus, Daniel (2002) "The 'O' in *Othello*: Tropes of Damnation and Nothingness," in Philip C. Kolin (ed.) Othello: *New Critical Essays*, New York and London: Routledge.

Walkington, Thomas (1607) *The Optick Glasse of Humors,* London.

Wall, Wendy (1993) "Our Bodies/Our Texts?: Renaissance Women and the Trials of Authorship" in Carol J. Singley (ed.) *Anxious Power: Reading, Writing, and Ambivalence in Narrative by Women*, Albany: State University of New York Press.

Wallace, Andrew (2003) "Placement, Gender, Pedagogy: Virgil's Fourth *Georgic* in Print," *Renaissance Quarterly* 56 (2): 377–407.

Weed, Elizabeth (1994) "The Question of Style" in C. Burke, N. Schor and M. Whitford (eds) *Engaging with Irigaray: Feminist Philosophy and Modern European Thought*, New York: Columbia University Press.

Weeks, Andrew (1997) *Paracelsus: Speculative Theory and the Crisis of the Early Reformation*, Albany: State University Press of New York.

Whitford, Margaret (1991) *Luce Irigaray: Philosophy in the Feminine*, New York: Routledge.

Whitford, Margaret (1994) "Irigaray, Utopia, and the Death Drive," in C. Burke, N. Schor, and M. Whitford (eds) *Engaging with Irigaray: Feminist Philosophy and Modern European Thought* , New York, Columbia University Press, 379–400.

Whitford, Margaret (2003) "Irigaray and the Culture of Narcissism," *Theory, Culture & Society: Explorations in Critical Social Sciences* 20, 3: 27–42.

Whitman, Jon (1987) *Allegory: The Dynamics of an Ancient and Medieval Technique*, Cambridge: Harvard University Press.

Wiggins, Peter DeSa (2000) *Donne, Castiglione, and the Poetry of Courtliness*, Bloomington: Indiana University Press.

Wilson, T. (1994) *The Art of Rhetoric*, P. E. Medine (ed.), University Park: Pennsylvania State University Press.

Wittig, Monique (1992) *The Straight Mind and Other Essays*, London: Harvester Wheatsheaf.

Wofford, Susanne Lindgren (1987) "Britomart's Petrarchan Lament: Allegory and Narrative in *The Faerie Queene* III, iv," *Comparative Literature* 39 (1): 28–57.

Wofford, Susanne Lindgren (1992) *The Choice of Achilles: The Ideology of Figure in the Epic*, Stanford: Stanford University Press.

Wood, C. (1981) "The Doctor's Dilemma: Sin, Salvation, and the Menstrual Cycle in Medieval Thought," *Speculum* 56: 710–27.

Wright, John P. and Potter, Paul (eds) (2000) *Psyche and Soma: Physicians and Metaphysicians on the Mind-Body Problem from Antiquity to Enlightenment*, Oxford: Clarendon Press.

Wright, Thomas (1620) *The Passions of the Minde in Generall*, London.

Young, I. M. (1997) "Asymmetrical Reciprocity: On Moral Respect, Wonder, and Enlarged Thought" in *Intersecting Voices: Dilemmas of Gender, Political Philosophy, and Policy*, Princeton: Princeton University Press.

Ziarek, Ewa (1998) "Toward a Radical Female Imaginary: Temporality and Embodiment in Irigaray's Ethics," *Diacritics* 28: 60–75.

Ziarek, Krzysztof (1999) "Love and the Debasement of Being: Irigaray's Revisions of Lacan and Heidegger," *Postmodern Culture: An Electronic Journal of Interdisciplinary Criticism* 10, 1, 29 paragraphs.

Žižek, Slavoj (1992) *Enjoy Your Symptom! Jacques Lacan in Hollywood and Out*, London and New York: Routledge.

Works by Luce Irigaray

This bibliography lists the writings of Irigaray cited in this book. It proceeds from early to late pieces; it includes information on both individual essays and the books in which they are collected; it provides original French or Italian publication data. Where the French or Italian texts are discussed by our contributors, they receive a separate entry.

Irigaray, Luce (1974) *Speculum. De l'autre femme*, Paris: Minuit.

—— (1977a) *Ce Sexe qui n'en est pas un*, Paris: Minuit.

—— (1977b) "Le marché des femmes" in *Ce sexe qui n'en est pas un*: 167–85.

—— (1977c) "Des marchandises entre elles" in *Ce sexe qui n'en est past un*: 189–93.

—— (1977d) "Quand nos lèvres se parlent" in *Ce sexe qui n'en est pas un*: 205–17.

—— (1984) *Ethique de la différence sexuelle*, Paris: Minuit.

—— (1985a) *This Sex Which Is Not One*, trans. Catherine Porter and Carolyn Burke, Ithaca: Cornell University Press.

—— (1985b) "Commodities among Themselves" in *This Sex Which Is Not One*: 192–7.

—— (1985c) "The 'Mechanics' of Fluids" in *This Sex Which Is Not One*: 106–18.

—— (1985d) "When Our Lips Speak Together" in *This Sex Which Is Not One*: 205–18.

—— (1985e) "Women on the Market" in *This Sex Which Is Not One*: 170–91.

—— (1985f) *Parler n'est jamais neutre*, Paris: Minuit.

—— (1985g) *Speculum of the Other Woman*, trans. Gillian C. Gill, Ithaca: Cornell University Press.

—— (1991) *Marine Lover of Friedrich Nietzsche*, trans. Gillian C. Gill, New York: Columbia University Press. (First French publ. 1980, *Amante marine. De Friedrich Nietzsche*, Paris: Minuit.)

—— (1992) *Elemental Passions*, trans. Joanne Collie and Judith Still, New York: Athlone Press. (First French publ. 1982, *Passions élémentaires*, Paris: Minuit.)

—— (1993a) *Sexes and Genealogies*, trans. Gillian C. Gill, New York: Columbia University Press. (First French publ. 1987, Sexes et parentés, Paris: Minuit.)

—— (1993b) "Belief Itself" in *Sexes and Genealogies*: 25–53. (First French publ. 1983, La croyance même, Paris: Galilée.)

—— (1993c) "Divine Women" in *Sexes and Genealogies*, trans. Gillian C. Gill, New York: Columbia University Press: 55–72. (First French presentation 1984.)

—— (1993d) "Flesh Colors" in *Sexes and Genealogies*: 151–65. (First French presentation 1986.)

—— (1993e) *An Ethics of Sexual Difference*, trans. Carolyn Burke and Gillian C. Gill, Ithaca: Cornell University Press.

—— (1993f) "Sexual Difference" in *An Ethics of Sexual Difference*: 5–19.

—— (1993g) "Sorcerer Love: A Reading of Plato, *Symposium*, 'Diotima's Speech'" in *An Ethics of Sexual Difference*: 20–33.

—— (1993h) "Wonder: A Reading of Descartes, The Passions of the Soul" in *An Ethics of Sexual Difference*: 72–82.

—— (1994) *Thinking the Difference: For a Peaceful Revolution*, trans. Karin Montin, New York: Routledge. (First French publ. 1989, *Le temps de la différence: Pour une revolution pacifique*, Paris: Librairie générale française.)

—— (1995a) "Questions to Emmanuel Lévinas" in *The Irigaray Reader*, ed. Margaret Whitford, Oxford: Blackwell: 178–89. (First French publ. November 1990, "Questions à Emmanuel Levinas," *Critique* 522: 911–20.)

—— (1995b) "'Je – Luce Irigaray': A Meeting with Luce Irigaray. An Interview with Elizabeth Hirsh and Gary A. Olson," trans. Elizabeth Hirsh and Gaëtan Brulotte, *Hypatia* 10, 2: 93–114. JAC Online 16, 3 (1996); http://www.cas.usf.edu/JAC/163/irigaray.html

—— (1996) *I Love To You: Sketch of a Possible Felicity in History*, trans. Alison Martin, New York: Routledge. (First French publ. 1992, *J'aime à toi: Esquisse d'une félicité dans l'histoire, Paris: Grasset*.)

—— (1999) *The Forgetting of Air in Martin Heidegger*, trans. Mary Beth Mader, London: Athlone Press. (First French publ. 1983, *L'oubli de l'air chez Martin Heidegger*, Paris: Minuit.)

—— (2001a) "Daughter and Woman" in *To Be Two*: 30–9.

—— (2001b) *To Be Two*, trans. Monique M. Rhodes and Marco F. Cocito-Monoc, New York: Routledge. (First Italian publ. 1994, *Essere Due*, Bollati Boringhieri.)

—— (2002a) *Between East and West: From Singularity to Community*, trans. Stephen Pluháček, New York: Columbia University Press. (First French publ. 1999, *Entre Orient et Occident*, Paris: Grasset et Fasquelle.)

—— (2002b) *To Speak Is Never Neutral*, trans. Gail Schwab, New York: Routledge.

—— (2002c) "The Rape of the Letter" in *To Speak Is Never Neutral*: 121–36.

—— (2002d) "The Setting in Psychoanalysis" in *To Speak Is Never Neutral*: 193–204.

—— (2002e) "The Utterance in Analysis" in *To Speak Is Never Neutral*: 95–108.

—— (2003) *The Way of Love*, trans. Heidi Bostic and Stephen Pluháček, New York: Continuum.

Index